MW00399607

Widow's Key

Widow's Key

INNOVATIVE APPROACHES
FOR OVERCOMING PERSONAL LOSS

Linda Lindholm

Glue Pot Press

Widow's Key: Innovative Approaches for Overcoming Personal Loss
Copyright © 2011 by Linda Lindholm
All Rights Reserved

First Edition

Designed by Max Marbles

Published by Glue Pot Press
http://gluepotpress.com
Printed in the United States of America

No part of this book may be reproduced or transmitted in any form or by any means, electronic or mechanical, including photocopying, recording, or by any information storage and retrieval system, without prior permission in writing of both the copyright owner and the publisher.

For information address:
Glue Pot Press, 1313 Mill Street SE, Salem, Oregon 97301

Widow's Key website: http://widowskey.com

ISBN 978-0-9831616-0-8

Library of Congress Control Number: 2010917280

This publication is designed to provide accurate and authoritative information in regard to the subject matter covered. It is sold with the understanding that the publisher and author are not engaged in rendering legal, accounting, medical or other professional services. If you require legal or financial advice or other expert assistance, you should seek the services of a competent professional.

Widow's Key is dedicated to three people who have enriched and changed my life... my son Andrew Brown, my daughter Kate Brown and my brother Max Lindholm...for all they did to validate, facilitate and encourage this written endeavor.

Table of Contents

First Few Days *Checklist Regarding Home and Family Matters *Eulogy, Finding the Right Words *Elements of Writing and Presenting a Eulogy *Funeral Celebrants *Memorial Services *Requiem Mass *Living Funeral *Funerals in Religious and Cultural Context (Jewish and Christian)

Introduction

Like a storm, death can overtake you, often fiercely and without warning. Your whole life changes in an instant. If you are reading this book, you have probably lost someone very dear to you. Whether you are a widow due to the terminal illness, injury or the sudden and unexpected death of your husband, you are about to go through one of the most profound emotional experiences life can throw at you. Such a loss can shake the foundation of your beliefs and lifestyle to the very core. My sincere heartfelt sympathies go to you upon the death of your loved one. As new widow, you need solace, comfort, understanding, validation, information, guidance and most importantly, hope.

In my trust and estates law practice, I have worked with a multitude of grieving widows. They all have questions and need individual help dealing with problems created by their widowhood. Based on over twenty years of legal practice, personal experiences, extensive research and interviews, I created *Widow's Key* as a comprehensive guide to answer those pressing questions and provide solutions for a widow's unique problems. I have seen tremendous first-hand results and life-altering changes occur when a widow is given the relevant information, strategies and innovative approaches that she needs to survive, strive and actually thrive in her new world.

Being a widow is part of the universal human story. There are books written by psychologists to serve the mental health aspect, books written by accountants and investors about financial security, books written in legalese by lawyers on estate planning and administration, books written by clergy and counselors on life transitions, faith and more. Until now, I never had one single source of information and written guidance to offer my widowed clients. The *Widow's Key* resource book combines several fields of knowledge applicable to your widow's journey before, during and after the loss of your loved one. Concepts in *Widow's Key* can provide you with direct, honest and practical solutions for coping with the changes and challenges brought on by your losses.

Widow's Key offers various beneficial processes and new adaptive techniques that I discovered over decades of assisting widows. My present and past clients have been my teachers when it comes to death, grief and life. Dealing with the pain and realities of loss, they demonstrate the frailty, resiliency and strengths of which people are capable. You too can access your heart's deep power and ability to heal.

Grief is difficult work, but moving forward after the death of your loved one should not be harder for you and your family than it has to be. Your feelings will be validated and your needs addressed through the knowledge and principles found in this book. Use the information and the innovative approaches that fit your own life and recovery. Weathering the storms of your widowhood starts right here with guidelines to help you discover renewed hope, health and happiness as you reconnect with life. You will emerge from your grief journey a stronger person with positive memories to cherish and a promising future ahead of you. Your transition from widowhood to selfhood begins here.

> What lies behind us and what lies before us are small matters compared to what lies within us.
> - Ralph Waldo Emerson

Chapter One

INITIAL REACTIONS AT THE TIME OF DEATH

Life has a way of changing your plans. It is a simple and sobering fact that most people are not prepared for death. Grief and healing are very personal journeys filled with raw emotions and realities. Words are not sufficient to describe the shock, pain and emptiness that you experience as a widow. Words alone cannot alleviate your pain, sorrow or confusion.

Death of a loved one is a life-changing experience. At the beginning of the grieving process, you may find yourself unable or unwilling to think about what happens next. It's ok to not be ok for a while. This section can help you understand what is happening to you and how to cope. The first step is to find a way to stabilize after the initial shock. Take stock of the situation and assess what you are ready or not ready to handle yet. Most importantly, acknowledge your feelings and be very kind to yourself.

Realization or News of a Death

No, no, nooooooooo! That can't be. There has to be some mistake. You're wrong. I just can't believe it! Tell me it's not true. Oh my God, Why? I just saw him a few hours ago, he can't be dead. This isn't really happening. This is a bad dream. Wait a minute. I can't breathe. My heart is pounding out of my chest. What is this crushing weight on me? I'm dizzy. It feels like someone just hit me in the stomach. I'm going to be sick. I'm going to die right here. This pain is unbearable. I'm shattered and in pieces. I have been split in half. I feel like I'm in a cold gray tunnel. Why can't I wake up from this awful dream? I need someone or something to hold on to. Help me. This is going to destroy me. This is going to kill his mother. How could this happen? Why him? Lord, take me instead. I can't live without him. I'm so devastated I can't even speak. This isn't right. It's not fair.

Why is this happening to me? Is this my fault? What did I do to cause this? Not yet. I'm not ready for this. I never got to say goodbye or I'm sorry. I needed to let him know how much I loved him. There is something I have to tell him. We didn't have enough time. I'm not ready to let him go yet. We never planned on this. Please, just one more day. Damn you, I'm so angry with you for dying. How could you do this to me? I'm afraid. I can't deal with this. I'm confused. I can't think straight. There are no words to express my despair. It wasn't supposed to happen this way. I'm going to fall apart right in front of everyone. I can't stop crying. Why am I not crying? How am I going to tell the kids? Give me strength. I'm too young to be a widow. I'm all alone now. I'm lost. I'm scared. I'm terrified. This is going the break me clean in two. Who am I without him? What do I do now? What happens now?

Do you recognize any, several or all of the feelings in the paragraph above? You know that your life will never be the same again from the moment of your husband's death. The initial shock or realization that someone you loved has just died will directly hit you emotionally, physically, mentally, socially and spiritually. The impact of loss is so profound that it touches the very core of one's being and affects every aspect of life. It is almost too much for the human spirit to endure.

Common Reactions to Death of a Loved One

Death is the most concrete of losses. The wound you experience when you learn of the death of your loved one is like a physical injury. Western cultures readily treat physical wounds, but tend to neglect mental or emotional ones. While everyone's experience is unique, traumatic news of a death can bring on overwhelming mental despair and physical collapse.

It is important to get an overview of the common reactions in response to the death of a spouse so that you and others around you realize that these reactions are normal in such a traumatic situation. You do not have to explain yourself, because what is happening to you is a natural reaction to your great loss. Knowing that other people have similar emotional, physical, mental, social and spiritual reactions should bring you some peace of mind.

From very personal experiences and years of working with widows, doctors, funeral directors, hospice, law enforcement, scientists, attorneys and ministers, plus reading their reports and studies, I have found the following to be normal and common reactions to one of life's greatest traumas.

Emotional Reactions: Common emotional reactions include a degree of shock, numbness, disbelief, anger, guilt, fear, paranoia, depression, anxiety and denial. A majority of people cannot accept the impact of the loss immediately. Unconsciously or consciously, you may deny its reality and spin into a spiral of disbelief and avoidance of the truth. It is mentally impossible to believe or comprehend what has happened. At first, the mind splits, with one part acknowledging the death, and the other part of the mind denying it.

Denial is a shock absorber that helps your mind assimilate the reality of the loss more slowly. The more sudden and traumatic the loss, the more likely you are to deny its reality. Normal feelings of stability, security, safety are broken, leaving you feeling suddenly unstable, insecure and unsafe. The person that defined continuity and purpose to your life was suddenly taken from you. You feel out of balance with the separation-anxiety and isolation. Emotional wounds are real, painful and debilitating. When faced with the unbearable, the mind and body balk and go into a form of shock to protect themselves from painful news.

Physical Reactions: For a moment the whole world may seem to stand still, timeless, with no movement, no sound. Body chemistry and body functions react instantly and put you in a state of shock. One of the most typical physical reactions to the shock is for an excessive amount of adrenalin to release into the bloodstream. The physiological signs of shock bring on primal fear response actions known as "fight or flight." The mechanisms of the body and mind are designed to declare a biological 'red alert'. Anytime the body senses a threat or danger, it involuntarily releases chemicals that stimulate the heart to beat faster and which force more oxygen into the bloodstream. This inordinate amount of adrenalin and oxygen in the system can cause rapid heartbeat, elevated blood pressure, dizziness, tingling in the lips or extremities, involuntary shaking of the muscles or hands and difficulty breathing.

Upon hearing the news, some literally run, scream in anguish, shake uncontrollably, hyperventilate or pass out. Others begin fighting, hitting or physically attacking the news bearer or those nearby or pounding on objects. That is one reason why police officers, doctors and clergy will often tell people to sit down before presenting the bad news.

Other common physical reactions may include: digestive track complications, difficulty swallowing, muscle spasms, severe headaches, fatigue or insomnia, changes in appetite, frequent urination, profuse sweating, distress pangs, crying and rashes. Any or all of these reactions are to be expected after a loss.

Crying is another of the body's healing and cleansing devices. Tears contain one of the brain's natural pain relievers, leucine-enkephalin. Tears also contain prolactin, a hormone that supports the secretion of tears. Women cry more readily because they have more prolactin in their systems than men. Dr. Joyce Brothers, in her book *Widowed*, describes tears as 'emotional first-aid'. Crying is one of nature's stress releasing pressure valves. Knowing what causes these temporary bodily reactions can keep your additional fears to a minimum.

Classic psychiatric studies describe crisis grief reactions as universal and remarkably uniform all around the world. While expressions of emotions and grief can differ from one cultural group to another, widows in all societies experience both mental and physical reactions. Upon notification of a loved one's death, people everywhere consistently experience and report tightness in the throat, muscular limpness, shortness of breathe, a need to sigh and loss of appetite. Loss grief ambushes with physical responses and symptoms like exhaustion, bone-dry mouth and tearfulness.

Shock steps in to cushion you from what you cannot yet handle. It is just part of the body's chemistry and natural defenses. Survivors feel numbness and shock like when the actual physical body is injured. Nature is a powerful ally who will help you survive. Poet Emily Dickinson describes this first crisis grief reaction as 'the hour of lead' and relates it to freezing persons recollecting the snow, first chill, then stupor and then the letting go. Don't fight the necessary survival and healing mechanisms. Accept how loss physically and mentally feels like and know that it will pass as the shock buffer wears off and the grieving process begins.

Later when the reality of the loss sinks in, the protection of shock diminishes as you are more prepared to handle the pain than you were the first few hours or days. Physical and psychological attributes of shock and denial are only temporary blessings. When the thin veil of numbness begins to lift, you will replace denial with the reality of grief in order to gently leave the state of shock and face your life and its new challenges.

Mental Reactions: When widows see or are told of their loved one's death, many describe a dreamlike state of mind, watching, rather than experiencing, what is going on around them for days. They feel anesthetized, numb and mechanical. Life seemed surreal, with other people appearing shadowy or far away. The unconscious mind can act illogically at this time. Sometimes this crisis reaction state of clouded consciousness is referred to as a 'cocoon of shock.' It is like being inside a protective cocoon, bubble or behind a clear shield where reality can't quite touch you. It is almost like mentally floating above the scene and watching as an observer.

Confusion and the inability to concentrate or remember are very common mental reactions to the loss of a loved one. Many widows report replaying certain life scenes in their minds like a DVD stuck on play, reliving of past events, obsessive preoccupation with the deceased, assigning blame, vivid dreams and visual and auditory hallucinations. Many experience exaggerated fear, panic attacks, pessimism, depression, high anxiety, indecision, bitterness, emptiness, loss of motivation, regrets, inability to plan, loss of humor and frustration.

In the case of violent victimization or murder of a loved one, it is common for survivors to feel rage and think about seeking revenge. Everyone feels angry…everyone. However, it is not ok to hurt someone or yourself. There will be times when you perceive yourself as being without appropriate feelings and sometimes feeling nothing at all. That is just another characteristic reaction response to a significant loss.

Know that these mental reactions are common and play a crucial role in the overall process of recovery and healing. You can be filled with reactions, thoughts and feelings that you have never experienced before and don't understand. It often becomes difficult to mobilize inner resources and just cope with daily tasks. Rest assured that you are not going crazy or losing your mind. You and those around you during this period should be aware of these temporary mental reactions in order to help understand your grieving state.

Social Reactions: Many bereaved want to withdraw, escape and just be left alone. Finding it difficult to interact with other people, function at work or in social settings, or even take care of yourself or your own basic responsibilities, you may tend to isolate yourself. Some widows do the opposite of withdrawal and become overly active, involved and busy to fill the void. Since the idea of being alone at home is intolerable, you may spend time in coordinating the services, social outings, church activities, shopping and entertainment venues.

As a widow, you may observe that after the funeral you feel ignored, avoided, exclude from gatherings and treated differently. "When I was married, I was Mrs. Somebody. Now that my husband is dead, I am nobody!" cried a widowed client. Sadly, too many widows feel lonely, misunderstood, betrayed and abandoned socially.

Even at the funeral or later when out socially, people may avoid any mention of your deceased husband following the loss. Generally, people avoid someone to whom they have trouble talking to or don't know what to say about a difficult topic. Death as a social subject is upsetting, alien and taboo. At the opposite end of the spectrum, others folks want you to relive the moment with questions of what, when, who, where and how it all happened. As a result, people may do or say insensitive things. Don't make negative assumptions, don't take awkward attempts at distraction or sympathy personally and don't feel individually rejected.

Realize that any social isolation is usually because other people do not want to think about their own mortality. They do not understand and are uncomfortable with the topic of death or dying. These kinds of social reactions by others can result in reinforcing the self-imposed isolation of one widow or encouraging overly forward and outgoing behaviors of another widow. Find your own healthy balance.

Many societies' customs expect a widow to stay by herself and follow certain mourning traditions and mandates. Additionally, in several cultures, widows suffer the compound problems of stigmatization and are ostracized. For example, in India's Hindu tradition, they believe the taboo of death clings to the widow, so widows are considered unclean and forbidden to attend social events. The effect on the stigmatized is shame and social isolation. In Western culture, this cultural separation is not usually the case. Widows are honored and left alone to grieve until they are ready to be reintegrated into society.

Spiritual Reactions: "Oh God, why did he have to die?" A common spiritual reaction to the death of a loved one is to question or become angry with God or Allah or the Universe for allowing the loss to happen. Going through the "dark night of the soul" often leads to a temporary withdrawal from religious activities, prayer, practices, faith or beliefs. "How can I believe in a God who would let this happen?" is a common refrain. A spiritual crisis often occurs in which guiding assumptions and core values get called into question. Many mourners then experience guilt for being angry toward God, themselves or their deceased spouse.

> The hardest part of faith is the last hour.
> - David Wilkerson

A recent loss can reactivate anger over a prior loss or prior feelings of anger. Some widows feel furious and abandoned by God and the deceased. "How dare you leave me?" Working through the feelings of abandonment, desolation and anger are normal and essential to the healing process. Anger, even if displaced, is an indication that you are beginning to accept the facts and reality of the death.

One of religion's most significant tasks is to enable its adherents to cope with the death of others and their own demise. Many religious faiths profess that the deceased is now in paradise or heaven or will be reincarnated, but when the widow cannot comprehend the unknown, she may questions her faith and bemoan her fate. Phrases like "It was God's will" or "He's in a better place" or "I'll pray for him" may torment the widow. To which a widow may respond, "Will prayer bring him back?" Widows may feel that religious practice, especially if it had been a kind of "make a wish" religion, has failed them at this point. If one is too confused to concentrate on scriptures or if the words fail to comfort and relieve the suffering, some widows start to disbelieve the power of the religious texts. In various cultures, it is the spiritual leaders themselves who judge and degrade the social and economic status of the widow causing fear, anxiety and additional traumatic losses.

> If God lived on earth, people would break his windows.
> - Yiddish expression

On the other hand, widows often claim that the experience of loss and grief brought them into a deeper, more personal relationship with God or their deity. Several books about death and dying, such as *Instantly a Widow* by

Ruth Sisson, are full of the faith-enhanced experiences of others. Bereaved widows often move toward a more mature, realistic and personal faith by honestly examining their values and beliefs during the grief process.

The assistance of clergy and an organized service can provide comfort, a sense of order and gratitude for a religious community during this passage. Rituals, meditation and prayer give direction to a confused mind and lessen the pain. People tend to seek out God or a higher power when death intrudes into their life.

Widows often speak of feeling the presence of a holy spirit or the deceased beside them. Persons in deep distress over the loss of a loved one have reported mystical experiences like seeing the primary deity, saints or avatars of their religion, such as Jesus, Buddha, Mohammad, Virgin Mary or Quan Yin. Sometimes mourners report that the loved one or a spirit came to assure them that all is well and it gives them positive comfort. This spiritual outreach is a way to make sense of something senseless. A widowed client once described her comforting sense of faith as similar to being wrapped up in a warm blanket. Whenever she felt overwhelmed by situations, she would literally wrap a fuzzy blanket around her shoulders and return to her safe place of love.

Impact of Loss

The impact of loss is so profound that it reaches to the very essence of your being and affects every aspect of your life –emotionally, physically, mentally, socially and spiritually. These obvious reactions are to be expected during and after a loss. Don't try to understand or rationalize all that is happening during the clusters of reactions. They are a natural part of your body and mind's healing processes doing their jobs to protect you. It was an identifiable traumatic event that brought on the symptoms and these reactionary manifestations will disappear in time as you progress thorough the healing process.

Widows behave and react in a number of ways to individual and private sorrows. The death of your spouse, one of the most intimate attachment relationships, poses profound challenges to your adaptation as a living being. Be kind to yourself and realized that this lightening bolt of grief and pain will lessen over time. Just know that whatever you are thinking or feeling, that another widow has thought it, felt it, lived it and survived it.

Chapter Two

FINAL MOMENTS AND RITUALS FOR THE DYING

Final Moments

Attitudes on how we care for the living are reflected in our attitudes on how we care for the dying. Medical staff, clergy and officials generally maintain respect and cultural sensitivity when dealing with the deceased person and his family. Being with and caring for a dying loved one promotes the healing process for you and those left behind.

Many times the last days of life take place in the home, a hospital, nursing facility or in hospice care. Hospice is a program or center that provides special palliative care for people whose conditions are terminal when they are in their final days of life. Hospice also provides support for the families of the ill person during the process and after the death.

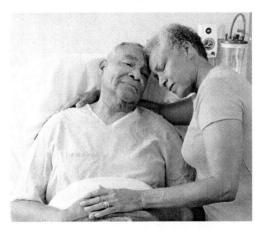

Vigiling, staying with one on the verge of dying, focuses on the person dying. Even though you are suffering, reclaim the last days, hours or moments of dying for the person going through it. Offer your loved one an opportunity to experience his passing with love, respect, care, calm, quiet comfort, honor and sacredness.

As Jesus said to his disciples when their lives were threatened by a raging storm on the Sea of Galilee, "Where is your faith? Don't be afraid." This is the comforting message that last moment rituals and prayers convey, that the person is to be at peace and address death without fear.

> There is no greater gift of charity you can give than helping
> a person to die well.
>
> - Sogyal Rinpoche

As someone is dying, the various traditions and religions observe several sacraments such as last rite and communion. These dying rituals are basically, confession and absolution to sanctify the body to make it ready for death. Often dying rituals involve creating a space around the person that contains the sacredness of the moment.

Death is a time to honor religion, cultural and family rituals. Rituals can help you and your dying loved one make the transition from life to death. The last moments and the dying experience can be infused with a spiritual and yet personal element. Rituals connect all involved with the spiritual and offer peace and reconciliation. The priest, rabbi, iman, poojari, clergy, monk, shaman or other religious leader can conduct ceremonies near the time of death or immediately after.

Traditions such as Extreme Unction or Last Rites, the Sacrament of the Anointing of the Sick are commonly administered to the dying, for the remission of sins and for the provision of spiritual strength. In modern times, their uses have been expanded to all who are gravely ill or are about to undergo a serious operation. Religious rites are used as a secondary effect of the sacrament to help a person recover his health.

The following is an introduction to the customs and rituals surrounding death and dying in two of the world's major religions, Judaism and Christianity. This summary about how religious rituals may deal with a person's final moments of life should be of help, to you, as the widow, family and friends of the dying person

Last Moments of Life Ceremonies or Last Rites

In Judaism, the *Shema* (declaration of faith) and *Vidui* (confession) are said together with the person that is about to die, if the person in conscious and in a lucid state of mind, according to the Code YD 338.1 of Jewish

Law. The patient may require a rabbi to recite prayers and facilitate the recitation of the confession on a death bed. If the person is not in a condition to say anything it is customarily said by those around him on his behalf. When death is imminent, the dying person should not be left alone. Transition begins when it is recognized that the person is dying, and falls in the category of being a *goses*.

During this *goses* period, there are specific directives for the behavior of the family and community of the dying person, including recitation of Psalms and confession of sins (*vidui*). The *goses* is considered a living person and this has implications for the Jewish arguments against euthanasia or organ harvest. Making funeral arrangements or beginning to mourn one's loss before the death occurs is considered inappropriate.

Christian Catholic ministrations to the dying are known as the *last rites*. Last rites are the final prayers and ministrations for Christians given only to people who are extremely ill and believed to be near death or at the time of death. The last rites go by various names and include different practices in different Christian traditions. Last rites include two distinct sacraments: Penance and the Eucharist, the last of which, when administered to the dying, is referred to as *viaticum*, a word whose original meaning in Latin was "provision for the journey."

The normal order of last rite administration is first penance or confession. If the dying person is physically unable to confess, absolution will take place as part of the effect of anointing. Next is the anointing and then viaticum. Like Confession and Holy Communion, the Sacrament of the Anointing of the Sick can be repeated as often as is necessary. Families often supplement the last rites with their own prayers and farewells.

Christians, in particular Anglicans, Lutherans and some other Protestant communities use a rite of Anointing the Sick, without necessarily classifying it as a sacrament. The Episcopal Church includes Unction of the Sick as among other sacramental rites and it states that unction can be performed with oil or simply with laying on of hands. Christians often follow many of the traditional Catholic traditions, but also try to ease the pain of death with prayers, the reading of scriptures and soft sacred music for the dying, but also for their families and friends and for the nurses and doctors who care for them. The patient may wish anointment by a minister or priest. Prayers are often recited. When death is felt to be imminent, many Christians will want to receive Communion.

Other Peaceful Farewell Rituals

Joyce Rupp, author of *Praying Our Goodbyes* (1988), *Your Sorrow Is My Sorrow* (1999), and *Walk in a Relaxed Manner* (2005), describes a popular non-religious "Go in Peace" ritual that has brought comfort to the dying and the living.

During the "Go in Peace" ritual, those family and friends with dying person bless and thank the various parts of his body (head, eyes, ears, mouth, arms, hands, heart, feet, etc.). They recall what his body had done for him and thank him for how he used that part of his body in some way as a gift or blessing to others.

For example, when praying a blessing for his head (the dwelling place of his brain and mind), several persons standing nearby placed their hands on the head and mentioned how he influenced their lives by his beliefs, attitudes, and values, and thank him for sharing dreams and hopes. Then those around the bedside added personal ways his head had helped them. After each part of his body was blessed, the group spoke together: "You will always be a part of our hearts. Go in peace."

Sometimes the names of saints or Jesus or those who passed away before are mentioned and said to be waiting. Listening to renditions of favorite music and being in the quiet presence of loved ones compliments and completes the farewell rituals.

Chapter Three

THE WIDOW'S FIRST FEW HOURS

From the first moments after your husband passes away, just when you are trying to deal with the shock and reality of the situation, you seem bombarded with questions, decisions and forms to fill out. In the middle of the shock, you are asked to make choices, deal with hospitals, funeral directors, morticians, family, friends, and sometimes reporters. You are suddenly faced with strange new responsibilities and that can be very frightening and unsettling.

Dealing with the first few hours and days after the death of a husband can make even the most organized woman feel incompetent, like a total amateur. You are not crazy. You are a widow. The best way to handle this duty is to take care of only the most urgent and necessary functions one at a time and take on the rest later.

Whether you have shared your loved one's final moments after a long illness or received a phone call with news of an expected or unexpected death, you still feel bewildered and in shock when someone dies. When death occurs, you and your family will need to make lots of very personal decisions. The formalities and details that need to be taken care of right away by the survivors seem particularly overwhelming during such an emotional time.

Immediately Upon Death

A variety of things must be completed in the first few hours and days. Among your tasks, you need to notify family, friends and clergy, arrange for the care of the body, organize funeral and burial ceremonies, prepare obituaries and alert various government agencies and business entities. There are some things to handle immediately and other decisions and actions, like settling the estate, which you can tackle in the coming months.

Initial Tasks - What to Do First

In this section, I will walk you through the maze of details in the first few hours and first days. The other tasks can just wait a bit until the most necessary obligations are over and you are more stable. I know you would rather just curl up and cry right now, but it is up to you and other family members to arrange a funeral service, handle visits, calls and such. You can get through this, maybe with the help of others, but you can do it.

What to do first depends on the circumstances and location of the death. In the United States, about thirty-two percent of deaths occur in hospitals, twenty percent occur in nursing homes, and half occur in other places.

Death at a Hospital or Care Center

If the death of your spouse occurs in a hospital, nursing, hospice or similar care facility and you are the first to be aware of the death, alert the hospital or care center staff. Give yourself adequate time to process and experience what has just happened. You have witnessed a profound event. You might need to spend some quiet or reflective time with your deceased husband. You may want to touch or hold your loved one and say your personal good-byes. Say farewell in your own time and in your own way. Family members, friends and clergy may want to have a few moments with him to perform rites, accept the death and begin the grieving process together or separately. The funeral home or mortuary need not be contacted immediately.

When you have said your goodbyes, it is time to surrender the body of your loved one to the funeral home. The hospital staff will usually help or take care of some arrangements and will contact the funeral home of your choice. If you are not present at the time of death, the hospital staff will notify you or the next of kin as instructed. The body might be moved temporarily to the facility morgue while transportation is arranged.

If you are present when the morticians arrive, they will need to ask a few questions in order to complete the death certificate forms. They will then prepare your loved one's body for transport. If your spouse has any jewelry you would like to keep, ask the funeral home personnel to remove it and give it to you. If you have any questions for the funeral home or coroner such as where the body is being prepared and a time when you will meet to plan the services, ask them. As professionals, they understand that this is a very difficult time and are usually very sensitive to your situation.

In the absence of any conditions that would necessitate the presence of the coroner or medical examiner, and after pronouncement of death, the hospital or care facility staff can contact a licensed funeral director for you or the family. If it is necessary, they will arrange an autopsy. Most state statutes do not permit a hospital, nursing home or facility based hospice to release a body to a funeral director or family member unless the facility has a signed death certificate and receives a removal notice.

Organ Donations

Decisions are extremely difficult right after your life partner passes away, but permission for organ donation must happen almost immediately. If it was the written or declared wish of the deceased that the organs or body are to be donated for transplant or medical research purposes, the doctor will have to be contacted as soon as possible. It is likely that the hospital staff will approach you if the circumstances are likely to favor transplant.

Organ donations in the United States for 2009 totaled 14,631 (8,021 from deceased persons and 6,610 from living donors). The designated donor consent rate was 74% in 2009. Many potential recipients in need of transplants go unmatched and pass away for lack of donated organs.

While organ donation is a very personal or religious decision, when someone dies you have an opportunity to save someone else's life by making a tissue, organ or artificial body part donation. Many widows feel that a part of their loved one lives on when they give the gift of life through an organ donation. Just know that when organs and tissues are removed, the procedures are similar to surgery and all incisions are closed, and an open casket is still possible after donation. There is no cost to you, the family or the deceased's estate for organ donation. Additionally, there is no financial compensation to the donor's estate or donor's family for the organ donation. Consider donations an act of charity.

Death Certificate

Federal law requires that the attending physician, a coroner or medical examiner must pronounce death. Authorities require a certificate from a physician or coroner to identify the deceased and validate the cause of death, generally within forty-eight hours. The funeral practitioner who assumes custody of the body will get the personal data from you or the most qualified person or source available.

The information needed by the funeral home staff for the death certificate will include:

- Full name of the deceased
- Deceased's residence address and telephone number
- Deceased's Social Security number
- Time of death
- Current location of the body such as facility name, address and telephone number
- Attending physician name and phone number
- Father's full name and birthplace; Mother's full maiden name and birthplace
- Veteran information
- Occupation
- Spouse's name, address and telephone number
- Information source's relationship to the deceased

The physician at the hospital or nursing home or a medical examiner will sign the cause of death and begin filling out the death certificate. This death certificate is given to a licensed funeral director to file in the state and county where the deceased has passed away. The funeral home staff in charge of final disposition arrangements will complete the non-medical paperwork and submit it to the proper government vital records authority, registrar or health department to issue certified copies.

Funeral directors generally are required to submit the documents and information to the proper government registrar within five days after the death in order to get official death certificates for you or next of kin. Each state government dictates the proper form of the document for use, timelines and the procedures necessary to produce a legal death certificate.

Certified death certificates, which include a government seal, can be obtained within days from the funeral home and thereafter more copies can be obtained through the state's official government authorized service and secure ordering system.

Sometimes called a medical certificate of the cause of death (MCCD), the death certificate is a document issued by a government official that declares the date, time, location and cause of a person's death. In the United States, death certificates often do not specify the full cause of death, generally referring to it as 'natural' unless the death was homicide, suicide, accidental or declared in absentia.

Death certificates may also be issued by executive order or court order in the case of individuals who are declared dead in absentia. Missing persons and victims of mass disasters (such as Hurricane Katrina) are issued death certificates in one of these order manners.

One purpose of the certificate is to review the cause of death to determine if suspicious causes or foul play occurred. The medical examiner's findings can rule out murder or accidental death. When the cause of death appears obvious like old age, accident, documented medical disease, and foul play is not suspected, an autopsy is rarely performed. If there is a chance that drugs or alcohol played a role in an accident, autopsies are common.

It is compulsory that a death certificate for each death that occurs in state will be submitted, within days after death and prior to final disposition, to the county registrar where the death occurred, to the Center for Health

Statistics or as otherwise directed by the State Registrar. Proof of major life events like a birth, a divorce, a marriage or a death are only issued by an official government agency. Additionally, public health offices use death certificates to compile statistical data on numbers and causes of death.

A death certificate is required for legal purposes to arrange a burial or cremation, to provide evidence of the fact of death. Original copies of the death certificate are needed for bank account amendments, claims on pension or life insurance, transferring investment accounts, title changes, processing other estate documents or starting probate. Be sure to order a sufficient number of death certificates from the funeral home so that you have them on hand for future business matters and administrative purposes. It is common to request a dozen or more certified copies, depending on the complexity of the estate. Photocopies will not be accepted in most cases.

Death at Home and Expected

If the death of your loved one happens at home and he was under medical care, be sure to notify the doctor. If you don't know the doctor's name, it can often be found on prescription bottles or medical bills. The deceased's attending physician can explain the condition of the deceased to the Medical Examiner. This will allow the Medical Examiner to give authorization to release the body, thereby expediting the process. If hospice is involved, notify the hospice organization on-call nurse. The hospice or home health care provider will notify the physician, the medical examiner's office if necessary and the funeral home.

Sometimes the funeral home will notify the proper authorities and the police may not need to go to the residence. When you or they call 911, be sure to inform the operator that the death was expected. Responding emergency medical personnel may attempt resuscitation unless there is posted notice or bracelet with a "do not resuscitate" declaration. Any death occurring without a licensed physician or medical personnel in attendance must be reported to the police. The police and emergency personnel will examine the situation and determine the next appropriate steps.

Coroner/Medical Examiner

State laws vary regarding which cases required investigation by a coroner or medical examiner. In certain situations, the coroner is contacted.

Generally, the local coroner will investigate a death under the following circumstances:

- Unattended deaths — no licensed physician was in attendance at the time of death or for a period prior to death
- A physician is unable to state the cause of death
- Suspected homicide
- Suspected suicide
- Accidental death
- Suspicious or unusual circumstances are involved
- Death occurring during medical procedures
- Death due to food, chemicals or drug poisoning
- Death suspected to be due to occupational causes
- Death suspected to be due to known contagious diseases constituting a public health hazard
- Death by drowning, fire, etc
- Deaths occurring while in prison or in police custody
- Suspected sudden infant death syndrome

After the coroner's examination, the body will either be transported to a funeral home of your choice or to the morgue for a post-mortem examination or autopsy, depending on the circumstances of death.

Unexpected or Unattended Death at Home or Work

If no one is present at the time of death or the death was unexpected, the first person present should call 911. The police and emergency personnel must be notified and respond to the residence or location before the deceased can be moved. These notifications are made to determine what caused the death and insure that there is no evidence of any wrongdoing.

If your loved one's death occurred in an accident, in a manner that violent or suspicious, or in a situation in which law enforcement authorities must retrieve criminal evidence from the body, do not move the body or disturb the surroundings. Many of the state laws regarding investigation by a coroner or medical examiner apply under these circumstances. In many states, the body cannot be moved until an officer is present and the local medical examiner gives authorization to the funeral director to remove the body of the deceased. If you discover a body or the death is sudden or unexpected, you should contact the police first. When you suspect that a death was not due to natural causes or an accident, do not touch or remove anything from the scene. The police may call in the coroner or medical examiner to investigate the death before contacting a funeral home or taking the body to a morgue for a post-mortem examination. The authorities will also find and notify the nearest relative. The police or doctor may ask you for permission to carry out a post-mortem examination of the body, which can find out more about the death, but this should not delay a funeral.

If Death Occurs in Another State or Country

When someone dies abroad, the death may seem more distressing because of the complications of being away from home and dealing with strangers, but you can get help. If a spouse, close relative or friend dies while you are abroad, report the death to your country's nearest Consulate. They will ask the hometown police to inform you or the next of kin. If you are not present and hear of the death from someone else, for example a tour operator, you should contact the American Embassy in that country. The web site for American Embassies abroad is www.usembassy.gov.

The consular staff will keep in touch with you, the family and the consulate abroad until burial or cremation overseas or until your deceased spouse has been brought back to his country of origin. They will also tell the foreign authorities of your wishes for the funeral and take details of who will be responsible for paying the costs involved, such as bringing his body back home.

If your husband dies while you are abroad with him, the Consul will support you by offering practical advice and help with funeral arrangements and other formalities such as inquests. If your spouse died while on a package holiday, the tour operator may be able to contact funeral directors and consular staff for you.

You will need to register the death in the placed where the person died according to local regulations and get a death certificate. The local police, consul or tour guide can advise you on how to do this. When registering the death, you should take information about yourself and the deceased including full name; date of birth; passport number; where and when the passport was issued; and details of the next of kin, if you are not their closest relative. You can also often register the death at the American Consulate as well, but this is not necessary.

Contact a funeral director in the state or country of death to work with the mortuary in the town where you want the deceased to be buried or cremated. The local funeral home can also assist with details of disposition and transportation of the body. Airlines have regulations regarding body transport. Airline representatives or funeral home directors can help you with these rules and logistics.

If there is a pre-paid funeral plan, check the policy for travel protection benefits. Some airlines have bereavement or compassion rates for relatives traveling to make arrangements, attending a funeral or accompanying a body home. When you purchase your ticket be prepared to provide documents regarding your relationship, hospital or funeral home contacts, a copy of the death certificate and other relevant details.

EXCLUSIVE READER ONLINE RESOURCES

A password hidden in *Widow's Key* allows you to receive extra reader resources. When writing this book, there was so much more information I wanted to include but there just wasn't room. But now you can get access to items, checklists and other valuable resources not in the book.

Here are just a few topics available to *Widow's Key* readers only:

* Comprehensive Funeral Planning Checklist

* Expanded Practical Home and Family Matter Checklist

* Top Ten Necessary Contacts (Social Security, VA, Hospice, Credit, etc.)

* Specific Example of Dealing with Death in Another Country

* Funeral Rituals in Other Religions and Cultures

Visit the *Widow's Key* companion website at www.widowskey.com. Follow the simple instructions to find your password in the book and get your extra reader-only information.

Chapter Four

ARRANGEMENTS AFTER DEATH

Whether the death occurs in a hospital, at home or far away, the loss is traumatic. While in the midst of shock and grief, you have to make decisions and arrangements for final services. After the first few hours and once the body is moved, you need notify family and friends and to begin planning the funeral or memorial service in accordance with the wishes of the deceased and dictates of your religion and society. The following sections contain outlines and checklists to help you get through the hours, days and weeks immediately following the death of your loved one.

Just take care of the most immediate tasks that you need to do right away and address the others in the weeks to come. In most cases, there really isn't any reason to rush. Be assured that after the initial blur of activity, you have plenty of time to pull yourself together, gather the information you need, weigh the options and make good decisions. Just remember, first things first.

Notify Others of the Death

You may feel pressure to get on the phone immediately and start letting others know of your husband's passing. If you need some quiet reflective time alone before facing this task, it is fine to wait a while or to ask someone else to make the first calls. You will need to notify close and extended family members, friends, family doctor, hospice, employers, social organizations, funeral home and your estate attorney. Be sure to notify your pastor, priest, rabbi or other religious leader for guidance and support.

Don't be shy about asking for help with calling and other tasks. The burden of relating the news does not have to be yours alone. Request that other reliable relatives or friends make phone calls to specific people. The job is much easier if you prepare a form in advance that lists people to call, telephone numbers and emails. If repeating the news of passing and the resurgent emotions are too difficult, tell the listener that you will talk later or turn the task over to someone else.

Grief teaches the steadiest minds to waver.   - Sophocles

Your faith, social, service and professional organization communities can help spread the word among their memberships. Sometimes you can consult with other family members and look in address books or computer files for other persons to contact. Announcements of the death can be posted through emails and in the newspaper. If possible, have one telephone number or email as the main contact for all funeral service, other necessary arrangements and questions.

Obituary – Public Announcement of Death

As part of the notification process, it is traditional to publish an obituary in the local paper and newspapers where your loved one spent significant portions of his life. A standard obituary includes a biographical outline, possibly pictures of your deceased husband and information on the date and location of the services. The usual obituary runs in a newspaper or online and announces the death. Newspapers charge for obituaries based on the length. Funeral homes will usually write and place a brief death notification at your request.

Death notices report the basic facts without including biographical information. Some newspapers publish death notices free; others charge. Better known or somehow unique people may have longer feature articles written by reporters who gather the profile information from you, family, friends and other sources.

There are a growing number of large specialized online obituary websites. They are easy to find with a search term of obituary or memorial tribute. They often include online services such as guest books, where readers offer their own memories and comments related to your deceased spouse. Be aware that you may receive a wave of ads or sites that try to take advantage of grieving families. Delete them as spam and be careful.

In your husband's obituary, the basic information must be covered accurately and completely. As well, an obituary can be a compelling story of a life. For many people, their obituary may be just about the only thing ever written about them in their whole life and death. The obituary can be the defining statement about your special loved one for the family, friends

and community. An obituary can be read now by all and saved for many generations. That historic genealogical aspect is all the more reason to make those last words lively, personal and significant.

You want to write an obituary that is accurate, memorable, does justice to the life your husband lived and avoids identity theft. An obituary text is many things in one: a notice of a death, a story of a life, a record of the extended family, relate information about a funeral service, a thank you to those who helped and a request for memorial or charitable donations.

As early as possible, begin compiling the necessary information for the obituary. Friends, family and funeral directors can help you write a proper obituary that honors your loved one. Sometimes your deceased spouse has already written his own obituary or included it in a Letter of Instruction along with other funeral wishes. However, if you are starting from scratch, here is a template for you to use as an outline, checklist or sample format for writing an obituary.

This format, from sources like obituaryguide.com, outlines what is covered in a typical obituary so that you can select what you might like to include.

OBITUARY OUTLINE:

Name and Announcement
- Full name of the deceased, including nickname, if any
- Age at death
- Residence (for example, the name of the city) at death
- Day and date of death
- Place of death
- Cause of death

Life Details
- Date of birth
- Place of birth
- Names of parents
- Childhood: siblings, stories, schools, friends
- Marriage(s): date of, place, name of spouse
- Education: school, college, university and other
- Designations, awards, and other recognition
- Employment: jobs, activities, colleagues, promotions,
- Places or locations of residence
- Hobbies, sports, interests, activities, and other enjoyment
- Charitable, religious, fraternal, political, affiliations & positions
- Achievements, unusual attributes, humor or other stories

Family -- Survived by (and city-state of residence):
- Spouse
- Children (in order of date of birth, and their spouses)
- Grandchildren
- Great-grandchildren and/or Great-great-grandchildren
- Parents
- Grandparents
- Siblings (in order of date of birth)
- Significant other or life patner
- Others, such as nephews, nieces, cousins, in-laws
- Friends
- Pets (if appropriate)

Predeceased by (and date of death):
- Spouse
- Children (in order of date of birth)
- Grandchildren

- Siblings (in order of date of birth)
- Others, such as nephews, nieces, cousins, in-laws
- Pets (if appropriate)

Services
- Day, date, time, place
- Name of officiate, pallbearers, honorary pallbearers, others
- Visitation information if applicable: day, date, time, place
- Reception information if applicable: day, date, time, place
- Other memorial, vigil, or graveside services
  if applicable: day, date, time, place
- Place of interment
- Name of funeral home in charge of arrangements
- Where to call for more information (even if no service planned)

Ending
- Memorial funds established
- Memorial donation suggestions, including addresses
- Thank you to people, groups, or institutions
- Quotation or poem
- Words that sum up the life

When you have finished writing the obituary, you should revise, edit and proofread it several times. As with any writing, revising improves the final product. This process not only spots errors, but also improves the style. Give yourself time to let a text develop. An excellent way to improve a text is to set it aside for a day, then look at it with fresh eyes, your own and someone else's. A well-written obituary is all the more reason to prepare something ahead of time, instead of rushing between the death and the funeral.

Obituary Pitfalls to Avoid:

- Making the obituary more about the people writing the
  obituary, rather than the deceased
- Making the obituary more about the death and funeral
  than about the life
- Use of clichés that make his life and information sound
  like all the other obituaries.
- Avoid the "She is walking with Jesus" or "He went home
  to be with his Lord" and clichés such as starting with "the

family regrets to announce" or "With mixed emotions
we announce the passing of our mother"
- Don't make reference to the deceased through the obituary
writers. For example, avoid saying "Dad" and instead write
about the deceased in the third person as an individual
- Avoid saying "after a courageous struggle…" Do not
describe just the final period of life and death.
- Mostly include information about the person's lifetime,
accomplishments, interests, connections to family and groups.

Sometimes it is appropriate to end an obituary or eulogy with a few memorable words to summarize the life such as: "Always entertaining, often inspiring"; "Travelled each and every highway"; "I wouldn't change it a bit"; "Supported the sublime with uncurbed enthusiasm"; "Down the trail"; "Found great happiness in insignificant details"; and even humorous "Never really finished anything, except cake." Taken from primatologist, Dr. Jane Goodall: "Forest peace, sharing vision, always optimistic".

But our golden ones sail on, sail on to another land beneath another sky.

- James Taylor

Practical Matters to Take Care of the First Few Days

Additionally, there are numerous other more immediate practical matters for you to consider and act upon while your dying spouse is hospitalized or soon after the death. Other less immediate, business and estate matters are outlined for you and discussed later. Each item on this practical checklist will have more or less relevance or importance depending on your circumstances and situation.

Following is a general checklist of the mundane, but very necessary, home and family matter chores to handle or delegate to others in the first few days and weeks after the death. Don't try to do everything yourself.

Checklist for Home and Family Matters

• Evaluate the emotional impact on yourself, family and close friends and arrange for support, privacy, quiet reflective time, rest and regular meals
• Arrange for care for pets, if any
• Notify family, friends, physician, attorney, clergy, employer, co-workers, social, sports, fraternal and professional clubs
• Contact your late husband's lawyer for special requests or additional information on last wishes
• Obtain a dozen death certificates from funeral home director
• Appoint people to handle calls and emails for information and incoming condolences
• Make arrangements for child care as necessary
• Evaluate the need and arrange for security or house sitting at the home residence, during the hospital stay and funeral services. Ask your neighbors to be vigilant for suspicious activity.
• Request police patrols during the funeral or memorial services and in the weeks that follow
• Rearrange or cancel home deliveries
• Hold mail at post office or pick up mail and newspapers
• Find perishable foods and arrange for care or disposal
• Arrange for house cleaning, housekeeping, food preparation and yardwork in anticipation of company
• Get help with travel and accommodations for out-of-town visitors
• Ask others to provide prepared meals and shopping to cover the first few weeks

• Arrange for care of indoor plants and yard work
• Organize or purchase clothing for funeral services
• Notify agent under any power of attorney or estate executor
• Notify insurance agent and Social Security Administration of the death. Details for notifications are in following sections.
• Locate the documents and information needed immediately for the death certificate and obituary
• Locate will, letter of instruction or documents held by attorney pertaining to funeral or burial
• Distribute extra floral arrangements to nursing homes, hospitals, family and others
• Pay current everyday household bills and loan payments, but consult your estate attorney before other debts are paid, benefits collected or any items are donated, distributed or given away
• Begin gathering documents and recording home and assets on dated video and with photographs for inventory and security
• Do not permit distribution of any property or assets until authorized by estate attorney or probate court
• Don't hesitate to ask for help and to delegate tasks to other responsible persons.

Chapter Five

FUNERAL AND MEMORIAL SERVICES

Funerals are the celebration and observances marking a person's life and death. A funeral is a sacred ceremony held before the burial or cremation of the body. The funeral rituals, behaviors and ceremonies vary for each culture, country and religious affiliation. The complex beliefs and practices used by people to remember and honor their dead are reflected in their funerary customs. Funeral rites are as old as human culture itself. There are examples of burials with flower and gift offerings as far back as 300,000 years ago, suggesting that even the ancient Neanderthals believed in honoring the dead.

Purposes of Services

It seems that religion plays the greatest role in how a funeral is conducted because religion deals with the spiritual concept of a human being. Since death is seen as the beginning of a spiritual journey, different religions dictate certain ceremonies and practices to help the person's spirit on their eternal path. Even though there are great cultural and religious differences in funeral services, the common purposes among funeral practices are generally to help the soul of the dead person in finding eternity and to provide emotional support to the wife, family and friends left behind.

Funerals are part of a culture's need to make a ceremony out of important times of transition. There seems to be an innate need to mark these points with personalized ceremonies. During a funeral, you and others will reflect back on the time spent with your departed loved one and begin to condition yourself to the idea that he will no longer be with you.

Cultural groups and religions' funeral rituals can be divided into three basic parts: visitation, funeral, and the burial service. It is important to acknowledge and celebrate the meaning of major events in our lives with ritual. When you wish to mark life's passages, to celebrate or to mourn and say farewell, you hold gatherings such as a funeral or memorial service.

A usually solemn ritual such as a funeral services can be an uplifting and meaningful acknowledgement of the passing of the soul. The service can have an emphasis on freeing the departing soul from the bonds of the earth, on the journey to the experience of union with the Beloved. Spiritual rituals are specifically designed to convey blessings and give comfort and understanding to you and others who loved the person who has passed.

The planning process of the funeral helps with the grieving and healing process. Even if you fear the severe test of holding up and having the strength to get through the funeral, the narcotic effects of shock and the positive movement forward generally supports you. At the funeral, you will be surrounded by the concern of others. The importance, meaning and gravity of the occasion will prevail to see you through the funeral rituals and gatherings.

There are usual steps and decisions associated with a funeral and burial or cremation preparations. Following are general guidelines, a sample checklist of funeral related decisions and then another checklist of some necessary practical things that need to be tended to right after your spouse dies. In respect for universal variation in funerals, a section describes the funerals practices, rites and ceremonies held by two mainstream religions.

Planning the Funeral

The funeral is an important life passage event, a special occasion, a production that takes planning and detailed execution. Arranging a funeral is a very emotional obligation done in a short period. It is important to realize options for the various decisions and to understand the variety of services that are available to you. If the deceased left specific funeral or burial instructions in his will or a letter of funeral instructions, locate these expressed wishes and comply as best as possible. If there was no pre-plan, you can make the necessary decisions.

Where do you begin? Funeral planning is a process often fraught with emotional stress, financial decision making and uncertainty. Without some guidance, the options and information surrounding funerals and arrangement planning can seem overwhelming at an already complicated time. In many cases, the professional funeral home and director can help you obtain death certificates, select a casket, urn or grave marker, arrange the funeral, locate cemetery property and deed, memorial service, burial service, prepare the obituary, help notify family and others and offer grief support or direct loved ones to other resources.

The average family spends approximately $10,000 on goods and services such as funeral home, cemetery and grave markers. Planning a funeral that needs to take place in a matter of days is not the time to be shopping around. This is not to say that one should not be cost conscious and make practical decisions. When purchasing a funeral, guilt and other emotions should not factor into your financial decisions. Avoid being susceptible to up-selling. Work with your funeral director as a realistic consumer.

Funeral Director

A professional funeral home can be of tremendous assistance and support. Directors have several years of studies that include microbiology, pathology, psychology, grief counseling and ethics, in addition to a two-year apprenticeship. Consoling mourners means navigating through complicated emotional territory. Funeral home directors and staff are compassionate people who are willing to do everything in their power to make this difficult time and process a little easier for you and your family

A funeral director's role is to advise you, take care of the body, work out details and coordinate the service and burial or cremation. The funeral director serves as an advisor, an administrator, a supporter, and a caregiver. When a call comes in to the funeral home that a person has died, they immediately begin arrangements. They take responsibility for the body of your loved one, and gather the necessary information needed for the legally required death certificate.

The funeral director consults with you to discuss your wishes, assure legal compliance, and arrange the observance of the customs that you desire. They coordinate the details of the funeral service and may help arrange for the clergy, music, special ceremonies, other resources, cemetery arrangements and the memorial stone or appropriate marker. The funeral director is responsible for ceremonial and administrative details and logistical matters such as transportation. The funeral director aids you and your family before and after the funeral in completing any necessary paperwork, including obituary notices, Social Security claims, veteran and insurance benefits. At a time when the emotional impact of a death makes it difficult for you to concentrate on the details of so many legal forms, you can call on and appreciate the funeral director's expertise.

Ideally, some pre-arrangements were made in advance with a known funeral home or you can get referrals from family or friends and move forward with the funeral plans right away. Many people say, "I have already told my family what I want done…they know what to do." In my experience, if wishes are not in writing, those verbal instructions may not be understood, interpreted or remembered in the same way by each person who was told those wishes. The result of verbal instructions, especially with multiple loved ones in a very stressful situation trying to assist, is similar to having multiple witnesses to an accident. Each person sees, hears, recalls and interprets the information differently. A lack of specific written instruction results in an unfortunate and unnecessary amount of family discourse and misunderstandings. When you combine family personalities, opinions, stress, and emotions, then you have the secret recipe for funeral mayhem.

Hopefully, you discussed the arrangements with you late spouse or have a written funeral plan guideline or letter of instruction to eliminate the tension and stress of your decision making. If there was no advanced planning, the following guidelines will assist you making those difficult decisions.

General Guidelines for Funeral Arrangements

Remember:
- There is no legal requirement for any funeral ceremony
- There are no legal statutes governing what kind or form any ceremony should take.
- You are not required to use a clergyman.
- The funeral service does not have to be in a licensed building it can be held in your home, garden, seaside, park or other sacred or special place.
- The only rule about a memorial service is that it should provide a loving and positive remembrance of the deceased.
- Consider using personal items like photographs, diplomas, golf clubs, art, military medals, crafts or favorite foods to reflect the person who has died.

• Using humor or even untraditional lively music can add wonderful moments to the service if they reflect the individual you are trying to memorialize.

• Create a visual life history display or presentation in a slide show, Power Point presentation or photographs.

• Find a role for children if the deceased was a special person in their lives. Young children or grandchildren can hand out flowers or programs.

• A funeral or memorial service need not be costly. There are dozens of ways to keep the cost down and still provide a perfect tribute to your loved one.

• Many communities allow "green burials" for those who want to bury loved ones in an environmentally sensitive way without using a sealed casket or concrete liner or vault. Returning quickly to the source, with burial directly in the earth, is gaining popularity.

• Services are for the living, so plan what is most meaningful and helpful to your mourning.

This all seems like a lot to consider and decide, but the funeral director and others will assist you all along the way. If there are no specific written instructions at the time of death, it is up to you or the next of kin to make the arrangements. Planning a funeral means there are many decisions to make and carry out.

Here is a series of items for you to consider and use as a checklist for funeral planning tasks.

Funeral Planning Checklist:

• Funeral home preference
• Choice of burial or cremation
• Embalming or early burial
• Check on policies for prepaid funeral insurance or death benefits
• Selection of casket, urn, grave liner, green burial linen shroud and natural casket or container
• Direct burial or cremation with no visitation and no services
• Funeral service to be held at funeral home, church, temple, mosque, indoors or out or other setting special to the deceased or family
• Obituary composition and publication in newspapers and internet online websites
• Visitation or wake beforehand

• Calling hours at funeral home
• Name of church/temple/mosque where service is to be held
• Clergy and/or celebrant for guidance and to preside over services
• Memorial cards with text, picture and perhaps an emblem of remembrance like a sprig of rosemary or posies of flowers
• Special readings, scriptures, poems
• Eulogy, tributes and memorial speakers in planned order
• Music, vocal, instrumental at visitation, funeral and burial site
• Special musical selections to personalize the service
• Open casket or closed casket
• Clothing, glasses, jewelry, affiliation pins
• Family history, photographs, video, album displays
• Floral arrangements and placement
• Items or props that reflect or represent some of the interests and accomplishments of your deceased husband
• Memorial contributions to charities or funds
• If veteran, flag on casket or folded
• If fraternal orders, social organizations, military, law enforcement or firefighter, honor brigade
• Special ceremonies
• Seating arrangements
• Ushers, program distributors, alter servers, coordinators and guest book attendant
• Names of pallbearers
• Burial services at cemetery
• Transportation to grave site and/or reception following
• Location/purchase of cemetery property and deed
• Type of property: burial, crypt, vault, mausoleum, niche, urn
• Grave marker or memorial
• Wake, reception or special gathering to celebrate the life of the deceased after the service
• Arrangement for after-service gatherings such as location, invitations, food and directions
• Accommodating out of town relatives and friends

Creative Funeral Ideas

There is no specific format for funeral or memorial services. In fact, services can be as innovative and unique as the individual. People are moving away from preconceived notions of traditional services and creating personalized services that focus on the life of the loved one rather than his death.

Today's boomers do not want cookie cutter funerals or burials. Many people are arranging different, more personalized exits. Folks want end-of-life celebrations and services that reflect their life. A personal stamp creates a memory. There are several ways to make the funeral or memorial service you are planning a creative, unforgettable and meaningful celebration of the life of your late husband. Consider using creative funeral ideas to personalize a funeral or memorial service.

Think About and Consider:
- A unique location that meant something to your husband
- Music that truly reflects the individual one you are memorializing
- Creating a true celebration of his life
- Multi-media sound and photography or video life story shows
- Including symbolic gestures like candle ceremonies
- Planning the service around a theme
- Using unique ethnic rituals in the ceremony
- New Orleans style musical parade to funeral or burial site
- Scottish bagpipes playing Amazing Grace or other tunes
- Military, law enforcement or firefighter honors, 21 gun salutes, taps, or airplane or jet fly-bys
- Providing meaningful mementoes reminiscent of your loved one to those attending the life celebration ceremony
- Other approaches specific to your culture and beliefs
- Whatever your vision of an ideal farewell might be, don't hesitate to ask the funeral director, clergy or family.

Music Types and Trends

Music is a vital element in funeral rituals. The use of music at funerals goes back to ancient times, when noisemaking and chanting were performed to drive away or pacify spirits. Beginning a funeral service with music and ending the service with music creates natural bookends for the event.

Music's universal language can be healing, calming and unifying as people gather to pay tribute to the deceased. Music has the potential to encourage, uplift, and console the grieving. Music can convey feelings and words that a community of mourners to may not be able to express. It may also provide needed hope, solace and comfort.

In a situation where you are choosing funeral music, keep in mind that the occasion is designed to help you, friends and relatives to accept the reality of the loved ones passing. Music provides an opportunity to include a song that held particular meaning during your husband's lifetime or that conveys a message of faith and hope after he has passed away.

When choosing music for funerals, keep in mind the location where the service is held. The music appropriate for a ceremony in the chapel of the funeral home may not be appropriate for a full Catholic Mass celebrated in a cathedral. The church organist or musical director may have some suggestions as to what is appropriate. The funeral director is a valuable resource about who provides the musical atmosphere and other guidance.

In the past, generally somber serious songs were played during a funeral in western cultures. Beethoven, Mozart, Bach and Chopin selections were commonly used as a musical backdrop. Organs and pianos are common instruments used to play these songs when the funeral is held in a church, private home, funeral home or nursing home chapel. Other common instruments include the violin, flute, clarinet, French horn, trumpet, saxophone and guitar.

Bagpipes are traditionally played at a veteran, military, firefighter or police officer funeral. Sometimes, if there is no one to play live music, recorded music is used. Whether played by community musicians or made available on CD or iPod, there are many options from jazz, a Bach organ concerto, a New Age harp or modern pop. To enhance an occasion, family may request a person to sing a solo or to play musical selections during the service. Even a grandchild's imperfect guitar or piano rendition of *Somewhere over the Rainbow* is likely to be forgiven when it is offered with love.

Many of the traditional songs played and sung at funerals include hymns of the particular faith. At times, the entire congregation may be asked to join in and sing a stanza or two of the song. Occasionally, soloists or choirs sing at funerals. The traditional religious songs played and sung, are:

- *Amazing Grace*
- *Jesus Loves Me*
- *The Lord's My Shepherd*
- *When the Roll is Called Up Yonder*
- *Sweet Chariot*
- *Abide in Me*
- *Be Thou My Vision*
- *I'll Walk With God*

- *The Strife is O'er*
- *O God, Our Help in Ages Past*
- *Be Not Afraid*
- *The King of Love My Shepherd Is*
- *On Eagles Wings*
- *Joyful, Joyful We Adore You*

Other classical options for funeral music include:

- *Laudate Dominum* by Wolfgang Amadeus Mozart
- *Jesu, Joy of Man's Desiring* by Johann Sebastian Bach
- *Prelude No. 1 from Book 1 of the 48* by Bach
- *Prelude No. 12 from Book 2 of the 48* by Bach
- *Moonlight Sonata* (piano), 1st movement by Beethoven
- *Symphony No. 7 in A, 2nd movement* by Beethoven
- *Prelude No. 6 or Prelude No. 7* by Chopin
- *Prelude No. 15, The "Raindrop"* by Chopin
- *Symphony 1, 3rd movement extract* by Mahler
- *Symphony 5, 4th movement extract* by Mahler
- *Song Without Words Op. 85 No. 2 - The Adieu* by Mendelssohn
- *Scherzo from "Death and the Maiden"* String Quartet by Schubert

Over the years, music has changed, and instead of the more traditional songs played at funerals, you may want to select new ones to personalize the service. According to funeral service corporations, sixty-eight percent of its branches have noted an increase in the number of requests for playing pop songs. These newer songs are often mixed with the old favorites. Some of the more popular songs of today performed at funerals include:

- *Wind Beneath My Wings* by Bette Midler
- *I Will Remember You* by Sarah McLachlan or Amy Grant
- *One More Day* by Diamond Rio
- *I Can Only Imagine* by Mercy Me
- *My Heart Will Go On*, theme song from *Titanic*, by Celine Dion
- *I Will Always Love You*, Whitney Houston song by Dolly Parton
- *What a Wonderful World* or *When The Saints Come Marching In* by Louis Armstrong
- *Bridge Over Troubled Water* by Simon and Garfunkel
- *Have I Told You Lately That I Love You* by Rod Stewart
- *May It Be* or *Only Time* by Enya
- *I Hope You Dance* by Lee Ann Womack
- *Field of Gold* by Sting
- *To Where You Are* by Josh Groban
- *Let It Be* by the Beatles
- *The Gift That You Are* or *Annie's Song* by John Denver
- *The Prayer* or *Time to Say Goodbye* by Andrea Bocelli/Celine Dion

Songs with humorous lyrics are even finding their places in modern funerals. You may want to pay tribute to your loved one by adding something less conventional as a way of honoring and personalizing the service. Those who have been ill for any length of time before death, often select songs they desire to have played at their funeral. Depending on their age, musical tastes and mood, they may choose something light and fun. *Another One Bites the Dust*, by the British band, Queen, is one such song. My uncle Elmo wanted Fats Waller jazz records from his collection played at his funeral.

While funeral songs can be joyful, there are times when a loved one will write his or her own song in memory of the deceased. Sir Elton John personalized *Candle in the Wind* for Princess Diana of Wales' funeral in 1997. Following suit, those with musical talent may write and play songs especially created for their loved one.

Bagpipe Music

Bagpipe music tends to tug at one's heartstrings when played at a funeral. Scottish, Irish and English pipers can add a special touch to a funeral. Bagpipe music is especially appropriate at the funeral of an armed forces, veteran, firefighter or police officer. Here are suggestions for bagpipe music at such a funeral: *Amazing Grace, Dark Isle, Danny Boy, or Flowers of the Forest.*

Jazz Funerals of New Orleans

In the United States, there is a unique funeral tradition that originated in New Orleans, Louisiana. The tradition combines French musical traditions, African spiritual practices and African-American cultural influences. The jazz funeral typically begins with a jazz band, the family and friends marching to the cemetery, starting from the home, funeral home, or church. The band plays solemn dirges on the way to the graveyard.

Once the final burial ceremony has taken place, the funeral march continues from the cemetery to a gathering place. The somber music is replaced by loud, upbeat, raucous music and dancing. This dance is known as the "second line" because onlookers are invited to join the celebrants in a dance-march to celebrate the life of the deceased. The dancers frequently raise their hats and umbrellas brought along as protection from intense New Orleans weather and wave handkerchiefs above their heads; hankies that are no longer being used to wipe away tears.

Guide to Funeral Flowers

It has long been customary to send flowers as a symbol of respect for the dead and solace for the family. Floral arrangements add brightness and beauty to an emotional solemn event. Any type of flowers can be sent for memorial and funeral tributes. However, there are certain flowers that are more popular and commonly used in arrangements, sprays and wreaths.

Chrysanthemums are used worldwide in funeral floral arrangements, with white being the most popular color, denoting truth and honesty. Also, mums can be sprayed any color that is specifically requested. Carnations are also traditional funeral flowers due to their great visual appeal, especially when massed. However, they are more expensive than chrysanthemums, so are not included as often.

Because of their timeless beauty, roses are a very popular funeral flower. Red roses are the most traditional flower used, followed by white, yellow and pink. Another traditional funeral flower is the lily. White longiflorum lilies in its trumpet shape, Cali lily and other types of lilies are often found in arrangements.

The floral tribute decision should reflect your heartfelt personal feelings for the deceased and your choice should send a sincere and appropriate message. Note that it is considered inappropriate to send flowers to a Jewish funeral, since they see flowers as a symbol of happiness.

Sometimes people send live plants that can you can take home or give to family, attendees or donated to nursing homes, hospice, military care centers or hospitals. If donations were requested for specific organizations or charities in lieu of flowers, you generally receive a notification from the charity as to who made the donation.

> While we are mourning the loss of our friend, others are rejoicing to meet him behind the veil.
>
> - John Taylor

Eulogy - Finding the Right Words

The word *eulogy* comes from Greek, literally meaning 'words of praise'. Eulogies are a common form of memorializing your loved one at a funeral service. A eulogy's intent is to show respect for your deceased spouse and show sympathy for the feelings of those in the audience. As the widow, you may choose to give part of the eulogy or ask others to speak in honor of the life lost.

A eulogy doesn't have to follow the formal rules of speech making. The person who delivers a eulogy is usually not accustomed to speaking in front of an audience, and it may be especially difficult since they are in mourning. Therefore, no one is expecting a eulogy to be particularly eloquent or perfect. Some of the best eulogies are conversational and rambling. It is the personal and sincere memorial that makes a eulogy good and memorable. It is important to be as open and honest as possible. At many funerals it is the touching eulogy that folks remember the most.

Elements of Writing and Presenting a Eulogy

Following are some basic elements of writing and presenting a eulogy that you or other presenters might want to consider as a starting point:

1. Gather material by talking to other close relatives and friends, looking through memorabilia and photographs, walking through the house and yard and identifying your loved one's unique interests and qualities. Take note of hobbies, life's passions, special sayings, poems, or songs, characteristic gestures, habits or stories. Remember humorous items like his insatiable love of chocolate, sports playoffs or voracious reading.

From this research, prepare a chronological outline of the deceased loved one's life. Write as you would speak, avoiding a formal written speech. Consider using notes only in presentation in order to avoid a stilted unnatural verbatim reading.

2. The eulogy needs a flexible outline that includes a beginning introduction, middle life portrait and a conclusion that ties all your themes together and a final farewell. There should be a distinct purpose to each section. A good eulogy should take no longer than five to ten minutes.

3. In the introduction, welcome and thank people for attending this celebration of your late husband's life. Introduce yourself and the immediate family. Present the theme of your eulogy with a quote or theme such as: "My husband, though outstanding in his professional life, defined his success by a life well-lived with his family and friends" or "Alexander was a natural born leader" or "Micheal was a man nobody can replace...at least not in my heart" or "Bruce was a positve funny type of guy you couldn't get enough of" or "Frank was a loving partner and faithful friend." The introduction and conclusion need to be brief and powerful.

4. In the main body of the eulogy, briefly outline a portrait life history. Note three or four standout qualities and accomplishments of the deceased, then illustrate with examples or short anecdotes. What makes you proud to have known such a man? What touching event sticks in your mind that represents his individuality?

What things did other people tell you about the deceased that resonated with you? Don't just say that he was a good father or hard-working; show that trait through a story or example. Praise and honor your spouse in a caring and honest manner. The eulogy should be both uplifting and inspiring.

5. It's okay to very briefly mention some negative quality of your late husband, if handled very judiciously. In some eulogies, this will add levity to the funeral proceedings and will make the good points more plausible if done tastefully and affectionately. Some of the best memorial services are filled with fond remembrances and laughter.

If possible, you can even use his own words, such as regrets he had or things he admitted he could have improved on. Something like how he could never get the BBQ cooking times right, but everyone ate his well-done steaks without complaint. The idea is to provide a true account of who the man was, and why you loved him. There is no need to assign sainthood. Do not make it a complaint session.

6. Relate two or three good stories that illustrate some of the best qualities or even finest moments of your loved one. Recollect some memories that stand out and highlight your themes. How did you first meet? What did he do that made other people happy? What did you most admire? What was the funniest thing that ever happened between you? What was the best or strongest thing he ever said or accomplished? Use quotes or short stories told to you or shared by friends and relatives.

7. Some of the simplest thoughts are deeply touching and resonate to all present. What will you always remember or miss most? "I'll miss that mischievous smile of his", "I'll always remember his contagious laughter", or "I'll sure miss those corny jokes" or "Who could forget those songs in his wonderful tenor voice?"

8. In the conclusion, you want to make your last words count. Tie all the themes together with a last story, poem or quote and end with a final farewell. For example, "My dear husband, you will always be remembered and you will always live in our hearts. I love you so much"; "You will be forever missed and forever loved"; Good night sweet prince"; "If love could have kept you here, you would never have gone", or "Loving you was easy."

People will not expect a eulogy to be perfectly delivered. The most important thing is that the speaker give it straight from the heart. Just remember to practice, practice, practice beforehand and to breathe. You might even stray from the speech you initially wrote if you feel moved by the moment. Others certainly understand if your voice cracks or if you break down. If you do choke up or cry during the eulogy, just take a moment to compose yourself and then carry on. If you find you are unable to recover, ask someone ahead of time to be ready to step in and finish from your notes. There is no wrong way to deliver a heartfelt, honest memorial for someone you love and who was loved by those listening.

Funeral Celebrants

A new trend at funerals is the use of professional certified Funeral Celebrants. The Funeral Celebrant's mission is to create a ceremony that reflects the wishes, beliefs, cultural background and values, both religious and non-religious, of your loved one and your family. A Celebrant funeral honors death and especially celebrates life. Ceremony specialists have a sound background in the history of ritual, ceremony and funeral traditions.

Funeral homes are now seeing the necessity of having someone available, either on staff or on contract, qualified to serve families that do not wish to use a clergy person or wish to supplement the services with a joyful celebration of life. They are recognizing the need to provide you with the opportunity for a funeral service that makes the life of your loved one significant, worthy of honor and helps families bond and heal. The celebrant fee is usually comparable to the fees charged by clergy for performing a funeral. The price ranges depending on your choices.

Funeral Celebrants have been drawn to this work by a strong realization that every life has meaning and deserves to be celebrated and celebrated well. Many have experienced grief themselves. All are convinced that funerals can be a valuable source of healing. Nothing can take away the grief, but a genuine, well-prepared tribute may ease the pain.

A Celebrant offers a personalized service for families either in addition to or in place of a traditional religious service. They have a wide library of resources for readings, music and other special ceremonies to help you design a special service. For those who may not be active in a church or synagogue, a funeral Celebrant trains to conduct a meaningful funeral service or tribute that reflects your deceased spouse's beliefs and lifestyle.

The Celebrant creates a very personalized ceremony after learning about the deceased in meetings with you or designated family and friends. Their job is to provide a funeral service personalized to reflect the personality and life-style of your loved one. A celebrant will incorporate those unique stories, songs and experiences of a loved one into the service.

In collaboration with you, your Celebrant will carefully craft a eulogy and create a ceremony with music, quotes, readings, unique symbols and rituals. No ceremony is delivered unless every detail of the eulogy and ceremony is checked and approved by you.

Then, with sincerity, compassion and great care, the Celebrant officiates at the ceremony at the location of your choice. After the funeral, the Celebrant may present you and your family with a beautiful copy of the ceremony as a keepsake.

Memorial Services

The memorial service is a time to focus on the memory of someone special to you who has died. It is a service given for the deceased loved one often without the body present, and as such, is often more convenient because the timing can be delayed to meet the travel needs or convenience of the family and friends wishing to honor the deceased.

Memorial services may take place after an earth burial, donation of the body to an institution such as a school, cremation, entombment, or burial at sea. Typically, services take place at the funeral home and may include prayers, poems, or songs to remember the deceased. Pictures of the deceased are usually placed at the altar where the body in the coffin or funeral urn would normally be.

Often memorial services are held when an object such as a gravestone, war memorial, landmark, memorial plaque, work of art, statue, sculpture, park, garden, scholarship or other object is dedicated to the deceased spouse.

After the sudden deaths of important public officials, victims of war or crimes, or well- known personalities, public memorial services have been held by government entities or communities, with or without any direct connection to the deceased. A state funeral is a public funeral ceremony, conducted under strict rules of protocol, held to honor heads of state or other important people of national significance. Generally, state funerals or memorial services are held in order to involve the general-public in a national day of mourning. For instance, memorial or state services have been held around the country after the John F. Kennedy or Martin Luther King, Jr.'s assassinations, deaths of other former presidents like Ronald Reagan or Gerald Ford, for Princess Diana of Wales, for the victims of September 11th or victims of school shootings, and for music icons like Elvis Presley or Michael Jackson.

In some cultures and religions, there are designated religious memorial services held on certain days and dates after the death. In Buddhism, for example, the family, friends and priests gather in prayer on the third, seventh, forty-ninth and one hundredth day to gain and transfer merits to the deceased to enable him to be reborn into the realms of happiness.

Requiem Mass

Mass for the deceased loved one, Requiem or Requiem Mass is a liturgical service of the Roman Catholic Church, the Eastern Orthodox and Eastern Catholic Church and certain Lutheran churches. The various texts request the repose of the loved one's soul and ask for eternal rest and absolution. Mass is often celebrated in the context of a funeral or is celebrated during a regular liturgy. Today the original black colored alter cloths and priest vestments have been replaced with purple in requiems. The Requiem Mass has inspired numerous musical compositions, such as the famous requiems of Faure, Verdi and Mozart.

Living Funeral

A Living Funeral is similar to a regular funeral, except that it revolves around someone who is terminally ill or will soon die. A 'family reunion' or 'celebration of life' is arranged while the person you care about is still alive and in attendance. Too often some of the most sincere and loving words are said at a funeral after the person has passed away and cannot hear them. Many funeral attendees express the sentiment that they wished they had the chance to tell him in person how special and loved he was while he was still alive. It can be very important to the dying person's psychological state and that of the person's family.

Therefore, the living funeral is held as a celebration of someone's life. It gives family and friends the opportunity to celebrate together and pay tribute. It can be a loving and uplifting way of showing appreciation and saying goodbye. Living funerals aren't meant to be sad and emotional. Living funerals often include: Power Point, slide shows or displaying photographs and mementoes; Participants remembering loving and funny times and stories; Spoken or written messages of friendship and love; and Sincere, reflective and humorous tributes. Services can be held anywhere such as a park, church community hall, chapel, home backyards, or clubrooms.

This living funeral reunion or gathering with your terminal family member or husband is a way to assemble the family and friends before the somber occasion of a funeral takes place. A famous living funeral was the one for Morrie Schwartz documented in the book and film *Tuesdays with Morrie*. While a living funeral is not for everyone, it is a growing trend that provides an opportunity to celebrate someone's life without unspoken words or regrets later.

> It is never good dwelling on goodbyes. It is not the being together that it prolongs, it is the parting.
> - Elizabeth Charlotte Lucy Bibescu

Funerals in Religious and Cultural Contexts

The following are summary examples of how two main religions, Jewish and Christians conduct traditional funerals. You can find more information on last rites, worldwide funeral rituals and other religious and cultures treatments of widows at www.widowskey.com.

Jewish Funerals

It is Jewish tradition for the burial to take place as soon as possible, even on the same day of the death, but no more than two nights after the death. Therefore, in this short timeframe, it is necessary for a Jewish widow to know what is required for a proper Judaic funeral. The first task when a Jewish person passes away is to contact the rabbi and the *Hevra Kadisha* or Holy Committee burial society. Representatives of the *Hevra Kadisha* will arrange for transporting your husband's body to conduct the burial preparations at their own facility or at a funeral home.

Tradition dictates that his body be covered with a sheet and that someone should stay with him at all times. This watchful guard, called a *shomer,* can be family members or others who know the person. Trained volunteer members of the *Hevra Kadisha* will bathe and dress his body with respect and care. There are three major stages to prepare a body for burial: washing (*rechitzah*), ritual purification (*taharah*), and dressing (*halbashah*). Blessings, prayers, and readings from Torah, and other Jewish scripture may be recited at several points. His body is uncovered, washed, thoroughly cleaned. The body is purified with water then dressed in simple clothing or a burial cloth with a sash tied in the form of the Hebrew letter *shin* representing the name of God.

According to Jewish law, embalming is not allowed, so no chemical of natural agents will be used to preserve your loved one's body. The only other item that may be buried along with your husband is a prayer shawl with one of the corner fringes cut to signify that it will no longer be used for prayer in life. Nothing of value is buried with the deceased. These burial customs reaffirm the irrelevance of wealth and stature in life, and enable a natural returning of his body to the earth.

The coffin, if there is a coffin, is prepared by removing any lining and other embellishments. Your late husband's body is then lifted into the untreated coffin and wrapped in the prayer shawl and a sheet. Soil from Israel, if available, is placed over various parts of his body and sprinkled in the coffin. Once he is dressed and in place, the coffin is sealed. Unlike other religions, in Judaism there is no viewing of his body and no open casket at the funeral, though you and the immediate family are allowed a visitation just prior to the coffin being sealed to pay final respects. Caskets are not used at all in Israel, with the exception of military and state funerals.

Funeral services take place at a funeral home, synagogue or at the gravesite. Many Jewish funerals are held entirely at the graveside. A rabbi or cantor will be the funeral officiate, preferably one who knew your husband and led the synagogue where he was a member. Generally, the rabbi will lead the funeral prayers, deliver a eulogy and organize the participation of you and other family members in the service.

The service begins with the rabbi cutting a black ribbon to symbolize your late husband breaking away from loved ones. A *minyan* of at least 10 Jewish adults, traditionally males, is required to recite prayers. Male guests are expected to wear a jacket and tie with a yarmulke as a head covering, which is available at the funeral home or synagogue. Women wear conservative apparel, a skirt or dress of somber colors, but they are not expected to wear a head covering. Mourners may recite the *Kaddish* prayer. A symbolic tear, called a *keriah*, can be made in your or other mourner's clothes, to symbolize a broken heart. To keep things as simple as possible, no flowers are brought or sent to the funeral. Rather, making a donation to a charity or organization is appreciated.

The funeral itself, the procession and the burial, are referred to by the word *levayah*, meaning 'accompanying.' *Levayah* means accompaniment because the funeral procession involves accompanying your loved one's body to his place of burial. It also indicates joining and bonding between the souls of the living and the dead. When his coffin is taken to the graveside in a Jewish cemetery, it is considered a great honor to shovel soil or gravel on top of the coffin to symbolize the acceptance of the finality of death. At the cemetery, more prayers are read. The Jewish insist on burial, also known as interment, to allow the body to decompose naturally, as the soul ascends to Heaven. Cremation is not considered a viable possibility.

Families have a customary meal after the funeral, called a *seudat havra'ah*, meal of consolation. It is traditional for the synagogue members, extended family or friends to arrange the meal for you and the other mourners. A pitcher of water, a basin and towel placed outside the front door of your home or outside the cemetery, is to be used by those returning from the funeral before they enter your home. Hard-boiled eggs are part of the consolation meal to symbolize the cyclical nature of life.

Additionally, this is the time that you light a large candle to burn in your home for the next week as you and your family sit *shivah*, a strict mourning period. In Jewish tradition, the period of mourning does not officially begin until the coffin is lowered into the ground and covered with dirt.

Seven immediate family members, the mother, father, son, daughter, brother and sister, and husband and wife, are expected to directly observe *shivah*, a mourning period of seven days after the funeral. During these seven days, the widow and other bereaved family members are not to wear leather shoes, shave, get haircuts, bathe, wear make up or use perfume, and no marital relationships are to take place.

Jewish families will also cover mirrors, burn memorial candles, or wear the cut black ribbon from the funeral. This break from daily routine symbolizes the disruption that death has brought to your life and demonstrates grief through self-sacrifice. Traditionally an official year of mourning occurs, and during this year, certain communities will have special customs that will take place.

Christian Funeral

It has been estimated that there are over 200 Christian denominations. Therefore, funeral rituals may differ from church to church. Generally, Christians believe in resurrection and the continuation of the soul, usually dependent on how the Christian person's life was lived.

In preparation for burial, the body of your late husband is prepared and preserved by embalming. His body may be dressed in uniforms, favorite outfits, ceremonial or best clothes and some jewelry to present him looking his best. It was a custom for years to bury men in their wedding suits or women in their wedding dress. Judy Garland was buried in the silver lame gown she had worn at her last wedding. At times, there are inclusions of grave goods like religious sacred objects, favorite items or photographs.

In the Christian faith the body is placed in a coffin or casket, which is in turn placed inside a burial vault in the cemetery. If the burial is a green funeral, the deceased person is wrapped in a linen shroud and placed in a wicker casket or placed directly in the ground without a liner. Christian burials are usually positioned extended, lying flat with arms and legs straight or with the arms folded across the chest and with the eyes and mouth closed. Historically, burials were positioned east-west, with the head at the west end of the grave in order to put the deceased in a position to view the coming of Christ on judgment day.

Over one third of Americans are cremated, not buried, and that trend is on a sharp increase. If your deceased husband is to be cremated, there may be no embalming process or coffin. You can request or rent a symbolic casket for the funeral service only. At the cremation, the incinerated body is reduced to ashes. The ash remains are placed in an urn for the services or interment.

During the visitations the day before the funeral, you may ask that the coffin be open so that family and friends can say goodbye to their loved one at a funeral home. Before the coffin is closed, you and the immediate family and their spouses and children are sometimes the very last to view your loved one. This opportunity can take place immediately before the funeral service begins, or at the very end of the service.

During the funeral and at the burial service, the casket may be covered with a large arrangement of flowers, called a casket spray. If your husband served in a branch of the Armed Forces, his casket can be covered with a national flag. Nothing should cover the national flag according to Title 4, United States Code, Chapter 1, paragraph 8i. The coffin is left at the funeral home or transported to a church, chapel or crematorium in a hearse, which is a specialized vehicle designed to carry casketed remains.

A funeral, held according to your choosing, may be from a few days to a week or so after the time of death, allowing family members to gather from various locations to attend the service. A funeral usually takes place at either a funeral home or church. A memorial or funeral service is often officiated by clergy from the decedent's or bereaved family's church or religion. At the designated location a minister or priest will read from the Bible or other inspiration works and offer words of comfort to the mourners.

Funeral services commonly include prayers; scriptural readings, other sacred texts or peotry; and meaningful hymns sung either by the attendees or a hired vocalist. Grief, tears and mourning is openly expressed at a Christian funeral. Testimonials and prayers including a rosary, ask for the soul's acceptance into in heaven.

Frequently, the clergy, you as the widow, a relative or close friend will give a eulogy, which details the decedent's life, happy memories and accomplishments. Family members or friends are often invited to say a few additional parting words about the loved one. These personal tributes are designed to commemorate his life and give comfort to the family and loved ones. Anecdotal stories, some humorous, to illustrate his qualities and achievements are common, however, commenting on his flaws, especially at length, is considered impolite.

In the United States, at a funeral, modest dark or muted colored clothes are traditionally worn out of respect for the solemn occasion. For men, a black suit is worn as a sign of grief. Some widows will occasionally request that attendees wear the deceased's favorite color or bright clothes as a celebration of his life. Noise, other than whispers, is considered disrespectful.

Family members often prepare videos of the deceased's life, photograph memorials, albums, special music and prized possessions, items or floral arrangements to be shared at the service. A common tradition is that attendees sign a guest book kept by the family to record who attended.

After the funeral service, the deceased loved one is usually transported to the burial site in a procession, called a funeral cortege, with the hearse, funeral service vehicles, and private automobiles traveling in a procession to the church or other location where the various services will be held. In a number of jurisdictions, special laws cover funeral processions, such as requiring other vehicles to give right-of-way to a funeral procession. Funeral service escort vehicles may be equipped with light bars and special flashers to increase their visibility on the roads. They may also all have their headlights on, to identify which vehicles are in the cortege.

After the funeral service, if the deceased is to be buried the funeral procession will proceed to a cemetery if not already there. If he is to be cremated the funeral procession may then proceed to the crematory. Sometimes the burial or cremation takes place the day after the funeral services and is attended by only immediate family. Funerals are often followed by a reception or meal at your home or the home of a close family friend, restaurant, church or meeting hall.

If your loved one was cremated there are different ways to memorialize his passing. Most ashes are kept at home or later scattered in a place close to the heart of the deceased. New trends and unique farewells include companies turning the ashes into a gem similar to creating synthetic diamonds for jewelry or blasting the ashes into outer space as they did to honor Jimmy Doohan, the actor who played Scotty on Star Trek. Eternal Reefs mixes ashes into an environmentally safe sphere ball and places it in the ocean to create a new marine habitat. Space Services can launch cremated remains into suborbital flight or arrange for a lunar burial. Creative Cremains packs remains into musical instruments, fishing rods or golf club shafts.

As mentioned, folks today do not want overly-traditional unoriginal funerals or burials. Many spouses are arranging more personalized services and memorials. The end-of-life celebrations and services reflect their loved one's unique life and personal signature to create a lasting memory.

Chapter Six

WIDOWS OF THE WORLD--THE WIDOW'S CLUB

At the moment of your husband's death, your life will never be the same again. In an instant you have been involuntarily drafted into an international group you did not want to join, the 'Widow's Club.' One day you are married and the next day you are single. When filling out forms you have to check 'widow' next to your marital status and 'deceased' next to your late husband's name. There is no more 'we' or 'us' in the present or future tense. Realizing the end of a relationship is a gradual process of extracting the 'I' from a vanishing 'we'. You have entered widowhood.

Widowhood: There is a word with only one definition and no synonym. That word is *widow*. A widow is defined as a woman whose spouse has died. The state of having lost one's husband to death is termed widowhood or occasionally viduity. Widow, vedove, viuda, veuve, witwe…all are words derived from the Indo-European base meaning 'to separate'. Widows are all too familiar with the sense of separation by death, because the nature of a marriage is for individuals to fuse. Many marriage vows include the words "two shall become one." You ache for the loss of your other half. Many widows describe themselves as incomplete. Additionally, the word widow in Sanskrit even translates as 'empty'.

Statistically speaking, death of a spouse will happen to over eighty percent of women in their lifetime. You are now suddenly a widow on your own in the real world trying to reconcile yourself to what has happened. Through no fault of your own, you are thrust into a strange group of women and into a role, you don't want to play. Adjusting to the unwelcome status, title and image is one of the first obstacles you face as a new widow. Life is taking a different course, one that you would not have chosen. The life that is wanted and familiar is replaced by that which is unwanted and unfamiliar. The very word 'widow' seems to conjure up harsh mental images of sorrow, grief, mourning, loneliness and poverty. Becoming a widow is a challenging journey in any language or culture. It doesn't have to be this way. From this point forward, you have a 'new normal'. You are now a widow and part of the universal Widow's Club.

Sadly, widowhood is not only a label assigned to a surviving wife, but is a social status as well. The traditional stigmas attached to widows persist. Unlike other bereavement-based statuses, this one is a permanently altered and can sometimes be a degraded social position. As is the case with all social statuses, there are normative patterns to its timing and behavioral expectations. In death-denying and couple-based cultures, there is a certain stigma to being widowed, one which is amplified by the fact that it is a status typically occupied by females.

Two reasons that over eighty percent of all women will be widows are the general pattern of older males marrying younger females and the females' eight or more years of life expectancy advantage. These facts often guarantee that a woman copes with the dying and death of a spouse, including the range of emotions associated with grief, and with singleness in a world of couples. In fact, widows often find themselves neither in the world of singles or of married.

As personal as your pain and as isolated as you may feel at the time, you are not alone in this state of widowhood. Death of a loved one occurs in everyone's life, regardless of nationality, race, creed, gender, and chronological age, level of education, wealth, vocation, religious beliefs or philosophy. Let's find out who the members of the Widow's Club are.

International Studies on Widows

The United Nations published a 2010 comprehensive research study called *Invisible, Forgotten Sufferers: The Plight of Widows around the World*. Cherie Blair, wife of the former British prime minister and Loomba Foundation president, declared, "At least 245 million women in the world have been widowed and more than 115 million of them live in devastating poverty. The plight of widows as an ostracized and disenfranchised group is a human rights catastrophe."

"On one hand, there are the humanitarian problems of abject poverty and widespread violence against women and children. However, on another, it is about the rights and role of women in certain societies, where their marginalization and dehumanization create environments that perpetuate abuse. Additionally, there are over 500 million dependent children of widows caught in the vicious cycle of disease, forced servitude, homelessness, and violence. Youngsters are denied schooling, enslaved or preyed upon by human traffickers." In these type situations, misery is heaped on grief.

"Across the globe, widows suffer dreadful discrimination and abuse. When their husbands die, some women are erroneously accused of murder, witchcraft, some are forced to marry another member of the family, many are disinherited and forced out of their homes and many are raped", said Blair asking the UN to officially recognize International Widows Day.

The respected Raj and Veena Loomba Foundation and charity, working with the United Nations bodies and leaders, are dedicated to fighting for the over 245 million widows worldwide who suffer dreadful prejudice and discrimination. They believe that gross injustices against widows could be reduced by promoting gender sensitive reform of national laws and policies; eradicating anti-widow superstitions, traditions and social practices; promoting gender equality and internatioal women's empowerment; implementing poverty reduction strategies; and promoting opportunities for the education of widows and their children.

"The world needs to pause and think of those innumerable faceless, nameless women who are forced to lead severely disadvantaged lives for no fault of their own. And then, perhaps, they would finally become the focus of some much-needed policy-making," says Raj Loomba. Evidence of the socio-economic and psychological vulnerability of widows will hopefully challenge many updated views about this invisible group.

Statistics on Widows

Statistics reveal eighty percent (80%) of all women in the world become widows. Forty five percent (45%) of women are widowed by age 65. Widowhood is significant everywhere in the world, from forty percent (40%) in developed countries to fifty percent (50%) in Africa and Asia. Almost everywhere around the world, widows comprise a significant segment of women, with reports ranging from 7 per cent to 16 per cent of all adult women. There are an estimated 245 million widows in the world, with at least 43 million in China and 42.4 million in India and 13.6 million in the United States alone.

In turn, widows are responsible for the lives of at least three or four others, including children and dependents. The proportion of widows within countries or regions varies with fertility levels, mortality rates, differences in age at marriage and patterns of remarriage.

Wherever there are conflicts, there are widows, many of whom are refugees. Two million Afghan widows and at least 740,000 Iraqi widows who have lost their husbands because of the ongoing conflicts face dire consequences. The Iraq War alone generates 100 widows every day. In Africa, the AIDS epidemic is leaving thousands of women widowed and their husbands' families can legally take their assets so they are left destitute.

Even in prosperous countries like Finland, Germany, United States and France, widows live in greatly strained circumstances, surviving for the most part on modest pensions or Social Security. Widows in other parts of the world figure among the most deprived sections of society, with little legal protections and few safety nets, whether they live in Syria or Somalia, Ireland, Canada or Israel. In all parts of the world, widows suffer discrimination and abuse. In too many cases they are pushed to the margins of society, trapped in poverty and vulnerable to abuse and exploitation.

United States Widows Statistics

According to the U. S. Census Bureau, the National Academy of Science and American Association of Retired Persons (AARP), approximately 800,000 American women become widows each year. Among people 65 and older, widows accounted for forty-five percent (45%) of the population in 2008; Thirty-two percent (32%) of women aged 55 and older are widows; while nine (9%) of men aged 55 and older are widowers. There are approximately 13.6 million widows in the United States, that is about one out of every five women over the age of twenty-one. Almost half of all women over the age of 65 will become widows. Eight out of ten married women are going to be widows, outliving their husbands by several years.

There are usually four times as many widows as widowers. Approximately 350,000 men annually experience the death of a spouse in the United States. Widowers on the average will remarry within one to three years of the death of their wives, while most widows tend be widows for an average of 14 years and remarry within five to fifteen years, if ever. Remarriage rates are lower for women partially because there are fewer available men in the appropriate age range. As baby boomers age (currently 43 million people nationwide are ages 55 to 74) the death rate and widowhood will increase significantly.

With instability in the world, we are experiencing death from more unusual causes like accidents, pandemics, natural disasters, crimes, war, and unrest in the country. Currently accidents are the fifth leading cause of death in the U.S. The demographic of death and numbers of widows is huge and soaring. The Social Security Administration reports that each year around one million Americans lose their spouses.

Widowhood can happen to married women of all ages. People are always surprised to find that the average widow in the United States is in her early fifties and that she is everywoman. Becoming a widow is a frightening prospect at any age. Widowhood is a very common experience in the life cycle of contemporary Americans, as well as in other countries. Given some thought, we all know someone who is a widow.

> All my work, my life, everything is about survival. All my work is meant to say, you may encounter many defeats, but you must not be defeated.
>
> - Maya Angelou

Myths and Facts about Widowhood

Until recently, lack of data concerning widows contributed to the persistence of certain misconceptions about the prevalence and condition of widowhood. For the first time myths about widowhood are being challenged by the international community. Two prevailing myths in particular being called into question: The first is that widows are elderly women whose children are fully-grown and the other myth is that widows can rely on extended family networks for financial and emotional support. Facts and experience show that these old perceptions are not true now or in history. Widowhood is more widespread and penetrating than it seems on the surface. Additionally, in many countries millions of widows are discriminated against and treated inhumanly. Findings reveal that the cruelties and biases meted out to these women are ordained in the names of religious beliefs and social practices. Example of these practices can be seen in the touchingly realistic Dharan Mandrayar film, *White Rainbow* or the movie *Water*. Studies only confirmed the widespread perception that widows in the 21st century get a worse deal than other women do.

Universal Status of Widowhood

The international and national studies and statistics about widows have been included here to emphasis that widowhood matters. You are not alone. You share in this universal status of widowhood with at least two hundred and fifty-four million of your female sisters who have lost their spouses. Most widows are comforted when they can connect with others in the same all too human struggles. There are surprising similarities and shocking differences in how becoming a widow affects you.

Cultural practices throughout history regarding widows can teach us the many ways in which all human beings, all cultures and civilizations, are alike and connected. Widows all wonder about the meaning of life, love, tragedy, and what if anything happens after they or their spouse dies. They have different answers to the eternal questions, and people invent different political and social forms to order their brief and toilsome time on this earth. All widows deal with the consequences regarding health, mortality, financial security, psychological well-being and social relations. At the foundation of it all, widows share a special common bond.

Common Elements in Religions Regarding Widows

Widowhood has been present since the beginnings of time. All societies and organized religions have some instructions and dictates about the treatment of widows and orphans. Examples of overall religious similarities are provisions such as guidelines for behavior, sound basic rules to live by, as well as a rational mind to learn how and when to apply those rules to our everyday life. Most all cultures and religions abhor murder, the arbitrary killing of innocent people. Similarly, there are mandates to tell the truth and not to take from others what rightfully belongs to them. People are to respect the dignity of every person and to help especially those who are not capable of helping themselves, such as widows, orphans, and the poor.

Many religions have a version of the "Golden Rule": doing to others what we wish others to do to us. Most religions foster modesty, moderation, and honest work and link religion and morality. Religion manifests by showing concern for the well-being and dignity of others, in a life of service to others, and in personal and social ethical behavior. Religions have more basic concepts in common than differences.

Christianity, Islamic, Hinduism and Buddhism are unquestionably the largest religions. Most lists of major religions also include Judaism, Sufi and Sikh and other religions that only number in the many millions because of their historic relevance. Many of the customs, biases and discriminations meted out to widowed women are dictated by religious belief, tradition and social practices. When people are comparing religions and cultures, they tended to focus on the differences between them. That type of comparison only emphasizes the distance between religions. It is not just Judaism, Christianity, and Islam, the so-called Abrahamic religious heritage, who have common roots and many common elements. Almost every form of religion or spiritual practice has similarities and common elements, especially where it comes to widows and orphans.

Ancient Scriptures and Texts about Widows

The earliest Hebrew writing contains inscriptions dating from King David's reign in the 10th century B.C. The ancient text written on a small piece of pottery reads, *Plead for the infant, plead for the poor and the widow.*

In Old Testament, Judaism has always recognized the special needs of the widow and orphan as among the helpless in society. *You shall not ill-treat any widow or orphan.* (Exodus 22:21) *Defend the cause of the widow.* (Isaiah 1:17) The support of the widows was a charity and they were to have gleanings of the cornfields, olive trees and vineyards. (Deuteronomy 24:19-22) There were bitter denunciations of their oppressors. Biblical widows such as Tamar, Naomi, Ruth and Abigail are studies of triumph, hope, love and courage respectively.

The life of the widow in the Old Testament was generally a hard one, and Christ refers to the widow's mite as an offering from the poorest of the poor. (Mark 12:44) There are numerous other references to widows in the New Testament. The support of widows was a special duty by the Apostles, who collected alms for them. *Pure and lasting religion means that we must care for orphans and widows in their troubles.* (James 1:17)

The Islamic Koran texts offer guides for a husband to leave adequate provision for the wife's maintenance after his death. (Surah 2 Al-Baqarah 240). The Koran allows remarriage of widows if they wait four months and ten days before they remarry. It wasn't until 2004 that second, third and fourth Muslim wives in a polygamous marriage could make legal claims to the estate of the deceased husband. Hindu Veda scriptures, philosophy and the patriarchal cultural support the loss of social and religious status for widows. There are laws that forbid child marriage and sati, sacrificing of the widow on the husband's funeral pyre. None the less, Hindu widows generally lead a life of severe austerity, ostracism and most never remarry.

Descriptions of various religions of the world, specific texts and how cultures deal with widows are intended to demonstrate that you are not the only one suffering in your widowhood state. There are hundreds of millions of other widows like you who are going through the most profound of all emotional experiences, mourning those lost and rebuilding their lives. You are emotional sisters in loss, grief and dismaying thoughts common to others in widowhood in general.

While your unique personal grief can be intense, perhaps your religion and culture do not additionally socially degrade you or impose harsh circumstances on you just because of your widow status. Count your blessings when you have family, society and faith to see you through the stages of widowhood because so many of your international sisters do not. Widows are bound together on the same journey of widowhood.

Chapter Seven

GRIEF --- THE NECESSARY PROCESS

Definitions and Dimensions of Grief

In its early French origin, the word *grief* was defined "a suffering, a distress or wretchedness, a pain, a burden or heaviness, a wound." Dictionaries define grief as "deep and poignant distress." The related word "grievance" refers to wrongs and injuries inflicted upon an individual by others.

People who experience grief are likely to feel many or all of the emotions that were inherent in the early definitions of the term. Grief is a highly personal and subjective response to a real, perceived, or anticipated loss. Grief as a type of stress reaction may occur in any loss situation, whether the loss is physical or tangible, such as a death, significant injury, or loss of property, or symbolic and intangible, such as the loss of a dream. The intensity of grief depends on the meaning of that loss to the individual. That your grief as a widow is more than the usual sorrow and emotional turmoil is universally recognized.

The psychology and mental health community pays particular attention to certain dimensions of grief.

1. Stress reactions include changes in physiological function that can increase one's vulnerability to illness and exacerbate preexisting physical problems.
2. Perception and thought are affected, with the increased possibility of making impulsive and potentially harmful decisions and becoming more at risk for accidents.

3. A spiritual crisis often occurs, in which guiding assumptions and values are called into question.

4. Family and communal response to loss, often neglected in the past, is a significant factor in grief and grief recovery.

5. Although the pain of loss may be universal, cultural heritage and influences and current support systems have much influence on the way one expresses and copes with stress.

> There is no way out of the desert except through it.
>
> - African saying

No one really knows how complex grieving a death is until you have to go through it yourself. Understanding some of the elements and phases of the grief process can give you a generalized map of the terrain you will have to cover. Each widow will take a different route. Each will choose her own landmarks and travel at her own unique speed.

An outline and examples of grief phases and suggestions to get through the maze provided here can help you to move forward. When you find familiar signs, you can know that "It's OK. This too is part of my journey. Others have gone this way before me and I will survive." The transition phase tips have been proven time after time to work. Give them a chance. Your culture, experience and faith will provide the tools you use to navigate. In the end, your journey changes you forever.

Grieving Devastating Losses

Suffering losses is an integral part of the human experience. In all of nature, loss sets the stage for further creation and recreation. Grief confronts everyone, often more than once in a lifetime. Grief experiences and intensity vary among individuals due to a variety of factors, including who the deceased person was, the nature of the relationship with the deceased, the circumstances of death, and concurrent stress.

The death of your loved one will fling you beyond security and familiarity into new difficult situations at any stage of life. Losing a spouse, life partner, child, parent or friend can thrust you into angst, deep sadness and puts your very sense of self in jeopardy. There is a diminished sense of your own existence when you lose the person with whom you have intimately shared your life. Death of your beloved is one of the most traumatic devastating events you will ever experience.

Grief is an equalizer that is no respecter of persons. Loss and the grief responses happen to everyone at some time in life regardless of race, gender, occupation, religious beliefs, life philosophy, financial status, education or age. A young woman whose husband dies in an automobile accident or an eighty-year-old woman whose husband dies in his sleep or after months of illness will both undergo their own process of hurt, anger and confusion. Grief is a normal healthy human response and a natural and necessary part of the healing process.

As the initial shock wears off and the reality of the death of your spouse takes hold, you can expect to come face-to-face with grief. Grief is a normal multi-faceted human reaction to any type of loss, separation, change or trauma, particularly the powerful loss of a loved one. Throughout your lifetime, there are many loss experiences, ranging from loss of personal possessions, employment, pets, business, home, vehicles, financial security, relationships, health, youth, reputation, innocence, dreams, or parts of the body through surgery. Generally, the most devastating loss is the death of a spouse. Losses of all types are grieved in various ways depending on the culture, personality, family ties, accumulation of losses, and spiritual and religious beliefs and practices. One common element is hope.

Grief not only has emotional responses, but also has physical, behavioral, social, cognitive and philosophical dimensions. Contrary to some views of grief, there is not one predictable order or one way to move through the grief process that works for everyone. While stages or steps can be useful to describe a process, stages can also be very misleading in its simplicity. Be forewarned that grief is not predicable, linear, self-contained or smooth progressive stages. It can ebb and flow in waves of varying intensity. When misapplied, descriptive theories of grief responses or stages can be foisted on a bereaved widow so that worries about "grieving correctly', can become stressors in and of themselves. Grief tends to make its own rules. Current grief theories and models of coping are characterized by a more individual approach, acceptance, balance, meaning-making and flexibility.

Differences between Bereavement, Grief and Mourning

As a widow, you will experience three distinct process categories: bereavement, grief and mourning. Even though people use the terms interchangeably, each is different from the other. Bereavement is the fact of loss and a state of experiencing the loss and the status allocated to survivors experiencing grief. Grief is the subjective personal response to that state of loss. Grief encompasses the physical internal responses and emotions, including sadness and depression triggered by the death of another. Grief can dislocate both the mind and body. Mourning is the outward, often cultural or traditional, demonstrations of the loss.

Mourning is a different process that grieving. Mourning has two interrelated elements: First, it includes your inner psychic process during which you gradually adapt to the loss, a process referred to as 'grief work.' Secondly, mourning also denotes a social process, the behavior patterns, norms and rituals through which you are recognized by others as bereaved and how you socially express grief. For example, people demonstrate mourning by wearing black, attending funerals, and sending cards and flowers. Mourning usually involves culturally or socially determined rituals, behaviors and grieving that a widow must do before returning to her normal social responsibilities or starting a new life cycle. Religious, cultural or social mourning mandates help make sense of the end of a loved one's life and give structure to what can be a very stressful and confusing time.

Disenfranchised Grief

Society does not equally grant the bereavement or grief status to all those experiencing the loss of a significant person. In the United States and many other societies, grieving rules limit grief to the deaths of family members. When a family member dies, a widow and close relatives are expected and allowed to grieve, often in specified ways. However, human beings exist in intimate networks that include bonds and attachment to fellow humans, animals, and even places and things, not just family.

Realize that there are other survivors, like close friends, work colleagues, club and church members, neighbors that loved and miss your late spouse. Also, nontraditional relationships such as cohabitation or same sex relationships, have tenuous public acceptance and limited legal standing, face negative sanction within the larger community, but they are experiencing a great life-changing loss too. These people may experience just as much grief-induced and profound sorrow, yet they are disenfranchised. Disenfranchised grief is what a person experiences when they incur a loss not openly acknowledged, socially sanctioned or publicly mourned. They are not accorded social recognition nor are they generally the recipients of condolences or help from others. This absence of grieving survivor recognition can compound the challenges of grief. As a widow, be aware that there are others outside the family who are also deeply grieving the loss of your loved one.

Chapter Eight

PSYCHOLOGY OF GRIEF AND MOURNING

Grief Theories

By introducing you to the basics of various psychological and scientific theories and models of grief, you can recognize your own symptoms as a widow and be better able to navigate through the grieving process. Knowing about the older theories, the current techniques, and the innovative methods of psychologically processing grief, you can avoid what will not work for you and utilize those transitional models that fit your needs.

Your grief experience is the period during which you make gradual and necessary adjustments to loss. You need to learn ways to cope with the changes that accompany your major transitions. You should have the information to make informed choices. This chapter outlines the history of grief psychology, various grief theories and models, current science on grief, followed by the latest effective adapting techniques for your review and use in overcoming grief.

Early Grief Psychology

Sigmond Freud introduced the notion of the "work of mourning" in *Mourning and Melancholia* (1916-17). Freud seemed to be particularly concerned with death and mourning in the middle of the First World War, when everyone in Europe was dealing with such losses. Freud saw the nature of acute grief as a normal defense against the trauma of loss. To Freud, grief was a psychological crisis. He outlined a trauma model of grief and mourning for those suffering personal losses.

The 'work of mourning' is a set of conscious and unconscious mental processes that start when you lose a person you love. Extreme pain, denial of reality, hallucination of the presence of the person, and awareness of the loss are often experienced. Freud noted that, in addition to the highly contagious feeling of sadness, a widow's mourning generally has three characteristics: loss of interest in the outside world, temporary loss of the capacity to bond or love, and the inhibition of all activity.

A kind of internal mental and emotional reorganization occurs through grief and mourning. Mourning is described as focusing excessive attention on your lost loved one and what will never again exist in order to come to terms with the fact that he is gone. There are other extensive studies on the complications and extremes of derangement brought on by grief.

> It is foolish to tear one's hair in grief, as though sorrow would
> be made less by baldness.
>
> - Marcus Tullius Cicero

While grieving and mourning work is in progress, a widow is gradually able, within an individual period of time, to separate from the lost spouse. Accepting the truth of a beloved person's death involves suffering. Freud compares the work of grieving and mourning to the work of the labor of childbirth. Any birth takes time and is the outcome of a creative process. The truth of a loss acknowledged is no exception to this rule. Eventually mental changes will occur that allow your attachment to new persons, interests and objects to develop.

Understanding grief, mourning and their numerous facets can help you confront the reality and deal with your feelings of loneliness, fear, despair and confusion. Grief and mourning are part of the methods you use to honor those you have loved and lost. Grief brought on by your loss is a physical, mental and emotional condition. It is your body's natural ability to heal injury. Grieving is not a passive process; it is a highly active one.

Although each widow handles grief differently, it is a necessary transition process requiring work, effort and cooperation. In particular, when you lose your spouse, it is vitally important to genuinely grieve the loss and incorporate it into the general framework of your life. Accepting your loss can help you recover, grow stronger and live a full life again. It is helpful to recognize and have some labels for what you are feeling so that you can discuss it and find solutions. Look at the various theories and models for phases/stages of grief, common feelings, symptoms and offer suggestions on how to cope and navigate through your own complex grieving process.

Grief Theory Models

Over the years, multitudes of stage and phase models have arisen from psychology, medical and spiritual theorists with various models attempting to describe what occurs during the grieving process. While the step stages or phase-based approaches explaining what happens during mourning are popular, current bereavement specialist note a few problems with the older models. Today, scientists and counselors find that:

(1) No particular stage or phase-based description or linear approach applies to all widows
(2) The uniqueness of each death is not recognized by the old models and there are no pre-determined standards for grieving
(3) The use of stages and phases imply that mourning is a passive activity rather than an active participation by a widow
(4) Stage or phase-based descriptions of grieving set expectations of what a widow's grieving is supposed to be like
(5) Overall, the personal complexities of your widow's mourning cannot reduce into simplistic dogmatic steps

Kubler-Ross' Five Stages of Grief

Perhaps the most well known model put forth for understanding the grief and mourning process was in the 1969 book *On Death and Dying* by Elisabeth Kubler-Ross, MD. She initially described psychological responses by dying people to news of their own terminal illness. She defined a grief cycle and outlined five stages: denial, anger, bargaining, depression and acceptance (DABDA). In a nutshell, Kubler-Ross described the dying patient's phases of grief as:
• Denial - having trouble believing what is happening to them;
• Anger - questioning the fairness of the loss;
• Bargaining - trying to make a deal with fate to gain more time;
• Depression - period when the person feels deeply sad;
• Acceptance - achieving some resolution to grief before believing in the ability to move on with life.

Even though it was not Dr. Kuebler-Ross' intention, some psychologists erroneously took those same stages and proclaimed that they also applied to grief and mourning after a loved one's death. When confronted with death and its emotional chaos, people will naturally turn to the idea of stages to serve them as some kind of outline or road map through an unknown territory. While the Kubler-Ross linear five stage model is now questionable in its usefulness to widows, it still remains a popular concept for a public yearning for clarity and clinging to any grieving guideposts. The greatest contribution of her work was to break the discussion barrier about death, loss and grief and to bring the psychology of loss into the public eye and bookstores.

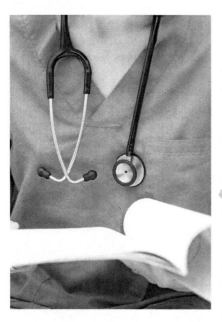

Current Science on Grief

For almost a century, Freud's grief-work model and later Kubler-Ross's five stages were the touchstones for grief psychology. More recently, scientists, doctors and psychologists believe that the idea of sequential 'stages of grief' oversimplifies the complex experience of losing a loved one. There are other, more descriptive and effective current models that better explain the process than the myth that grieving occurs in certain linear stages. Many of those newer scientific theories and models presented here give widows like you better maps of the grief territory and an understanding of the new techniques available.

In the 1990s, bereavement research pioneer and Professor of Clinical Psychology at Columbia University, George Bonanno, used rigorous scientific techniques to study grief and found that the five stages were not the same behaviors he saw in his research. He maintains that the emotional state of bereaved people are actually much more personal, simple and much less measurable. Research demonstrates that resuming healthy functioning is not repressing feelings, that it is just part of a person's resilient nature. No two widows mourn the same way or within the same timeframe.

In his 2009 book, *The Other Side of Sadness, What the New Science of Bereavement Tells Us About Life After Loss*, Bonanno overturns wide-spread assumptions and the five-stage theory of grief and argues that they do not represent what the majority of people go through when they lose a loved one. Bonanno shows how the accepted model for mourning discounts a person's remarkable capacity for resilience.

He found that most people, genetically wired for survival, get over even traumatic loss in a short time. That does not mean they don't suffer in an intense way, but that intense sadness can do its job faster than previously thought and that resilient people can do the recovery grief work in a matter of weeks and do it consistently over time. There may be a lingering sadness for years, but regaining the ability to rejoin life to work and concentrate, interact and be emotionally available to others again can happen quickly. Science shows if you are done with grief, you are done with grief.

Dr. Bonanno also discusses how widows can learn from the elaborate mourning rituals performed by cultures around the world, because traditions provide comfort and closure to help folks move on with their lives. He states that in the Western culture we appear embarrassed by traditional ritual or behavior because it makes us less individual and autonomous. He would like his writings to impact the traditional western ideas on bereavement so that people don't judge those who have lost loved ones just because they laugh, resume life activities or remarry after the loss.

There is no reason to label certain behaviors inappropriate or to prohibit a widow from being healthy and happy in her own way and time. Unfortunately, well-intentioned onlookers, dubbed "grief police" by bereavement expert Dr. Robert Neimeyer, a psychology professor at the University of Memphis, say things that imply to the widow that there is a 'right way' to grieve. Each grief journey is personal and unique.

The current science of bereavement can serve as useful corrections to a number of well-intentioned misinterpretations and out-dated grief theories. Modern psychologists do not minimize the acute sorrow widows feel when the one they love dies. While a small proportion of mourners, ten to fifteen percent, have long-lasting depression and distress and may benefit from counseling and medical intervention, most bereaved widows do recover and get better on their own without any professional help. To use Bonanno's key term, most widows are very *resilient*. They fluctuate between pain and happier emotions, seek comfort, maintain their equilibrium and, before long, find renewed meaning and pleasure in life. This is the proven scientific and human nature of grief.

Positive Sides of Grief

Believe it or not, there are some postive sides to grief and mourning. Grief can actually deepen interpersonal connections and, in many cases, leads to a profound new sense of faith, gratitude and meaning in life. In *More Resilience This Minute*, Professors Lawrence Calhoun and Richard Tedeschi claim that widows have the ability to grow through the greatest challenges of life, called post-traumatic growth. Additionally, the benefits of going through the processes of loss and grief include a greater sense of personal strength, spiritual growth, improved relationships, new possibilities and a greater appreciation for life. Resiliency experts say personal healing and growth come from a combination of five factors:

• Commitment to finding meaning or rightness in what happens to you. Creative psychologists call it 'creative construing'.

• Belief in your capacity to create a positive future. Telling yourself a story that includes not just the past and present, but a possible future that is easier and more hopeful.

• Willingness to grow and working toward something positive

• The choice to find ways to laugh, whether with friends or through funny books and movies

• Practicing gratefulness and increasing thankfulness. Gratitude has an awesome power to uplift and focus on what is good, whole and right in our lives right now.

Mourning Tasks, Adaptations and Challenges

Instead of grief stages, psychologists and scientists currently prefer to consider mourning to be a group of tasks, adaptation phases, challenges, meaning-making or life story revisions to be undertaken. The idea of tasks or challenges has the advantage of characterizing mourning as an active process requiring decision-making participation by the widow. As a bereaved widow, you may be told by others to expect and to follow the classic five stages of grief, only to discover that your own grieving process unfolds very differently. You would be better off discarding the notion that a linear sequence of stages of grief occurs among all who experience the loss of a loved one. Your grief is personal and needs a choice of adaptation actions, not a simplistic set of dogmatic steps. The number one rule of successful re-entry from widowhood is that there are no rules that fit everyone. Additionally, you need to be an active participant in your own grief journey. The following chapters on adaptation explain some of the different grief work models and practical tips available today to help you.

Chapter Nine

ADVANCED GUIDELINES FOR COPING WITH GRIEF

Among the leading grief theorists, Dr. Robert Neimeyer, Ph.D., is Director of Psychotherapy Research in the Department of Psychology, University of Memphis, where he also teaches and maintains an active clinical practice. He has conducted extensive research on the topics of death, grief, loss, and suicide intervention. Dr. Neimeyer has published over twenty books, including *Meaning Reconstruction and the Experience of Loss, Lessons of Loss: A Guide to Coping,* and is currently working to advance a more adequate theory of grieving as a meaning-making process.

The central process in grieving involves an attempt to reaffirm or reconstruct a world of meaning challenged by loss and bereavement, especially in its more traumatic forms. Highly individual processes of meaning making and adaptation are at the heart of grief dynamics. All surviving widows share the challenges that death presents, the tasks of processing the loss, coping with grief symptoms and revising the relationship to the late husband. Your relationship to the deceased and the nature of the death determine your lessons of loss tasks and their durations. For example, untimely or sudden deaths like accidents, homicides, war related, suicides, deaths in youth, tend to trigger more intense symptoms of disbelief, anger, depression and longer mourning.

Adaptation grief work can move you toward a satisfactory resolution of your losses. However, resolution does not mean that you put the experience of loss behind. Rather it means that even though life was irrevocably changed and the enduring sense of loss will remain, you can learn to cope with the grief and be able to move on with life.

Phases of Adaptation

Early models of grieving fail to fully recognize, that while death is a universal experience, the bereavement process is very individual. Grief, as a natural response to loss, unfolds in many ways. Grief theorists recommend that future models focus on each widow's unique experience of loss, concentrating on the task of reconstructing meaning and identity.

It is more accurate to think about and use the more advanced "Phases of Adaptation" as a resource, rather than rely on the earlier linear "Stages of Grief." While there is no one specific right way to manage grief, there are healthy, effective non-stage methods for you to cope and adapt.

You will find that Phases of Adaptation overlap rather than follow a sequence. Dealing with grief is a process, not a step-by-step program. The transition grief process discusses what you might be feeling and suggests tasks and experiences for you to try. Please note that completing the various phases or following the suggestions will not completely end your grieving process or totally heal your broken heart. Closure is for bank accounts. It is not for love accounts. When you have loved a person, you will always grieve them. It just needs to change over time.

> Grief isn't a disease, after all; it's a transition.
> - Dr. Robert Neimeyer

All surviving widows will experience the psychological challenges that death presents, from processing the loss and coping with grief symptoms through reformulating a relationship to the late loved one. These transition tasks can take lots of hard internal and external work. Healthy grief is not a passive experience. The act of dealing with your personal grief, mourning, requires attention and focus. You have to be active and take charge of your own grieving and mourning processes.

As a society, we have become accustomed to everything coming to us pre-made, pre-cooked or pre-packaged. Many things are ready to use with no effort required on our part. People expect change without all the work or going through the process. New widows especially desire results without going through the hard grieving process. Just know from the start that you cannot move from one level of mourning to another without the self-discipline, commitment and courage to work through your grief.

Let me remind you that grief experiences rarely happen in any specific order. Erratic symptoms come at you in any order, at any time or all at once. Grief does not follow a set course nor move neatly through proscribed progressive stages. There is no linear pattern to the adaptation phases and often you will take two steps forward and one back.

Instead of a straight line, the healing path seems zigzag and often loops back. Like a roller coaster, you level out for a while for a smooth ride. Then climb up to the sky only to plunge back down at lightening speed. Your stomach comes up to your throat and you cannot breathe. You feel powerless, thrown around emotionally and physically and unable to stop your screams. You have lost control of your world and your reactions for a while. Grief is full of those types of up and down roller coaster symptoms of progressions and regressions. Just like the carnival ride, the crazy grief ride does slow down and let you off.

Individual Responses to Grief

The loss of your loved one poses significant challenges that linger long after the vivid emotional impact of the loss has faded. Grief is a very personal journey, so take the conditions and samples of grief therapy transition tasks offered in this book as a resource and guideline of what might be encountered on your road to recovery and reconstruction of your life. The practical hints and suggestions for coping, adapting and moving forward in healing come from various sources, observations through my years of legal practice and plain common sense. They are only grief guidelines and are not meant as a substitute for professional or spiritual assistance.

Each widow will find what works for her and discover new paths and techniques on the way. Like an athlete or musician, you must practice and use exercises to get the strength to grow through the widowhood experience. There are multiple pathways to follow through the bereavement maze. Some lead to surprising resilience and others that lead to hard grief work.

Studies are starting to point specifically toward what can be done usefully with that time in order to gain a perspective on the loss. The phases of adaptation suggested by Dr. Neimeyer and other grief specialists, explore grief as a deep disruption of the personal premises on which your life is lived and gives you a general process for making a meaning of it all. The adaptation suggestions discussed will help you learn to move through your challenges, be resilient and grow through the experience.

> Old models say that time heals all wounds, but research tells us that it is not what time does for the bereaved person that counts, it is what the bereaved person does with the time.
> - Dr. Robert Neimeyer

Effective Adaptation Approaches

Grief is not a simple stage-like process. Contemporary counseling theories say that working through the grief and meaning reconstruction are the central processes and challenges for grieving widows. Each widow's reality is unique and subjective. Human beings describe and organize their lives as the author of their own life stories, struggling to compose a meaningful account of the events and dramatically rewriting these when changed by unanticipated events such as the death of a loved one. Grief work is a tool to help you symbolize, articulate, renegotiate those beliefs and meanings disrupted by the loss, and regain some understanding and power.

Major death losses are significant disruptions to personally and socially constructed narratives, assumptions about the world and personal identity. Meaning-making following the death loss involves a complicated balance between redefining yourself and an implicit reweaving of how you engage with the world, explains Neimeyer.

Viewing mourning as a process of meaning reconstructions captures the nature of the experience. Your primary task is not one of returning to pre-loss functioning, but of developing a meaningful life without your loved one. To rebuild or reconstruct your world, you need to understand the concepts and take on a series of suggested tasks to help you rewrite the narrative about who you are and constructing a world in which you can live effectively afterwards.

You are the only one who can rewrite your life story. Start the process of challenges by changing your relationship with yourself.

> Every time you change the main character in your story, just like magic the whole story starts to change in order to adapt to the new main character.
>
> - Miguel Ruiz

Mental health professionals use an eclectic approach in counseling widows, integrating and combining many of the mourning theories and innovative, yet proven, modern techniques. Recognizing the individual nature of grieving and in contrast to the more traditional stage based approaches to grief, current process frameworks theories are characterized by acceptance, balance and flexibility. The emphasis is on interactive tasks and adaptations done by the grieving widow through the transitions.

A widow can take comfort in the fact that others have had the same feelings or initial lack of feelings and that their experiences are perfectly normal parts of the healing process. Let's get started on your transition.

Grief Transition Phases

Popular for its realistic approach and effectiveness are the transition challenges that Dr. Robert Neimeyer describes in *Lesson of Loss, a Guide to Coping.* These six challenging transition phases for you as a widow include:

(1) Acknowledge the reality of your loss
(2) Open yourself to the pain
(3) Revise your assumptions and world-view
(4) Adjust to the absence of your late husband
(5) Revise your relationship to the deceased
(6) Reinvent yourself

Following chapters are summaries of each grief and adaptation transition phase, what you might be feeling, tasks and coping hints to help you mentally (mind), emotionally (heart), physically (body), spiritually (spirit) and socially (connections) navigate through the maze of grief.

EXCLUSIVE READER ONLINE RESOURCES

A password hidden in *Widow's Key* allows you to receive extra reader resources. More useful information is now available to you online. Get access to professional links, items, checklists and other resources not in the book.

Here are just a few topics available to *Widow's Key* readers only:

* Links to Psychologists Neimeyer, Bonanno and Grief Author Mavens

* How Friends Can Really Help a Grieving Widow

* Writing Meaningful Sympathy Letters and Cards

* Resource Websites Dedicated To Widows and Grief

Visit the *Widow's Key* companion website at www.widowskey.com. Follow the simple instructions to find your password. The password hidden in Widow's Key gives you access to your extra reader-only information.

Chapter Ten

ACKNOWLEDGING THE REALITY OF THE DEATH

Transition Phase One

While it might seem obvious, the first thing that a bereaved widow has to understand and accept is that the death has actually occurred. Few people are ready for the hard hits that grief delivers to the human brain. Each individual's body and brain handles grief in different ways. Research shows that initial grief reactions of shock and denial are impacted by how a person's loss influences the view of themselves and their worlds.

Universally there is a difference between a deep emotional (heart) realization and an intellectual (head) realization. Intellectually you may accept the fact a death has occurred because you might have witnessed the death, observed the body or were told of the death by a reliable source. However, your heart was not yet ready to absorb the truth of what has happened. Your head and heart get out-of-synch.

Many early studies refer to 'denial' as a stage. Unless a person is truly delusional, denial is more symbolic than literal. Mentally and intellectually you know full well that the person is actually physically dead, but express it in rhetorical language of disbelief, as in, "I still can't believe he's gone" or "He can't be dead. I just spoke to him this morning." These are just figures of speech and not true denials of the actual death or denials of the reality of the death. When the term denial is included here, it refers to an emotional shock, not some stage of grief. Signs of denial are not indications that you are rejecting the truth or are totally removed from real world event.

For some widows, acknowledging the reality of death comes quickly, while others remain in disbelief for a longer time or in periodic bursts. Physicians will tell you that caregivers, who are constantly with their loved ones through their illness, often have the hardest initial response and desire for denial. They seem to have held onto a belief that by virtue of their determination, love and presence, they could keep the person alive. The inevitable death strikes caregivers as not only a loss of the beloved person, and their caretaking job and hope, but a kind of failure on their part. If you were a primary caregiver, you may have a hard time accepting that the death is now finally a reality and that it was not somehow your fault. Let go of that guilt and stop denial.

Additionally, for some, acknowledging a death can be even more difficult when there is no physical proof of the loss such as with an unrecoverable body from a drowning, air crash or explosion, a kidnapping or a Missing in Action (MIA) soldier.

Grief counselors say that the reality of your loved one's death is often disbelieved or denied at first because you do not want it to be true. Often the first word out of a widow's mouth is 'No!" When you initially experience or hear about the death of someone precious, your first reaction is physical shock followed by a sort of numbness and wishful denial. This natural denial response is to protect you from the sudden onslaught of the implications of the death for you and the rest of your life. Shock symptoms come in various degrees and forms dictated by how the death occurred, the meaning of the death, or a belief that the absence is only temporary. Your physiological sense of physical and mental numbness is often intermittent and gives way to lack of focus or concentration, but it is not a stage of grieving.

Disbelief and Emotional Denial

Short-lived, low intensity disbelief or emotional denial is a natural reaction to learning that a loved one has died. In Joan Didion's *The Year of Magical Thinking*, published memoirs about the death of her husband, she describes how she was able to discard all her husband's clothes except for a pair of shoes. Even though she mentally and intellectually knew he was dead, there was still an emotional part of her expecting him to walk through the door needing those shoes when he got home. She wrote about thinking like a small child, as if her thoughts or wishes had the power to reverse the narrative, rewind the tape and change the outcome.

Other widows have described instances where forgetfully they call out to their spouse in another part of the house or they try to phone their loved one, only to suddenly and painfully remember that person has died. It is only natural that you might act habitually since you have automatically been doing the same thing for many years. It takes some of these reminding sad experiences to help your heart realize what the head already knows; that your loved one is physically gone and not coming back. These occasions of momentary forgetting that your spouse has died are not a denial of the reality of the passing.

It may seem strange, the sheer number of times you are shocked back into the reality that your loved one is no longer with you. If you wake one morning feeling great, having forgotten that your loved one has died, don't feel guilty for your momentary solace. When your sadness sets in again, try to think of a happy memory associated with your loved one as you go about your routine. Memories will help you through.

C.S. Lewis, in *A Grief Observed*, wrote about grieving his wife's death, "I think I am beginning to understand why grief feels like suspense. It comes from the frustration of so many impulses that had become habitual. Thought after thought, feeling after feeling, action after action, had H. for their object. Now their target is gone. I keep on through habit fitting an arrow to the string; then I remember and have to lay the bow down. So many roads lead thought to H. I set out on one of them. But now there's an impassable frontier post across it. So many roads; now so many cul-de-sacs."

Extreme grief reactions and denial can become habitual and potentially harmful. A classic example of a complicated bereavement is how Queen Victoria required that after the death of Prince Albert, his clothes and shaving kit be laid out every morning as if he was still alive. Doing this for a short period might not be strange, but her actions lasted for 40 years.

Denial of a death can be in the form of trying to lessen the pain by fooling yourself that the deceased is really somewhere else, such as on a business trip, vacation, or in the hospital. You can't rewind this movie just because the ending was so tragic. Eventually, after enough confrontations with the fact that your loved one has died, you come to accept the fact that your beloved is actually physically gone. Your head and the heart become more in-synch. If you refuse or cannot come to that realization, professional help is probably warranted. Otherwise, you will remain stuck and unable to adapt or proceed.

What You Might be Feeling as You Accept the Death

For the first few days and weeks after your life partner dies, you might mentally and emotionally feel totally shocked that this event has happened, numb, in a hazy distracted dreamlike state, alienated from others, withdrawn and quiet, painfully lost, adrift or bereft of purpose.

It is common for a widow to feel unfocused, lonely, hazy confusion, sad but unable to cry, disorganized, helpless, anxious, distant, spacey, out of touch with your feelings, unstable, emotional, over-reactive, guilty or fragile. You may have extreme mood swings, panic attacks or memory gaps, misplace items or forget simple tasks. Other widows experience an aura of peacefulness, are calm, relieved that the struggle is over for the deceased and become competent organizers of the services and household needs. No particular response is better or worse than any other.

Physically you may feel weak, lethargic, fatigued, sick, aches and pains, have no appetite or insomnia. Some become hyperactive, energized and capable of multi-tasking at length. Widows often describe their feelings in physical terms. "His death just crushed me like a ton of bricks", "It knocked the wind out of me", "Hit me right between the eyes", "This has thrown me completely off my feet" are common examples.

To help you cope with the transition phase of dealing with the reality of your loved one's death, the challenges and tips in this section are divided into categories under Mind, Heart, Body, Spirit and Connection. These bits of philosophy and advice are your keys for transitioning through this first phase of grieving.

Practical Suggestions for Coping with the Reality of Death

Mind

- You may need to spend some time alone with your deceased husband right after the death, before removal by the funeral home staff. You might want to hold him, say parting last words and kiss him goodbye. These moments of quiet alone time and tenderness can provide primary acknowledgement of his death and offer some preliminary closure.
- Try not to use phrases like "passed away" or "gone" or "in a better place". Use the actual word "dead". Before the funeral, dedicate some alone time to the task of saying aloud to yourself: "___ is dead; he is dead." You need to hear yourself saying it with your husband's name in the sentence. Break through the denial.
- You will be dealing with lots of people and decisions, so you need to take time for solitude to reflect and feel refreshed. It is a self-preservation technique to take care of your mental and physical needs first.
- Don't have unreasonable expectations of yourself to be all or do all. This is not the time for you to play the wonder woman role or become the strong supportive trooper for everyone else.
- Use kind words and be patient in your conversations with yourself. Believe in, take care of and be good to number one.
- When self-doubting or disapproving inner voices chip away at your self-confidence, focus on the reality of your capabilities and worth. Call the destructive thoughts 'liar' and they actually will start to get embarrassed and go away. Negativity will soon begin to have less influence over your life.
- If you served as primary caregiver for your dying husband, you may feel bereft of purpose, an undeserved sense of self-blame or guilt and at a loss. Your life had a job-like routine before and now you may feel adrift. This is when you need to go easy on yourself and replace that scheduled life with more you-focused time. Your new purpose or new role at first can be the planning of the services and dealing with other mourners.

Heart

- You have permission to feel whatever you feel. It is okay not to cry or to cry when you have a need to, even at inappropriate moments.
- Don't repress or hide your feelings. You do not have to apologize or explain yourself to anyone.
- Don't be afraid if you feel lonely, frightened or uncontrollably sad. Even crying hysterically will not harm or destroy you. Carry tissues and just let it out.
- Expect the unexpected. Your world will feel turned upside down. Feelings and emotions will range from low lows to high highs.
- At this time, you need to be in touch with your feelings and aware of what is happening within and around you. Medications, drugs, tranquilizers, alcoholic or other intoxicants only numb you for a short time. The residual dehydration, illness and lack of clarity will make things harder on you and all others concerned. Avoid excesses of any kind. As painful as it may seem, you need to experience the reality of the loss fully. Clear memories of the services and concern of others will help you in your grief work down the road.
- Acts of closure are very important to you and everyone who knew and cared about your late spouse. Don't deny yourself or others the opportunity to experience the rituals of death and have a chance to express love, share memories and say goodbye.
- If you cannot deal with all the service plans and details, recruit others to help rather than forego the ceremonies and rituals necessary for facing the reality of the death.

Body

- First, recognize that the physical shock and numbness from an overload of emotional energy have a purpose to protect your mind and heart until you can deal with the reality and pain. It is physically, mentally and emotionally difficult for your mind to absorb the finality of death in those first few hours or days.
- The physiological reactions of shock send adrenaline into your bloodstream and you may feel chilled or shivering. Put on a shawl, sweater or just wrap yourself up in a cozy blanket. It is a proverbial cocooning method of comforting yourself.
- Go home or back to where you are staying and take a long bath or warm shower. The religious and cultural rituals of bathing and ablutions are there for symbolic but valid cleansing reasons. Quite

literally, washing away the stress, tightness and tears of the day away and down the drain will help.

• Although you may have little or no appetite, eat something regularly to keep your body chemistry, blood sugar levels in a normal range. You will need all your strength and energy. Drink lots of water and healthy natural fluids.

• Get at least seven to eight hours of sleep every night. Getting enough sleep is as important as eating right and exercising. It is a critical element to your physical and mental well-being. A body without sleep is anguished both physically and mentally. You put yourself at risk for injury, health and behavior problems if you don't get enough sleep every night.

• Get sufficient rest, but don't use excessive sleep as an escape from the reality or the accompanying responsibilities.

Spirit

• Closure rituals such as the funeral, memorial services or burial are very important for accepting the death of your spouse. The planning of funeral services and other spiritual, religious and customary acts are there to provide you with a sense of purpose and meaning.

• As difficult as it seems for you to make decisions and go through the social motions, the ceremonies and rituals are designed to help you cope with the loss. Traditions generally center around spiritual beliefs of connection to the afterlife and connection between the living and the dead. There is something enormously comforting about traditional rituals and mourning practices.

• Research shows that if you are a surviving widow with a spiritual life, you should practice your faith tradition at this time. Turning to your religion and faith tends to break through the denial phase and help you absorb grief more quickly.

• Generally, through religious faith and texts, you can find some kind of meaning in your loss and are better able to cope with it.

• A spiritual or religious community, rituals, prayers and meditation can become a source of solace and support to you throughout the grieving and recovery process.

Connection

• Overcome those feelings of isolation, unreality or distance by reaching out to family members and close friends. They can be your touchstones and you can be theirs. Hold and hug each other. If anyone asks if there is anything they can do, say yes. They mean it and really want to help in some way.

• If you can handle it, make the notification calls or delegate this task and other helpful household or service jobs to others. Having something meaningful to do helps you, family and close friends deal with the reality of the loss and feel closer to each other.

• Don't hesitate to talk about what you are experiencing and reminisce about your loved one. Put the emphasis on his life rather than his death. Use his name. Telling the stories and sharing memories can help honor your late husband.

• Writing the obituary and eulogy are ways of recounting the life and experiences that you shared with your spouse. It reinforces his connection to the community and other loved ones. This is a productive way for family to come together to celebrate and grieve.

• Prepare a photograph or power point presentation for the wake, funeral or memorial service. The selection of favorite pictures, memories, personal items, favorite music and such will help the memories flow and probably a few tears also.

Chapter Eleven

OPENING UP TO YOUR PAIN - Transition Phase Two

As that shock of the death slowly subsides, you will begin to experience more of the physical, mental, emotional, spiritual, and social pains related to your loss. After the primary phase of benumbed disbelief, you move to a transitional phase of intense mental and emotional pain.

Mark Twain, at the loss of his beloved daughter, claimed, "It is one of the mysteries of our nature that a man, all unprepared, can receive a thunderstroke like that and live." Pain is inevitable, but unnecessary suffering is optional. Suffering is basically an argument with the past. You have a major choice as to what to do with your pain. Don't hold it all inside, ignore it or try to tough it out. The healthy choice is to be open to it and work with it. Getting through the most difficult painful times in life is a bit like skiing. It doesn't really work if you are standing still. It is necessary to be enough out of control to keep you going down the slope, but you have to find a balance and keep moving.

> The deeper the sorrow the less tongue it hath.
> - Jewish Talmud

Sorrow is not a state, but a personal process. Impermanence and loss are indeed part of the lifelong human condition. You adapt to the losses in your lives through grief and mourning. Grieving is something you do, not something any one else can do for you. Humans are incredibly resilient and have a natural ability to heal, so rest assured that when you open up to your pain, it will subside and healing will happen.

Pain and Grief as Personal Journeys

You can't deny grief any more than you can deny a broken bone. It is understandable that someone engulfed in the sorrows of loss will ask what to expect and how long the pain will last. Sadly, there is no typical loss and there are no typical pains, responses, stages or timelines. There are also no shortcuts through grief. Pain is the cost of living.

Loss of a loved one is has been called a 'spiritual wound'. How quickly you will heal from a physical wound depends on the depth and nature of the injury; the same is true of the pain and grief. The course of your mourning depends on the unique personal, mental, physical, psychological and spiritual characteristics of your loss and resilience.

Mourning is highly personal and as individual as fingerprints. Each widow has to do her own inner pain and grief work and make adaptations to redefine themselves in new roles. There is no specific healing recipe, formula, surefire prescription, process or right way to manage the pain of grief. This is surely a case where one size does not fit all.

> Only the wearer knows where the shoe pinches.
> - English Proverb

On the long list of ugly, losing your husband is right there at the top. One of the hardest tasks you will ever face is to open up to the emotions and pain experienced at the death of your loved one. There is no response more appropriate or more normal than grief. While pain happens to be a four-letter word, it is crucial in adapting to a serious loss. You must endure what cannot be changed in the great human cycle of death and rebirth. The psychological wounds experienced when a loved one dies are sometimes compared to a physical wound caused by a severe burn. Burn victims are extremely raw and susceptible to life-threatening infections. The only way to insure that no infection develops is a periodical scrub of the burn wound. This process is extremely painful, but necessary to assure proper healing. To neglect this painful scrubbing of your psychic and emotional wounds can delay healing and lead to other disorders or even death. You need to push through the painful grieving process to be healthy and happy again.

Know from the start that the mourning process does have a beginning, middle and end to it. You can be certain that you will get better and heal.

Trust in the process of grieving and recovery. You will have people tell you, that you just need some time, saying that after all 'time heals all wounds.' Time does not heal all wounds. The more appropriate advice is that it is what you do with your time that heals you.

Like any other aspect of life, mourning is an active, working process, not a passive one. Grieving is something you have to do for yourself. You will be a different person from the one you were before you engaged yourself in the mourning process. Your brain and body have the natural inner wisdom to heal themselves. Give them what they require to heal. Honest grieving seems to be the key.

> You can not heal a wound by saying it is not there.
> - Jeremiah 6:14

Early on in the grieving process, expect that overwhelming emotions will surface. There are healthy effective ways to cope. You cannot avoid painful grief for long, if ever, and you cannot dismiss it as quickly as other emotions. Think of grief as another expression of love that says how much you cared for the deceased and embrace it as a last gift. Pain shows that the loss was life changing and significant. Honor that meaningfulness by accepting the pain that comes with your loss and change.

Working through the adaptation grief tasks will offer you some options. If you take action and follow the suggestions in this section, it will help keep one of the most devastating experiences of your life from becoming worse than it already is. You are not expected to like opening up and facing your pain, but you will find out that these emotional first aid hints do work. Through grief and mourning, you acknowledge the pain, feel that pain and bit-by-bit progress and live past it.

What You Might Be Feeling as You Cope with the Pain of Grief

Grief is your body's natural ability to heal your emotional injury. Understand that the following symptoms are common and found in varying degrees in all grieving widows. You may feel or experience vulnerability, confusion, forgetfulness, mood swings, hyper-activity, fatigue, insomnia, weight loss or gain, deep sadness, tearful, fear, depression and helplessness. Widows talk of a sense of being crazy or out of it, sleepwalking, feeling inferior, indecisive, envious, experiencing isolation, anger, guilt, unstable, compulsive behavior.

You may be unable to focus, remember or be productive, clumsy, unable to give or feel love, anxiousness, paranoia, unable to concentrate on tasks or conversation, obsessive preoccupation with how your spouse died, having dreams or nightmares, calling out the deceased's name, treasuring or avoiding articles of the deceased. Are you having inconsistent thoughts, negative thoughts about yourself, reckless behavior, lack energy, feeling fragile, sad and blue, yearning and experiencing physical aches and pain? Believe me, there are creative antidotes for all these painful grieving symptoms. To help you open up to the pain caused by the death of your loved one, the following challenges and suggestions are in categories under Mind, Heart, Body, Spirit and Connections. These bits of philosophy and advice are your keys for transitioning through this second phase of grieving so that you are able to adapt to your pain and begin healing.

Practical Suggestions for Opening Up to Pain

Mind

• The only way out of pain is through pain. You need to think about your late husband, the experience, your sadness and your loss to experience the gamut of emotions and cry in order to break through the pain and grief barrier.

• As frightening as it may seem, you can jump into the pool of pain and swim around. It is not bottomless. Immerse in the hurt fully for a while; then get out.

• Do not try repressing or stuffing the pain and emotions brought on by your loss. The energy to keep it all together increases and the pressure gets to a point of explosion. For you as a grieving widow, explosions may occur as uncontrollable fits of anger, extreme anxiety, addictions, rage, clinical depression, or it may manifest itself in illness or other physical and emotional ailments.

• Work through your pain right away or it will stay with you and inevitably resurface later. You cannot outrun or escape the pain that is a part of you.

• Address your pain head on, perhaps in journaling or through physical exercise.

• The best way to deal with grief is acceptance. Accept that deep pain, fear and vulnerability are just a temporary part of your grieving process.

• Cut yourself some slack. Some craziness is the nature of widowhood. Expect highs, lows and setbacks as temporary conditions.

• Prioritize tasks. Envision a ladder, strong and simple to climb. Set your task items on each rung with the easiest on the bottom rung. Take them on one rung at a time. Climb as far as you can each day.
• Make and rely on lists, calendars and reminder notes in order to counteract any confusion or forgetfulness. Keep them handy where you can refer to them.
• Keep a list of phone numbers, addresses and emails with you in print or on your cell phone. It is usual for you to experience mental 'cognitive deficits' and temporarily blank out on even the telephone number that you have had for years.
• Use GPS to get to locations because remembering and following directions may escape you for a while. Give yourself extra travel time to get to places and events.
• Believe in yourself. Post positive affirmation notes or cards around the house, workspace, on the mirror, refrigerator or dashboard.
• Surround yourself with positive thoughts, humor, upbeat music, fun activities, uplifting people and influences. The power you possess is based on words. You can heal yourself or release yourself from pain with just your words and opinions.

We must embrace pain and burn it as fuel for our journey.
- Kenji Miyazawa

• Longing for the past and anxiety about the future are going to rear their heads daily. Giving your fears labels, names and talking to them as they arise takes away their power. Say "Good morning achy-breaky heart. I'll get through this day in spite of you and mend".
• Give words and expression to your sorrow to relieve the ache. As you hurt, talk to others. When it is hard to articulate your inner feelings or relate to others, anonymous writing can be liberating.
• Keep a journal or diary that becomes a private space to note your thoughts and feelings. You don't need to be grammatically correct, witty, smart or compelling. No one will read this, criticize or judge you. Expressing your feelings of self-pity, complaints, guilt, heartfelt poems, quotes, touching music, dreams and even daydreams, is a way of observing and recording the events, emotions, and eventually seeing your progress during change.
• You are the author and scriptwriter of your current and future life story. Writing is a good way to practice your new role and dialogue. Joan Didion's best selling book and play about her husband's death were based on her journal writings.

• If your grief feels like too much to bear, talk to a trained grief counselor or mental health professional. It doesn't mean you are crazy. You can work through intense emotions and overcome obstacles to your grieving with the help of an experienced therapist or counselor.

• Consider grief like a tapestry. If you focus on one piece, it may look dark and bad; but try to remember that it is a part of a bigger whole. Take in the full picture.

• Read books, listen to tapes and visit websites of other widows or counselors to find the common grief threads and solutions. But, don't expect any words of advice or comfort to suddenly and miraculously reverse your symptoms of grief. Books, tapes and resources are just tools. You have to take the initiative, work on grief tasks and take positive actions.

• Talk to others close to you about what happened and reassure each other that you did the best you could under the circumstances.

• Avoid obsessive thought patterns, such as re-living or going over in your mind all the things you could or could not have done differently. If the images of the death are traumatic, find ways to stop replaying the tapes that are running through your head. Discuss the memories with others who were there and reframe the scene to be the ones who helped your deceased loved one through pain and along his final spiritual path.

• Don't punish yourself with guilt, worry, condemnation and the proverbial "If only…" Stop any thoughts mid-sentence if they begin with "If only." Don't waste any more of your tears over words left unsaid and deeds left undone.

• Don't continue to insist on self-blame. Realize that on some primal level, blaming yourself, irrational as it is, sets up a sort of cause and effect rather than facing the terrible randomness of the death and feeling powerless. Assess the circumstances realistically and set blame aside. It is not your fault that bad things happen to good people.

• Don't beat yourself up with the guilt stick. You may feel guilty for being the survivor, having your health and life ahead of you. If your marriage was stormy, you were estranged or absent when the person died, you may have regrets and feel remorseful, but do not dwell on painful guilt. Guilt is fear and punishing yourself for being afraid.

• If you were the caregiver during an illness, you may secretly feel relief that the person is no longer suffering, that the physically and emotionally burdensome job of care giving is over and you can return to a normal life. Relief is normal, yet you may still be guilty for feeling this way and become angry with yourself. It is normal to feel two such conflicting emotions, relief coupled with guilt, at the same time. Stop judging or berating yourself for natural feelings.

• In Tibetan there is no word for 'guilt' and the very concept is foreign to the Buddhists of Tibet. Instead, if someone has done something they feel has hurt another or themselves, they feel remorse and pledge not to do that action or inaction again and move on with life. So get rid of any long-term perpetuating guilt. Experience remorse if you must; then forgive yourself forever. Guilt is just energy wasted.

• You are not being punished because of some error, omission or sin you have committed. Don't blame yourself for any real or imagined mistakes that may have caused your loss. Let pain-inducing guilt go because it serves no purpose and offers no comfort.

• Guilt creates anger and vice versa. Don't get caught in that vicious circle. More often than not, nothing you did or did not do caused or could have prevented the death. Forgive yourself right now for any actions or omissions you may feel you have done and forgive the deceased for his acts or omissions.

Heart

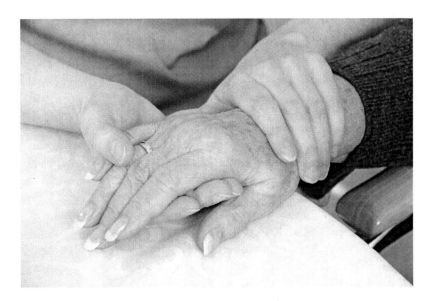

• Let yourself experience turbulent emotions rather than shutting them down. Don't deny, avoid, hide or delay your pain. Experience it and deal with it fully now.

• Take the time to retreat into and be ensconced in the pain. If you resist, it will eventually come back to plague you.

• Since there is nothing rational, fair or reasonable about losing your loved one, you cannot deal with it by intellectualizing the situation. Thank your emotions and feelings for helping you work through the grief minefields. Do this acknowledgment aloud. Once it is subconsciously noted, the brain and body know they are doing their jobs and can move on to other concerns.

• Even though grief is your constant companion, robbing you of joy and draining emotions, know that you have the strength and resources to get through this time, especially when shared.

• Practice the virtue of endurance. You cannot avoid, flee or hide from the pain. You need to endure what cannot be changed.

• It is human nature for you to mourn for yourself when you mourn the loss of your loved one. When self-pity becomes a full time focus or indulgence, it can become dangerous. Excessive self-pity can become your worse enemy according to Helen Keller, a blind deaf mute who should know. Survival depends on being resilient and functional.

• Find professional assistance if you get stuck for long periods dwelling on negative thoughts or acting out reckless or destructive patterns that might threaten your health or well-being.

• Redirect your anger. Anger is a primal, intense, white-hot emotional response especially to an untimely or violent death. Intense emotions can feel like a tangible powerful connection to the loved one. Letting go of the emotion can feel like letting go of the person again. Don't be so reluctant to let go of negative emotions like anger or guilt. Redirect strong raging feelings to fuel your passion about new projects and your new life.

• Putting all the theories, stages and counseling aside, there are going to be days when you think you doing better, and then bang, you just feel like hell. Expect big ups-and-downs.

• Carry tissues. Tears come when you least expect them. If you wear makeup, use waterproof mascara or makeup manufactured for athletes.

• You don't have to maintain false bravery with a stiff upper lip. Even Jesus felt deeply moved in spirit, troubled and wept over the death of his friend Lazarus.

• Don't let others we will call the 'grief police' make you feel guilty about not responding the "right way". There is no correct way to grieve. There is no timetable for healing. Each widow experiences her own unique pain and ways of expressing it.

• Don't listen to people who tell you such things as to snap out of it, stop being so sad or crying or that your actions are inappropriate. They are generally seeking their own comfort level, not yours.

• You never solve an emotional problem or escape its consequences by running away from it. You have to meet the pain of loss head-on and deal with it.

• Instead of simply treating your pain, it is important to retreat into it, so that you become attuned to your heart and pay attention to the needs of your spirit.

• Don't grieve alone. It is braver to seek support than to try to go it alone. It really makes a difference, especially if you were a caregiver at the end, to find a support group, therapist or close friend whose has been through something similar.

• It is helpful to communicate and associate with widows who are experiencing the same type things as you. Sharing your sorrow with others who have known similar losses can help you navigate painful and confusing emotions. The understanding and camaraderie of mutual suffering can ease the pain.

• Join a caring support group. Other widows can provide invaluable guidance and support. They are living proof that you can and will survive. The goal of grief counseling and support groups is not to make the feelings go away, but to help you embrace their purpose. To find a bereavement support group in your area, contact your clergy, local hospital, hospice, funeral home, your doctor, counseling centers or search internet connections.

Body

• Take one day or even one hour at a time. Focusing on the present, something immediate and physically present can help you hold onto a little piece of control. As you do things during the day, whether it is taking a shower, eating a meal or reading the paper, concentrate and be present fully in the accomplishment of those tasks.

• Completing simple objectives like a short walk provides a physical and mental shift from your painful grief. Physical awareness renews your confidence and reminds you of some of the blessings still present in your life.

• Tears are not a sign of weakness. They are a natural way to release intense feelings. Don't try to be brave by holding back tears when you're hurting so much inside. Each tear you shed brings some of your grief to the outside where you can better deal with it.

• Laughter is not only okay, it is healthy. Keep your sense of humor handy. If you are clumsy, forgetful, turned around or moving in slow motion, don't be frustrated or irritated; instead, relax and try to react with amusement or laughter. Smile and say "That was funny" or "Silly me!"

• Absent-mindedness or preoccupation is common. Be extra cautious. Driving or work involving power tools or heavy equipment can be extremely dangerous following the death of your loved one. Stop the car if you find yourself spaced out or preoccupied with thoughts of your late husband. Take a walk around and give all the tires a swift kick. Don't drive while under the influence of your emotions.

• Don't forget to just breathe, inhaling and exhaling fully. Breath is life. If your pain seems to center in a particular spot like the head or heart, place your hand on that spot and direct your breath and healing energy to that area.

• Get sufficient rest and exercise. Your body and mind need to slow down externally and get extra rest in order to heal internally. Sleep at least eight hours a night and take occasional naps as needed.

• Don't push yourself into exhaustion. Preserve your stamina. Oppositely, don't become lethargic or try to escape life locked up in your house or under the covers either. Balance resting with activities that you enjoy and that energize you.

• Reduce your physical and mental pressures by exercising, walking, running, swimming, recreation, hobbies, volunteering, social interactions, prayer, meditation, reading, counseling, yoga, hugging, art, sports, journaling and music.

• Put on that mysterious Mona Lisa smile of yours to get through the pain. The brain and body react to the stimulus you feed it. If you physically sit up straight and smile, the brain doesn't know it is not real and the body releases hormones to actually make you feel better. This neural plasticity gives your brain the exercise it needs to return to a natural more pleasant state.

• Make and keep regular medical checkups. Contact your health care provider if you have any signs of health problems. Be sure the physical aches and pains are not biological conditions. There is separation distress, depression and other medical conditions that can occur after losing a loved one, so be aware and take care of your physical and mental health.

• Eat healthy foods, take stress vitamins and drink plenty of water. Take extra care of your health because there is a significant increase in mortality and elevated risks attributed to cardiac disorders within the first year after a spouse's death, where the grieving widow literally and figuratively dies of a broken heart. Other factors such as drugs, alcohol, susceptibility to diseases like cancer, and suicide also contribute to these tragic outcomes.

• Avoid harmful substances or dangerous activities. Don't take risks like drinking heavily, taking drugs, driving under the influence, reckless driving or speeding or dangerous acts.

• Don't try to numb your pain with drugs or alcohol. It will simply make your pain last longer and can lead to serious consequences. Alcohol is a depressant drug. The term "crying in her beer" is a valid observation. Twenty percent of recovering alcoholics or drug abusers' initial addiction problems began because of some major loss. Rather than address the pain and grief head on, they tried to keep themselves numb in hopes it would just go away. It doesn't!

• Bring vibrant and alive things into your life. Maybe it is time for you to get that cuddly kitten you saw at the pet store, plant roses or a vegetable garden, put up a bird feeder, place a new green or flowering plant in every room, buy fresh fruit and vegetables for each meal, volunteer to rock babies at the hospital, hike through a city or state park, take pictures at a wild life sanctuary or invite family and friends to visit and stay for a while. Don't separate or isolate yourself. Embrace and make living growing things a part of your life.

• Go for nurturing massages. You need that physical contact, improved blood circulation, muscle relaxation and stress relief. Treat yourself to sense-reviving spa treatments.

• Take care of your appearance. Maintain hygiene regiments. Try scented bath salts, lotions and other soothing care products. Keep up with hair, skin and nail treatments.

Spirit

• Meditation and prayer are proven methods of calming the mind and centering the soul. Create time each day for reflections, prayer or meditation. By moving into a place of peace for even ten minutes of quiet can be restorative and productive.

• Find your own nearby "let things be" tree and go lean on it when you need to. Everyone needs a 'leaning tree'.

• Participation in and support from your spiritual community can be a great comfort. Try praying, talking with a spiritual advisor or leader in your spiritual community or studying the tenets of your faith as they relate to the end of life.

• The spiritual practices of prayer, meditation and service bring positive effects.
• Use your faith as a source of energy, inspiration and power. Explore using your spiritual resources, which might include dharma texts, scripture, clerics, songs, chants, icons, retreats, and prayer groups to help you work through your feelings.
• According to the Bible, God saves all our tears in a bottle. Invite other family members or people to cry with you.
• Some widows cope by writing letters, postcards, quotes, poems and drawings to the loved one or to God. Find a box and decorate it the way you think a mailbox to heaven or the universe would look like. Put your letters and other items in envelopes and address them to your late husband, God, Allah or higher spirits. Visualize your notes being picked up by an angel and delivered to the addressee. Imagine how happy they will be to hear from you.

Connection

• Don't take on additional social responsibilities, challenges, burdens, make drastic changes or put yourself in upsetting or stressful situations. Take it easy.
• Some widows try not to address the pain of loss by remarrying, moving, literally running away on extended vacations or by occupying themselves with hyperactive nonstop mental or physical activity. Some withdraw into being very antisocial, inactive or sleeping. These avoidance escapes are only transitory respites. As soon as these activities slow down or the inactive patterns wear out, the pain returns with vengeance. If you try to ignore it, it will not go away.
• You are living in a world, especially western culture, which does not allow your pain to interfere with business. People generally don't accept the fact that that your emotional pain, like a physical injury, not only hurts, but can be debilitating. Everyone seems to expect you to snap back to your old self, be cheerful, work as efficiently and energetically as before and still fulfill all your social and family obligations. Although others demand instant recovery, work through your grief and heal in your own way and in your own time.
• Many cultures aren't very skilled at dealing with grief, so they attach a social stigma to grieving widows. Don't hide your pain because you don't want to make others uncomfortable. By succumbing to pressures to suppress, ignore or dismiss your great loss, you are

interfering with your own healing process.

• Try not to feel betrayed or misunderstood if friends and relatives seem to abandon you as you try to cope with your loss. They may want to help but don't know what to say out of ignorance or anxiety. Others fail because they feel helpless and just don't know what to do to bind your emotional wounds.

• Reach out to others and keep communications open, because if you have strong support from family and friends you can handle loss better and recover more quickly.

• Build your own support system of emotionally healthy friends, family and professionals. Stay in contact by email, social networks, telephone, regular gatherings, meals, overnight visit or vacations. Lean on others until you can stand alone.

• Even at this time, people can say some very insensitive and foolish things. Realize that they may be afraid of what you represent to them; you might be the widow that they are afraid of becoming. A person's response to your grief or even to your progress on your journey of healing says more about his or her own life or fears than about yours.

• Be truthful and real with your family and friends. Not everyone handles emotional expressions well, so be patient and accepting of the way they handle your new reality.

• Spend time with your family and friends to practice caring, feeling love and closeness. One touch is worth ten thousand words. Don't underestimate the pain-reducing power of contact and touch. Tell family and friends that you need a hug or someone to hold your hand. They want to know your comfort needs and could probably use a big hug too.

• Avoid those people and situations that upset you or bring you down. There are always certain people who seem to bring out anger, resentment, negativity, irritation and ill humor in you at this time. If their presence and misguided sympathy expressions just make you want to scream, it is okay to stay away from them or cut conversations and time together short.

• If someone is full of "I think you should..." advice or wants to hold a 'pity party' every time you are together, close or put that relationship on the back burner. As they say, dealing with negative toxic people like this is not just a drain; it is a sewer.

• Use your deceased husband's name in conversations with others. Not saying the loved one's name will cause more pain. Tell folks not to be afraid to say the name of your late husband, because using general references tend to negate his existence in the first place.

• Ask for the help of friends and family at this time. It will make them feel empowered and relieved when you ask them to pitch in. Draw up a list of all the things that need to be done, especially things you can't seem to accomplish on your own. As these things are getting done you will feel better and it gives others an opportunity to demonstrate their support during this time.

• Don't try to go it alone. You shouldn't go through your pain and grief without outside help. It is not a sign of personal weakness to turn to others during your bereavement, grief and mourning. You may be uncomfortable or unaccustomed to asking for help, but if you are feeling overwhelmed, ask a family member, friend or business associate to assist you for a while. Allow others the gift of caring for you and helping you.

> Remind yourself that each problem carries within itself the seeds of opportunity to learn, to love, to increase your awareness and to be happy simply because you are alive.
>
> - Miguel Ruiz

Chapter Twelve

REVISE YOUR ASSUMPTIONS AND WORLD VIEW
Transition Phase Three

The death of a loved one shakes your sense of self and the world. Such a loss deeply challenges your personal world of meaning. When a traumatic loss occurs, you try to fit it into your view of the world and into the story of your life. To begin with, there are basic taken-for-granted thematic foundations on which your self-narrative depends. This view is called the 'assumptive world'. Jeffrey Kauffman explains this life meaning transition in *Loss of the Assumptive World*. The following are some of the key concepts in the seldom-mentioned major area of grief, your loss of assumptions about the world and life in general.

Assumptions and Core Beliefs

Kauffman's words have great applications for grieving widows. "From the time we are infants, we observe, experience, and learn about the world around us. From these observations and experiences, we form our own particular set of assumptions and beliefs about ourselves, the external world in general, and our relationship to that world. These assumptions, some of which we consciously know and others that become part of our core being, last into our adult lives sheltering our souls.

Even if we do not consciously believe it, three premises generally form the foundation of how we see the world." Specifically:

    1. The world is good: What underlies this premise is belief that the world is a relatively safe place. People are good, that all things

happen for the good, and there is a future with hope. If something bad does happen, there are powers that protect you (God, Allah, laws, governments, police, family ties). In other words, "God is in his heaven and all is right with the world."

2. Life and the world have meaning: This world meaning premise acknowledges a relationship between you and what happens to you. Part of this relationship recognizes that quality of life called 'justice.' Good, moral, decent people deserve to have good things happen to them, but those who are bad, immoral, and corrupt people deserve any misfortune they receive.

A world of meaning also suggests that there is some 'control' in what happens in the world. Either you control or an ultimate power (e.g., Allah, God, gods, the universe, karma) controls things so that everything comes out the way it should. Justice and control supports the idea that the world is orderly and that it can be comprehended. Life events are not random or absurd.

3. I am a worthy person: The final premise relates to the concept that you are a good, decent, and moral person who deserves having good things happen to you. You are a whole, knowledgeable person who can perceive dangers and act appropriately."

The relationships you have with others, especially those you love and are interdependent with, are a critical part of your assumptive world. Those who die then become an integral part of your past, your present, and your future. They were key components of your outlook on life, plus what and how you thought. They were part of your dreams, hopes, fears and how you lived life. In short, the unique relationship you have with each of those you love, especially a husband, helps define who you are and likewise, you define who they are.

Viewed from this perspective, loss of a loved one can invalidate the "core belief constructs" on which you have relied. The death of your husband profoundly undercuts your taken-for-granted senses of trust, predictability, security and optimism.

Grieving widows say things like, "I used to think that God was watching over us, but now I know that no god is going to protect me" or "I've lost all sense of trust, innocence or significance" "Why me?" "How can I feel safe in a world like this?" You may find yourself becoming cold to God, Allah, ancestors or spiritual beliefs. Faith based beliefs seem as lies. The invalidation of assumptions and abiding beliefs can take away the core illusions that once sustained you.

This loss of assumptions may also challenge your sense of self-continuity over time, making you feel shattered and wonder who you really are and what you can believe. In an instant, your world turns upside-down. Bad things do indeed happen to good people. Life doesn't seem fair, safe or just to you any more. You challenge and question your identity, world-view, faith and sense of control. You may have found yourself furious with fate or a higher being's judgment or felt helpless to stop the death and its consequences. You will continue to feel victimized by all that has happened to you until you let go of it as something that is out of your control.

> Expecting life to treat you well because you are a good person is like expecting an angry bull not to charge because you are a vegetarian.
>
> - Shari R. Barr

When loss and adversity that are inconsistent with your assumptive world occur, you have to make gradual changes to your beliefs and reinterpret your beliefs and assumptions. You are forced by fate to adapt and must learn to live in your new "real world" whether you feel ready to or not.

> I know God will not give me anything I can't handle. I just wish that He didn't trust me so much.
>
> - Mother Teresa

Revising Your Assumptions and Meanings

The fundamental challenge of grief and mourning is the challenge of revising your world-view assumptions and beliefs and creating a new assumptive world. There are three main areas of grief.

1. You grieve the loss of your loved one
2. You grieve all of the related secondary losses
3. You grieve for yourself and the world you assumed existed

A traumatic loss forces you to confront the essence of who you are, what your place in the world is, what your life is to be, and what it means to be alive. You strive to make sense out of what happened and to learn what you can from the experience. This is the transformative power of mourning. Widows learn that they will survive, perhaps "sadder, but wiser."

Turn your wounds into wisdom.

- Oprah Winfrey

Your human desire for certainty and stability are what make this change stuff so difficult. Rather than fear instability or the unknown, tell yourself that it is okay not to know why, how, when and what is next. Moving through the changes you are experiencing forces you to get familiar with the unknown, be more open and draw on your reserve of creativity. Actually changing your attitudes about certainty and stability may even become an exciting new path for you. Enjoy the mystery of the journey.

Making Meaning Out of Loss

Some life events are so significant that they interrupt the status quo of your life, how you define yourself and even perceive life itself. Transition is the way you let go of the status quo and how things used to be, accept how they are in the present and move forward to develop a new status quo in your life. Generally, cultures and religions do not realistically prepare you for working through difficult transitions such as the death of your loved one. Society expects you to accept and grieve losses in a relatively succinct timeframe, pick yourself up by the bootstraps without too much assistance, and get on with your life.

Few widows know how or are taught how to use this period of transition for personal development and growth. You can learn to move through absorbing the external loss and endings, acceptance, self-assessment and reorientation and forward to exploration and new beginnings.

The fastest way to adjust to major changes is to focus, observe and become aware of your life assumptions and beliefs. Your beliefs about what is happening to and around you will have a direct effect on how you find meaning in the experience and how you handle the grief process. If you believe that any change is unfair, a punishment and difficult, then you will have a difficult experience. On the other hand, if you can create new perceptions about change, such as seeing change as a learning opportunity that brings new beginnings or personal growth, then your transition will not be so frightening or overwhelming.

It is what you choose not to observe in your life that controls it.
                                                  - Lynn V. Andrews

In the wake of loss, in time you can learn to understand and manage your emotional and physical symptoms. You then take up the challenge to reconstruct and rewrite a meaningful narrative of yourself and your world at psychological, social and even spiritual levels. During grieving, you may struggle to affirm and reconstruct a personal world of meaning that has been shattered by your loss. Dr. Neimeyer talks of 'meaning-making' that involves a balance between redefining yourself and an implicit reweaving of how you engage with the world. The meaning of death and the meaning of your new life become part of your wider framework for living. Meanings are personal, but they are formed in a social context. The meaning of your life may be as simple as being happy and making others happy.

What You Might Be Feeling as You Revise Your World-View

The most common feelings as you adjust your assumptions and world-view include bereavement, childlike fears, abandonment, disillusionment, depression and loneliness. You may be experiencing fear, anxiety, stress, resentment, irritability, guilt, envy, embarrassment, isolation, sleep disorders, appetite problems and confusion.

Feelings of doubt, rattled core beliefs, lack of trust, anger, frustration, being overwhelmed, caught a blur of change, are often followed by acceptance, resolution, revised world views, sense of purpose, freedom, tolerance, deeper connections, renewed faith, optimism.

Practical Suggestions to Help You Make New Meanings

Mind

- Stop asking "Why". Instead, start asking, "What do I do next?" "How can I make the best of this?" Make peace with the fact that some questions will never have answers.
- You cannot comprehend, understand or figure everything out. An unexpected source of wisdom, the musical rock star Tupac sings, "You can spend minutes, hours, days, weeks or even months over-analyzing a situation trying to put the pieces together, justifying what could've, would've should've happened....or you can just leave the pieces on the floor and move the f*** on."
- Begin by watching, experimenting, taking some risks and exploring. This is a time of questioning who you were, who you are now, and who you want to be.
- Realize that life is sometimes about having to change, not know what is coming or going to happen next, about taking the moment and making the best of it. 'Delicious Ambiguity' is what Gilda Radner called this state of change and uncertainty.
- The only person who is around your entire life is yourself. See your world through your own senses, intuition and intellect. Be alive while you are alive.
- Give yourself permission to explore new ways of thinking and living. Discover what you really believe and want. Look into new philosophies, cultures, personal interests, lifestyles, relationships, locations and opportunities.
- No one has to accumulate education or knowledge to become wise. When you become world wise, you learn to respect your mind and your soul. You are on your way to creating new assumptions, new world-views and adjusting to losses.
- Bereavement prompts you to relearn the world and relearn many old and new things about yourself.
- Embrace change and personal growth. Life isn't about waiting for the storm to pass, it's about getting out and dancing in the rain.

Heart

• Don't rush yourself or the adjustment of your assumptions about life and your world view. Give yourself the luxury of time to create a new reality and adjust.
• Realize that your inner world is a construction zone and everyone knows that you need to slow down in work zones.
• Express your frustrations, doubts, fears and feelings. Holding emotions inside or pretending everything is normal can just create more problems.
• Find ways to wake up and be very aware of the world around you and find ways to please your senses.
• Return to awareness and regain your sense of awe.
• Search your heart for new questions and new answers. Don't make assumptions. Ask all those hard questions.
• Learn to love the world and have compassion for all people.
• Take care of your emotional needs by going to professional mental health care providers or clergy for wise experienced guidance. You need a safe and validating environment that includes a counselor and perhaps a peer support system. Bereavement counselors help you express and understand your feelings, adjust to your losses, rework your world assumptions, and create new goals.

Body

• Cherish your health. If it is good, preserve it. If it is unstable, improve it. If it is beyond what you can improve, get help.
• Revising your perceptions of the world is hard work. Good physical habits will give you the vitality and strength to move forward without getting stuck.
• Stay energized by getting plenty of rest, eating a variety of healthy foods, drinking plenty of water, avoiding addictive substances and exercising regularly.

Spirit

• Take a fresh look at the beliefs, assumptions and expectations you held before the transition-triggered event. Are they still valid and serving your well?
• Re-explore philosophical, religious, spiritual or psychological beliefs and seek out experiences that you find meaningful and suitable.

• Make prayer or meditation a regular practice. Silence is a discovering place.
• Find a regular time and place to be alone and reflect on the process you are going through currently.
• Consider a pilgrimage to a sacred place or journey such as walking the Camino de Santiago in Spain, a trip to Mecca, Konya, Lhasa or the Holy Land. Get in touch with your innermost thoughts.
• Reintegrate and participate with your spiritual community for support and comfort.
• Connect with your new or revived beliefs, faith and world-views.
• Drink precious spirit and life in with a heightened sense of reality.

Connection

• Renew your connections with family, friends, co-workers and spiritual groups.
• Hospice, religious leaders, bereavement support groups and other social service associations will confidentially help you deal with reconstructing the meaning behind the loss and the revised meaning of your life.
• Join support groups where you can voice your shattered assumptions and views. Others who have walked this path are willing to share their insights.
• Take opportunities to learn about new ideas, beliefs and ways of living. Discuss these with others.

Chapter Thirteen

ADJUSTING TO THE ABSENCE OF YOUR HUSBAND
Transition Phase Four

The death of your husband can produce a profound shift in your sense of who you are. Whole facets of your past shared with the deceased slip away forever. Your life will never be the same again. Death shakes your sense of self and of the world. Grief is a very personal intimate process that is inextricably linked with your sense of who you are and the meaning and purpose of life. This is neither the begining of your story, nor the end.

It is totally up to you to determine who you are and what life will look like now and in the future. Many widows tend to see no good in the forced transition, deny having any distress and just want to hurry on to the new life as quickly as possible. You have experienced an ending, followed by a period of distress and confusion, leading to a new beginning. There are both negative and positive aspects to the situation. Coping with endings and letting go of the past is an ambiguous task that takes internal and external work.

> We are made wise, not by the recollections of our past, but by the responsibility for our future.
> - George Bernard Shaw

Adjustment Guidance

During this time of transformation and adjustment, your focus shifts from basic biological reactions to subtly psychological ones. Use the mourning process as an opportunity to reconstruct self and world meaning. It is a frightening task to confront the ultimate concerns of existence, including death, freedom, isolation and meaning. Through guided reflection and trying out a variety of life roles, you can find fresh perspectives on the losses for yourself and others.

> Tears have a wisdom all their own. They come when a person has relaxed enough to let go and to work through her sorrow. They are the natural bleeding of an emotional wound, carrying the poison out of the system. Here lies the road to recovery.
>
> - F. Alexander Magoun

It is a difficult process to let go of your old situation or loved one, suffer the confusing in-between, and move forward again into your new roles and situation. Doing the work leading from disorientation to reorientation is part of the process of self-renewal. In times of personal transitions, it can become distressing if you do not have some clear goal and beneficial pattern toward the desired end.

Meaning reconstruction after loss recognizes that your goal is to gain new and fresh perspectives regarding your situation and to become engaged in life again. It requires an acknowledgement that you will never return to the good old days, pre-loss life, but that you must develop a meaningful life role without the deceased loved one. You have an avalanche of profound changes hitting you all at once and feel unprepared to cope with it alone.

You need a safe and validating environment, perhaps with a mental health counselor and support systems, in which you can tell and retell the stories associated with your losses. A counselor's primary role is to provide the therapeutic conditions of empathy, congruence and positive regard that is useful in increasing your awareness and insight. A professional advisor can assist you in reassessing and reorganizing the patterns and assumptions of your life. Counseling theorists advise that you should fully experience the anxiety appropriate to your life circumstance. Use that anxiety to adjust your life and transcend the past and present in order to reach the future.

Grief or bereavement counseling is a special type of professional help, which is often available through hospice services or health care provider referrals. Grief counseling reduces the level of transition distress that you go through after the death. It can help you adjust to your new life without your husband and help you move more easily through the phases of grief.

Adjustment to the absence of your loved one does not mean that the pain is over. Your old life is gone and you need to mourn its losses. You grieve not only the deceased person, but also losing the future you planned and expected with that person.

Adjusting to Absences

After the funeral and burial, your life's responsibilities and everyday patterns must eventually resume, but they do so in an altered form. There were roles that each of you played, yet now all of the responsibility has fallen on you as the surviving spouse. Cultural, personal and familial contexts all influence the reconstruction of your life.

A relationship with a husband is an exclusive and critically important one. Your husband was one of the key people who defined who you are and affirmed your identity. You now have to explore and find out who you are beyond the interdependent marital role and relationship. You have to learn what it means to be 'me' without 'him' and accept there is no longer an 'us' or 'we.' Your sense of self and security require gathering new social validation for your character. You are trying to learn about your new world and relearn yourself. Death losses invariably involve both loss-oriented and restoration-oriented stressors and pressures.

> It is not the strongest of the species that survive, not the most intelligent, but the one most responsive to change.
> - Charles Darwin

Additional Loss-Oriented Stresses

The grieving process can be very painful and difficult as you come to terms with the death by recognizing what the loss means to you in actual day-to-day life. First, there are loss-oriented stresses related directly to the death of your spouse. These include the ending of the physical relationship with the deceased, the lack of companionship and social interaction and the disintegration of your plans for the future.

Yearning for your lost spouse is common as you are weaned into aloneness. The desire to remain connected to your deceased husband and the need to move on with your life are in conflict. This loss of the main person in your world and witness to your life takes a specific type of coping and strength.

Your secondary loss stresses are created because the responsibilities, roles, additional household chores and financial burdens now fall on you. Feeling confused and helpless occurs especially when the division of labor roles and responsibilities had been clearly or traditionally, defined by gender or mutual agreement. Your reintegration into daily living requires a redefinition of roles. Expanded duties amplify the feelings of confusion, abandonment, isolation, loss of control and loneliness. Studies show that widows who were dependent on their husbands for male-stereotyped tasks like finances, car and home maintenance were at higher risk for anxiety.

Additionally, you deal with a decrease in financial resources, increase in responsibilities and altered communication patterns with relatives and friends. Social isolation may occur, as many gatherings were had been based on couples and groups find it difficult to adjust to your new status and identity as a widow. Your professional and personal life may suffer because your mind and heart are elsewhere.

There seem to be a maze of decisions to consider. Coping involves dealing with the estate administration, financial problems, parenting alone and other new or overwhelming tasks. Obtaining professional help and favors from family members and friends where necessary is a wise coping technique. Losses in the life circumstances and home environment are more amenable to external adjustments and outside help.

You will come to know and accept the reality of the losses and all it entails slowly over time. For example, months or years after your spouse dies, you are reminded of your late husband's absence at every holiday, anniversary, excursion or an event he would have been expected to attend. This can bring back strong emotions, and may call for mourning yet another part of the loss. You adjust to the absence and to daily life without the deceased as the initial grief and pain become less intense. Handling the daily roles and routines or delegating tasks to others becomes a new way of life.

In time, there is reclamation of the emotional energy that you invested in the relationship with your deceased spouse to use in other ways and relationships. One day you will realize that your grief has begun to subside and you have been transformed by the experience in ways you never imagined. Be secure in the progress you have already made and in your gratitude for having known the loved one you lost. You will be able to accept that your loved one is still living through you and then you'll know that your life is moving forward.

Individuals who have suffered losses are naturally inclined toward growth and are self-regulating. Health is defined as a person's awareness, recognition and paying appropriate attention to desires and needs as required hierarchically. As they arise, you address and attend to the most pressing needs. For healthy individuals, this creative adjustment process is fluid and focus can shift rapidly when faced with changing demands. You will become more creative, resilient and address losses more quickly.

> No one's death comes to pass without making some impression, and those close to the deceased inherit part of the liberated soul and become richer in their humanness.
>
> - Hermann Broch

Phase four adjustment challenges and tips are divided into categories under Mind, Heart, Body, Spirit and Connections. These suggestions and philosophy are keys for transitioning through the fourth phase of grieving so that you can begin to adjust to the absence of your late husband.

What You Might Be Feeling at the Absence of Your Husband

The most common feelings as you adjust to the absence of your mate include yearning, intense longing for the one who died, bereavement, childlike fears, abandonment, disillusionment, depression and loneliness. You may experience separation anxiety, stress, resentment, irritability, guilt, envy, embarrassment, anxiety, isolation, sleep and appetite problems.

Feelings of lack of trust, doubt, disorganization, incompetence at new tasks, unfamiliarity with roles, anger at the desertion, frustration, overwhelmed by day-to-day living, caught in an avalanche of change and conflict are often followed by acceptance, resolution, new reserves of strength and determination, revised self-worth, freedom, independence, forgiveness, competence, deeper connections and renewed optimism.

Practical Suggestions to Help You Adjust to Absences

Mind

- Take things one day at a time. Put one foot in front of the other until daily life routines feel more doable, comfortable and natural again. Be patient and kind to yourself.
- Start with short-term goals. You counteract the feeling that your

life is out of control when you set goals and accomplish them.

• Make lists of quick simple activities or tasks such as answering a letter, going to synagogue, preparing a favorite meal or making an appointment. Set timeframes for completion and congratulate yourself when you reach the goal.

• Take baby steps and inch toward new ways of doing things.

• Jot down some long-range goals and set time limits for reaching those goals. List some of the plans you could develop for the future such as trying a new hobby, going back to school, taking a trip, redecorating, learning a new skill, exploring a career change and other meaningful goals. Just daydream and have fun.

• Check your progress periodically. You certainly can always reexamine your priorities and adjust short or long-range plans.

• Expect times of anxiety; expect many of your old fears to be triggered; and expect others in your life to be threatened by your transitions and changes.

• Quiz yourself: "If I was not afraid, I would _____. Be creative and brave.

• Make physical, spiritual and mental adjustments to your life so that thoughts of your deceased husband are accompanied with less pain. The goal is to derive a measure of comfort from memories in time. Believing tomorrow will be better can make it so.

• Keep learning. Learn more about the computer, legal and estate matters, finances, communications, gardening, car mechanics, maintenance, or whatever is needed to deal with the multiple losses and fulfilling your new roles. Never let the brain idle.

• Congratulate yourself on learning new skills or the completion of even simple tasks.

• Appreciate those special moments, even if they are short, when you felt like yourself again.

• Look back and focus on all the things you do right so you can keep building on them. Celebrate your achievements today and celebrate your life always.

• Discover or rediscover old interests and satisfying activities. Join a volunteer effort that is of interest to you, resume club memberships, attend religious and spiritual gatherings, try sports or hobbies, and use any body of knowledge you find inspiring, uplifting or comforting.

• Don't take on more responsibilities or jobs that aren't yours. Stop being a control freak trying to do everything. The Jewish Talmud reminds you that 'the sun will set without your assistance.' Let go of some tasks and don't be too proud to ask for help and delegate.

• There will be days when you feel unable to start and other days when you feel unstoppable. Take it at your own pace those days because even tiny steps will move you forward.

• You are created with an inherent ability to heal and be blessed by grieve experiences. Lynn Brookside wrote, "Finally, I grabbed my grief by the neck, shouting 'I will not let you go until you bless me!'"

Heart

• Don't hesitate to talk about the past and the loss in order to accept the reality and adjust to the new identity and role you are living.

• Remember to carry tissues for unexpected bursts of healing tears. The tears happen, so endure, grieve, blow your nose and move on.

• Enjoy the simple things and experiences that give you pleasure. If you love long walks, concerts, playtime with the grandchildren, reading, travel, scrapbooking, fresh flowers, yoga class, painting, writing, cooking, entertaining, singing at church, do them.

• Surround yourself with what you love. Whether it is plants, pets, pictures, hobbies, family, keepsakes, music or anything that brings joy and hope. You get to make the decisions about your environment. Your home is your refuge.

• Regain your sense of awe. Be aware of your surroundings. Notice the sunsets, savor the smell of fresh roasted coffee, enjoy the softness of your child's skin and hair, visit art galleries or attend concerts. Find ways to please all your senses.

• Don't take guilt trips. Take a trip to the shopping mall, even to the next town, to a foreign country, but not to where the guilt is. Guilt is the most useless emotion there is.

• Fight off any survivor guilt you may be harboring. You are allowed to be fulfilled and productive. Your beloved would want you to go on with life and be happy.

• Savor moments of joy, humor and satisfaction. Things can seem funny again and it is alright to laugh long and loud until you gasp for breath. No one is meant to live in perpetual mourning. Laughter is very healing to those with emotional or physical injury.

• Working one-on-one with a professional counselor or clergy and in grief support groups can provide you with emotional and practical help with coping with the death of your spouse.

• Make a special effort to help others who are bereaved. You are in a unique position to share your experiences and insights. Service to others provides a sense of meaning and well-being.

• As you find new reserves of strength and determination, you will begin to believe in yourself and a bright future.

Body

• Healthy habits are the foundation for handling all those change coming your way. There will be times when you don't want to take a walk, eat your vegetables, get out of bed or when a cocktail sounds better than a tall glass of water. Make good choices.

• Continue to expect tears. Grief is like peeling the layers of an onion until you reach the core of your feelings and essence. There will be crying in both cases.

• Do not expect that you can medicate your pain away or block out memories. When someone has a true chemical imbalance depression, certain antidepressants have a place in their recovery. Antidepressants or sleep aids can impede your grieving process. Drugs cannot remove the cause of the sadness or yearning.

• Be alert to signs of health problems like consistent pains, difficulty sleeping, lethargy, headaches, heart conditions or eating disorders. Make and keep your doctor's appointments.

• Get into the habit of hugging, touching and holding hands of loved ones. It is advisable to give and receive three hugs a day for survival, five for maintenance and at least eight for growth. If no one is around, go ahead and hug or caress yourself.

• Breathe. Breathing is central to health and healing. Practicing slow, deep and steady breathing can help you relax. The more relaxed your breath, the more relaxed you feel in your mind and your body.

• Keep regular sleep hours. Hope rises with the sun each morning.

Spirit

• Practice daily prayer or meditation. Silence is a discovering place.
• Be alone and reflect on the losses and transitions you are going through. When you are alone, you are with an interesting person.
• Reach out for comforting people or a spiritual community to be with and share your thoughts and feelings.
• Reconnect with faith, spirituality, joy and life.
• Create personal rituals and use objects to honor your husband.
• The life potential and spirit inside you is too precious to waste. Do not let your spirit or potential die with your loved one.
• Remember that what is real never ceases to be, according to the Bhagavad Gita and other sacred literatures.
• Do things on a larger scale. Live with a heightened sense of reality and spirituality.

Connection

• Ignore the grief police who tell you it is time to get over it and get back to your old life. Don't let others put additional stressors on you to mourn 'correctly' or do too much.
• Ignore well-meant advice that misses the mark for your situation.
• Avoid making any major decisions like selling everything and joining the Peace Corp until you recover from your loss. Too much change has already taken place.
• Watch out for con artists or vampire relatives while you are in a vulnerable state. Conferring with your attorney on big decisions will slow down sudden impulses and eliminate illicit requests from others that are not in your best interest.
• Don't become reclusive or confine yourself to your home following the death of your mate. Get out of the house regularly to attend services, work, visit with friends and family, go shopping, volunteer, socialize or at least take a long walk.
• Reestablish friendships and family connections that you have found nurturing in the past. Tell the people that you love that you love them at every opportunity. Don't isolate yourself.
• Baby girl, you are never as alone as the think you are. You've got more people that love and care for you than you know. Nothing will ever change that.
• Develop an empathetic support system. You were never meant to grieve alone.

• Stay away from toxic people, situations or things. Be around positive forward-looking people. Keep only cheerful emotionally healthy friends. The grouches will pull you down. Don't worry about dropping some people from your past. There are good reasons they won't make it into your future.

• Learn new skills and hobbies. It will lead you to experiencing new interactions and relationships.

• Seek and recruit help with practical jobs. Unfamiliar duties like paying bills, doing yard work, fixing things around the house, maintaining a car, cooking and so on can overwhelm a grieving person. This added stress makes the loss and pain more frustrating.

• Ask for and accept offers of help. Friends and relatives want to help but often don't know what to do. Even small odd jobs, activities or visits can make difficult times more bearable. Have specific 'honey-do' lists of tasks for volunteers to pick from. Request help from those trustworthy folks who are physically able to do a few chores.

• For complicated grief with feelings of despair, worthlessness, hopelessness, deep depression that persist, you should seek professional medical help and explore the options. A psychiatrist familiar with grief can discuss your situation and evaluate the best course of action. Some complicated grief and severe depression, like other illnesses, may require medications.

• Organizations like AARP Widowed Persons Service (888-687-2277) and Parents Without Partners (800-637-7974) and the local chapters of Hospice Association of America (202-546-4759) offer personalized help especially geared toward widows.

Chapter Fourteen

CHANGING YOUR RELATIONSHIP TO THE DECEASED
Transition Phase Five

In discussing all your challenges of grief and mourning, one of the most forward moving is how to reconstruct your relationship to your husband who has died. Traditionally and culturally, many times the advice given to widows who lost a spouse was to "forget the deceased, move on with life, and find another relationship to invest yourself in." Grief specialists describe this type of simplistic advice as treating love as if it was money to redirect from one investment (relationship) to another.

Psychologists and counselors realize that 'forgetting and reinvesting' is bad advice. You should not follow this mentally unhealthy path of fast relief mourning. Instead, follow what you are naturally drawn to do; and strive to maintain and then restructure the relationship with your deceased loved one. Just as it takes time for a broken bone to mend, it takes time for a broken spirit to mend. Grief work has a great transformative power.

Transforming Your Lost Relationship

You know what made him laugh; he will always be a part of you. You didn't just lose your husband; you lost your best friend, confidant, lover and knight in shining armor. The goal of grieving is not one of letting go and forgetting the deceased spouse; the goal of grieving is to find a less painful way to hold on and honor the memories. Memories are very important, but you should not use them as a shield against the present. Grieving is the process of learning to live your life without someone you care about. It is a lifelong journey.

Every widow has a different grieving style. Some widows appear visibly shaken while others never show outward public expressions of anguish. Obvious emotional grief and remaining distraught for a long time is not evidence of how deeply you loved your late husband. The depth of your sadness is not necessarily a measure of the depth of your love or dedication. You do not have to prove that love to anyone. All responses, whether refrained or intense are simply how you are actively processing your loss. Transforming and changing your relationship to your deceased husband is a testament to your resilience and recuperative powers.

Attachments and Bonding

An effective theory of grief, developed by John Bowlby, is the attachment model. This approach emphasizes that attachment or bonding is a needed instinct and functional survival mechanism found in many of the social animals. Attachment is necessary for the survival of the species, especially given humans' prolonged periods of infancy and dependency. When a person who was the object of attachment dies, there are instinctual biological behavior responses to that loss. These behaviors include crying, clinging, yearning and searching. Humans actively seek to maintain the attachment and restore the lost bond. When bonds are permanently severed by death, the behaviors continue until the attachment is divested of significance and emotional meaning.

Additionally, grief and morning behaviors expressing distress tend to engage the care, support, and protection of the larger social unit. This psychobiological model sees grief as a natural response to a loss or major transition in life. This continues until the bond is restored or the grieving person sheds the bond. Bonds between the grieving individual and the lost object of affection will continue after the loss, but in a different form.

Creating Healthy Connections

As the Bowlby attatchment study shows, you are instinctually unable to forget someone you bonded with in love even though he is dead. You attached to that person and he was an important part of your life. Recovery from your loss entails finding methods to maintain a certain bond with your attachment figure while simultaneously acknowledging that he is no longer physically available. It is biologically impossible for you to just walk away from those emotional bonds as they exist until the attachment is given a different meaning. It is paradoxical that the work of mourning requires you to pay exaggerated and excessive attention to your late husband as a subject in order to come to terms with his being gone.

The fact that widows maintain a type of relationship even after death is vividly demonstrated by how frequently widows (over 80%) say that they sense or perceive the presence of their loved one. Many also reported talking to their loved one. Feeling the presence, talking, hearing, smelling, seeing, or feeling the touch of the deceased is in the range of normal grieving behavior. Those who have perceived the presence of their departed spouse say these experiences are reassuring and pleasant. Many widows believe that this is how their deceased husband communicates that he is fine and that she should not remain fixated on the past.

It is important for you to maintain some feeling of connection with your deceased husband at first because it gives you, not only the tools to weather the stress of separation, but also an opportunity to revise your relationship with him internally. Healthy mourning involves transforming the old bonds and developing a new relationship with him. It is a way for you to reintegrate your loved one into your mind and heart. After actively doing the grief work, you can learn how to embrace your loved one, not in a physical way, but in a symbolic way so that he can always reside in your heart. It is possible to restructure love so that it transcends the physical world and resides within you. Often widows say that in many ways they feel closer than ever before to the one who died.

> Death leaves a heartache no one can heal; love leaves a memory no one can steal.
>
> - Irish Headstone

Different Cultural Grieving Customs

Cultures greatly differ in their grieving models and transformation methods. While the biological responses to loss seem to be universally hard-wired, the psychological and social processes of adaptation to loss are not universal. Each society specifies rituals, manners, social customs, dress, habits, actions and even attitudes that are expected from the widow. For example, the Hopi Indians of Arizona believe the death is not a linear path, but circular. Death is 'birth' into a new world. They value self-reliance and keeping emotions to oneself. The Native American widow is taught to stay outwardly calm and continue life as usual, because how they act after a death may affect or delay their spouse's journey into the next world.

In contrast, the Japanese widow is expected to maintain lifelong ties and interaction with the deceased and ancestors through religious rituals. The well-being of surviving family members is affected by how the deceased was cared for, visited and the upkeep of the gravesite. East Asian and Indian collectivist cultures have century old traditions, ceremonies and elaborate rituals to help surviving widows cope with the loss. The custom of widows wearing unadorned black clothing during periods of mourning dates back to the Roman Empire. Some widows will wear black for the rest of their lives. In India, the Hindu widows are set apart by their white attire and shaved heads. Many cultures and religions continue specific rituals and customary actions to express grief and hold periodic ceremonies to recall the deceased.

Relationships Don't End, But They Do Need to Change

Nowhere is it written or said that you must forget your husband. Your loved one is part of you and always will be. Love doesn't die because the body dies. Love continues even though it may change and be different from before. Nobody forgets a loved one or ever completely stops grieving. You face constant reminders of your time together and at first wonder how you will get through each day or the future without the person. Relationships don't die, they do need to change. An old spiritual hymn that says, "It's so high you can't get over it, so low you can't get under it, so wide you can't get around it...you must go in through the door." Accept the important truth that you will never get over, under or around the death of your husband, but you can always get through it.

Having this dimensional life taken away reminds you of the impermanence of life itself and is a call to appreciate life and all that it gives you while it is here. Your husband's death allows you to receive the magic and bounty of being alive and encourages you to live fully from the heart. You will have fond memories of the one you lost, you will discover a sense of gratitude for having known your loved one while he was alive and the experience will awaken in you a desire to live the rest of your life full out on his behalf.

When the one you love was living, he existed outside of you. Now that he is no longer here physically to maintain a connection, you have to reintegrate him into your inner being and create a special place in your heart where he can always be present. Even though your relationship ended in loss, you are still a wiser person for having invested in the relationship. Always strive to incorporate the death of your spouse into the tapestry of your life.

Grief is not a straight line with an endpoint. Grief is a response that involves processing and making adjustments. No one is ever completely finished with mourning or totally stops grieving for the loss. You will emerge from a phase only to have it repeat and reoccur, round and round. There will be triggers and anniversary mourning. In spite of the fact that your grief seems to sometimes double back and wind around like a spiral staircase, you do adapt to your altered circumstances and recover.

Grief changes over time and gets easier. You will learn that dwelling on the death, pain and suffering is definitely not the way to live a full life. There is a dual physical and mental process going on simultaneously. On one hand, you deal with the typical emotions and symptoms of grief, while at the same time, work is taking place internally to change the relationship with your deceased loved one.

You will still miss the one you loved who is no longer with you, but you will find that the gratitude for having loved him will help conquer the loss. Your challenge is to hold your late husband in your memory, conversations, life story and rituals in a way that is manageable rather than painful. Death ends life, not the relationship.

> God gave us memories so that we might have roses in December.
>
> - James M. Barrie

Inner Connections

There is a process that psychoanalysts call 'internalizing'. It is by making the deceased part of your inner world that you change your connection to him. Yes, the actual physical flesh and blood person is gone, the possibilities, dreams and promises are gone, the sounds of voice and laughter are gone, the knowing smile is gone, your life witness is gone, the hugs and touch are gone, the sharing of family events, parenting and grandparenting together is gone, sharing meals and a bed are gone. These things are no longer a part of your reality. However, when you make your late husband part of your inner world, in many ways you never lose him. "To live in hearts we leave behind is not to die." says Thomas Campbell.

Love leaves an indelible imprint on your heart, memories and actions. Having a shared love enriched your life. You can both keep your late spouse with you and let him go at the same time. By making him part of what you do, think, feel, remember and love, you can both carry him within yourself and let him go. When someone you love becomes a memory, the memory becomes a treasure. Honor and remember your late husband by living your life fully from the heart right now. The highest tribute to the deceased is not grief, but gratitude.

You can process the intimate loss of your spouse by retelling stories, visiting his grave, and assuming qualities, interests or projects to blend with his identity. For example, taking up causes like helping the less fortunate, continued travel or serving at church keep the memory, interests and values alive through your actions. Find your strength in what remains behind.

Your internal processing and external grief work changes the nature of bonds with the deceased, while also maintaining and developing other relationships and social outreaches. Your grieving is an ongoing action of reconstructing a personal world of meaning and reconstructing a new type of relationship with your late spouse. Counselor Alan D. Woldfelt advises that the unfolding journey through grief is not intended to create a return to an old normal, but the discovery of a new normal.

Rituals Maintain Your Bonds

There are healthy ways to maintain that love bond when your life partner is no longer present through ways called 'links'. The role of the physical possessions of the deceased, what to do with them, and the nature of linking are handled in a variety of symbolic and dynamic ways. Grief rituals and their accompanying symbols have been shown to help transform and reframe your relationship with the deceased.

Each culture and society has its own established and prescribed linking rituals surrounding dying and grieving. Grief healing rituals strengthen human bonds, honor the deceased and encourage expressions. One of the world's greatest artworks, the Taj Mahal in India, was created as a physical expression of an unfathomable grief.

Meaningful personal rituals to honor your dead spouse can help you redefine your relationship and recover. To create a ritual, you only need three things: a place, time and activities. Some use linking objects for their rituals. The objects can be as simple as placing your loved one's photograph beside a single rose or religious symbol or candle. Starting with an attitude of awareness and loving care, you can light a candle or say a prayer, pledge or affirmation like "I love and miss you." "You made me realize what a miracle life is." "I will honor you by creating a new fulfilling life." "Thank you for making me who I am and shall become." Fixing your loved one's favorite meal, using his tools, playing favorite music or wearing a saved sweater are also considered rituals. You may replace or discard the ritual or linking objects without feeling guilty when you don't need them anymore. Many different ideas and tasks, especially meaningful if you create them, help in restructuring the relationship with your deceased loved one. When you begin to feel hopeful, experience gratification, regain an interest in life and adapt to new roles, you are well on the path to internalizing the love connections and revising the relationship with your late spouse.

The fifth transitional phase revisions' suggestions and challenges are in categories under Mind, Heart, and Connections. These bits of philosophy and advice are your keys for transitioning through this fifth phase of grieving as you honor the past, but begin to change your relationship with your late husband and connect with your new life.

What You Might Be Feeling as Your Lost Relationship Changes

The grief work that you do to revise the relationship to your deceased husband may include feelings like longing for deceased, sadness, clinging, emptiness, loneliness and isolation. You may experience changes in sleep patterns, vivid dreams, and sensing a presence of the deceased. There may be a fear of forgetting, feelings of being disloyal, ambivalent, awkward, reflective and a fear of being alone or never loving again. You may start to recognize the faults and humanness of the deceased and of yourself, find forgiveness, face challenges and discover creativity, insights, ability to laugh, ability to cry, hopefulness and renewed interest in life.

Practical Suggestions for Lost Relationship Changes

Mind

- Reflect on the legacy of your late spouse. What were his life accomplishments? What gave made his life special, purposeful and meaningful? How did he influence and inspire you and others? Take up some of his projects or interests and make them your own.
- Note the good things you learned in your relationship. He taught you things that are still with you and part of your life, for example: gardening, how to cook gourmet foods and appreciate Spanish wines, how to use email and EBay, finding the best forest mushroom, how to dive, encouraged your interest in sailing and many more things.
- Continue to write in your diary or journal. This record will help you to identify and understand your current and desired future feelings. Writing lets you calm those rattled spirits and relieve your body and mind of stresses. It allows you to own your feelings and empowers you to walk your new path.
- Forgiveness means to release your late spouse's past faults and experience your newfound freedom. You need to do this right away for your own peace of mind and the quality of future relationships.
- Write a letter to your lost loved one today. No one will ever see this but you. Be honest and tell him everything you want to share. Then you could change hands and write back his response or your own feelings. The method of non-dominant handwriting allows your mind to free flow and the writing to appear to come as if another person is speaking through you and to you.
- When you fully realize that your late husband is not coming back, ever, you will see your world in a different light.
- Reframe photographs of your loved one. Hang a few around to stimulate memories and conversations. Scan and make copies of photographs, albums or CDs for family and friends.
- Donate or dispose of clothing and related personal items within six months or less. Keep some items such as jewelry, letters, artworks, degrees, awards or one-of-a-kind photographs or share some with

your children, relatives or close friends.

• Do not keep physical reminders and rooms in a museum-like or shrine condition. This is a classical example of denial and refusal to deal with grief. If you can't let go of some things yet, at least pack them up and put them out of sight in storage.

• Rather than dispose of all tangible reminders, you can rearrange some furniture, paint rooms in cheerful and soothing colors, landscape or redecorate certain areas to reflect your taste and renewal. Maybe recover and put his old recliner in a different place so you don't forget and expect to see him there out of habit.

• Make a video, power point, collage, or scrapbook of pictures of your life together. Look at these mementos, treasure the memories and assure yourself that you will have good times again.

• If you or someone you know does crafts or sews, you may be able to make a personal handcrafted item like a quilt, pillow, teddy bear, memory box or collage for you to keep near.

• Plant and dedicate a memorial tree or garden, something alive and growing. Keep growing live plants in your home as a symbol of life.

• Find joy and pride in your new normal life.

Heart

• Say "Thank You!" to your deceased mate. Gratitude is one of the most beautiful expressions of love. Just saying thank you will help you find closure and open doors to an abundance of life's blessings from all directions, but especially gratitude in your present and future.

• Forgive your deceased husband for his transgressions and faults. Sometimes the late spouse had a dark side that you knew or only discover later. Forgive him and forgive yourself for your own actions, omissions and judgment of his actions.

• If you experienced many trials with your husband because of problems with addictions, abuse or bad life choices, you may not be able to forget all the hurt and anger caused by him. Don't bottle up these feelings just because someone said never speak ill of the dead.

• Express the truth, derogatory memories and negative feelings in a supportive environment. Once you vent you can begin to forgive and remember some of the good times. Deal with the unresolved issues around difficult times and disappointments so that you can come to peace with it and learn from them.

• Visit his gravesite to face the reality of separation and share your private thoughts.

• Know that you are not being disloyal to the love you lost by moving on with you life. Hope is grief's best music.

• While the quilt of your life used to be in the wedding ring design, now it is time to fashion a new quilt design to comfort you.

• Separate reality from illusion. Reality is based on the absolute facts that make up your situation and surround your change. Illusion is the image you create around change and what you assume it might mean. For example, reality states: "My husband has died." Illusion cries out, "I'll be single for the rest of my life; I will never be loved or happy again." Differentiate reality from illusion.

• Isolate the facts and realize that while some things have changed, many parts of your life are still present and strong. Don't allow worse case scenario illusions to frighten and immobilize you.

• Strive for balance in your life between your happiness and any negativity that interferes with your happiness. A happier life consists of both work and play. It is up to you to develop a proper balance.

Connection

• Sharing stories and memories about the deceased allows you and others to continue a connection to him. Telling and retelling of stories of your late husband and your loss helps you get social validation for the changed story line of your new life.

• Stay with professional counselors and support groups because they are kindred spirits who can provide you a safe environment for sharing stories and expressing feelings without fear of reprisal. Others may say, "Don't feel that way" or "What good does it do to keep talking about it?" But, a group of people going through the same thing understands you. You can find new meaning through the telling your stories and plans.

• Continue to mark special dates, holidays, anniversaries, birthdays. Prepare your late husband's favorite dishes or raise a glass in toast. Share expressions of loss with others saddened by his absence.

• Create a memorial to honor the deceased. Some widows and family members set up scholarships, donate to charities, put up a park bench, erect a monument, marker or plaque, fund and name a hospital wing or college building, buy a church pew, dedicate a stained glass window or organ or other such lasting remembrances.

• Follow rituals like ceremonies or light candles and saying prayers.

• Plan memorials services to honor, express love, share memories or scatter the ashes.

Chapter Fifteen

REINVENT YOURSELF - Transition Phase Six

In the adaptive phases of grief, a section is necessary on how you can reinvent yourself after the loss of your loved one. You have been working through the challenges of (1) Accepting the reality of your spouse's death after the initial physiological and psychological shock, (2) Opening up to and using the pain of grief, (3) Revising your world-view assumptions (4) Adjusting to the absence of your spouse, and (5) Reconstructing your relationship to the deceased. Now you can get information and suggestions on how to reinvent yourself and write your new life story.

> In the midst of winter, I finally learned that there was
> within me an invincible summer.
> > - Albert Camus

New Life Roles

When someone you love dies, a part of you dies along with him. You take on and function simultaneously in specific roles such as wife, mother, sibling, father, child, husband and such, each with its own set of duties and responsibilities. You often naively take for granted that these life roles and relationships with those you care about will continue. Eventually, someone you love does die and a unique void is created within you. In an instant, your life is forever changed and your loved one is no longer around. Who can fill that person's role to share both memories and the present happenings of your life, or to join you in planning for the future? The roles you played in life also change. You go from being a wife to being a widow, from having a significant other to being single. Your world is challenged and you are forced to reinvent yourself if you are to survive and thrive in this new world. A key element of grieving is to gain a perspective on the meaning of the loss and to reconstruct a world in which you can live effectively afterwards. When your life story totally entwines with another, and that person dies, it is as if a main character of the book dropped out. As the author, how can you write the future chapters and scenes so that the book makes sense? There has to be a rewrite of your story because your life is not a history book, it is an ongoing narrative.

Revising Your Narrative Life Story

People organize their lives, their sense of reality and their perception of the world through a personal narrative story. You become the author of your own life story, struggling to compose, edit and dramatically rewrite these when unanticipated or tragic losses occur. The very person who played a starring role in your life story has been cruelly removed. The loss of one who was the intimate witness to your past can undermine even your basic self-definition. Your late husband, who was in the special relational position, is no longer there to remember and validate the unique database of shared memories of who you are and have been together. Your deceased spouse and your life together acted as definitions of who you were. You often define yourself by the roles and relationships that you have and by the circumstances of your life.

> Grief is more than an emotion; it is a process of reconstructing
> a world of meaning that has been challenged by loss.
> - Dr. Robert Neimeyer

Now that one of the main characters starring in your life story has died, there is a need to readjust and reorganize the story plot and rewrite the endings. The tendency is to organize the loss experience in narrative form, to construct accounts that make some sense of the troubling transitions in life and find some meaningful structure for the remaining chapters of your life story. Your new narrative includes the surviving main character (you) relearning about yourself and scripting your new role in the story. This new role encompasses adjusting to the loss, redefining your character, reorganizing the daily plot of your life and envisioning a fulfilling future.

In Lewis Carroll's *Alice's Adventures in Wonderland*, there is a passage that may describe your sense of being in transition: "Who are you?" said the Caterpillar…"I---I hardly know, Sir, just at present," Alice replied rather shyly, "at least I know who I was when I got up this morning, but I think I must have been changed several times since then." Ever felt this way?

Rebuilding Your Life

Death shatters and disrupts your life story. "How can I ever put my life back together again?" a widow cries. You are not Humpty Dumpty; you can be put back together again. Losing a loved one can make you feel like your purpose for living, the reason for your existence and your very life has been taken from you. Like the phoenix, you may feel reduced to mere ashes, waiting for the wind to scatter you. You will arise out of those ashes, but you must work at it. After the loss of a loved one, you can come back whole as a changed and stronger person. You can once again soar like the phoenix and see not only the smallest of details, but also the whole of life.

So, how can you reinvent yourself? Just as you learned how to live as a married woman, you will learn to live as a single person again. You will begin by watching, exploring, experimenting and taking some risks. This is a time of questioning who you were, who you are now, and who you want to be. Draw up a before and after plan. It will require reevaluating your priorities, facing challenges you didn't have before, different skills and establishing new relationships with others and yourself.

> If the future seems overwhelming, remember that it comes one moment at a time.
>
> - Beth Mende Conny

Loss can automatically cause what was once trivial until now to seem important and vice versa. You may ask, "Who will take care of me? Who will now do the things that my loved one did for me? Whom can I confide in? Will I ever be able to love again? How has the purpose and direction of my life changed?" It is very humbling to realize that much of your self-image was merely a reflection of how your husband saw you.

Learning to do something new, something your spouse once did may seem a trivial accomplishment, but these new skills and experiences are profoundly important if you never had to take on that role or responsibility before. You will find that you can make decisions alone, communicate and relate with others, learn new skills, do tasks for yourself, deal with challenges, and rightfully, you will be proud. Your small accomplishments mean that larger and more complex ones can be achieved.

Working through grief can actually deepen interpersonal connections and, in some cases, leads to a profound new sense of faith, gratitude and meaning in your reinvented life. Be patient with yourself.

> You cannot plant an acorn in the morning and expect that afternoon to sit in the shade of the oak.
>   - Antoine de Saint-Exupery

Self-reinvention and life story rewriting challenges and suggestions in this section are in categories under Mind, Heart, Body, Spirit and Connections. These words of advice and philosophy are your keys for transitioning through the sixth phase of grieving as you learn how to create your new life. Here are some ways for you to go from widowhood to selfhood.

What You Might Be Feeling During Your Reinvention Phase

As you are reinventing yourself and trying new skills and roles, you may experience feelings of being incomplete, lonely, bereft of purpose, grief, regret, self pity and directionless. There will be times of frustration, lack of skills, drained energy, self-doubts; times when you are feeling disloyal, scared, guilty, stuck, not your old self, distracted, immobilized, lazy, lackadaisical, isolated, vulnerable, irritated and impatient.

But on the other side, you will also have feelings of being creative, independent, informed, reliable, trusting, competent, have nesting instincts, motivated, compassion for others, restored, energized, transformed, courageous, special, sensual, proud of accomplishments, curious, daring, excited, balanced, strong and whole.

Practical Suggestions for Reinventing Yourself and Writing a New Life Story

Mind

- Be open with a beginner's mind. If you are open to receiving it, every experience has the seed of something good in it. There are many life-giving lessons for you to learn through this transition.
- Crisis actually means "crossroads or turning point." How you respond to your crisis and the decisions you make can determine which path you choose and consequently how you pull thorough.
- Live in your world under new sets of conditions and assumptions.

• Address the tough questions as you get into new meaning making. Write about what you have learned about yourself, the world and your relationship to the world and others in it. How have you made sense of it all through your loss and grieving experience?

• Stop asking yourself disempowering questions like "Why did this have happened to me?" or "Do I have what it takes to get through this?" Start restoring your confidence with a new line of empowering questions like, "What positive things or opportunities have come about because of this change?" or "What good people or things in my life haven't changed?" Remember that life is on your side.

• Work your dream. If you have always wanted to try or do something, take it on. Whether your dream is simmering possibility or a dawning reality, concentrate on making your visions and projects come true.

• Be open to learning new skills and ways of doing things that are now part of your new role and responsibility. Ask for needed help.

• Explore new interests or renew old interests. Sign up for classes in any topic that fascinates you, travel around the block or around the world, take up a new sport or activity, learn new life skills, read, attend concerts, or play the piano again.

• Journal or diary writing is still a great way to organize thoughts and express your self. Write out insights about your experiences and reflect on them to help you.

• Trust your own judgment. Do whatever research is necessary and make informed decisions. The time before a change or decision is always much harder than the actual decision itself.

• Congratulate yourself on facing a devastating loss with courage (at least most of the time), working through the pain, restructuring your inner and outer world and reinventing your self. However, don't get stuck on just being healed or surviving. Use this life changing experience as a springboard for growth and happiness.

• Engage in positive self-talk. It is within your control to fill your head with good thoughts, even if sometimes they are 'fake it, till you make it' affirmations. Confidently saying mottos like "I can do this!" become a self-fulfilling prophecy.

• Plan on, focus on and expect a positive outcome. Visualize life the way you want your life to be for the highest good. Energy flows where the attention goes. There is proof that the laws of positive attractions work. You may as well reinvent a special you.

• Give yourself permission to fail occasionally and also give yourself the permission to excel.

• Create and maintain a regular schedule, probably lighter than before, so that you have a sense of order, organization and something to rely upon. Keep a calendar and checklists.

• Be sure there are fun, relaxation and social time with others on your calendar and lists of things to do.

• Visualization is powerful. Create a picture-board collage to help you visualize what you would like to accomplish in life. Pictures cut out of magazines, drawings or photographs help you envision clear goals in ways that words simply cannot convey.

• Exercise control over words you say, dominant thoughts and feelings during the reinvention phase. Since you cannot control all your outside circumstances, you might as well control what goes on inside of your head. Be aware of the language you use to describe your self and your experience.

• You are what you say and what you tell people, so if you choose words of oppression over words of opportunity, then that will be how you experience change. Change oppressions and victim vocabulary for words that are empowering and encouraging.

• The mind is everything. What you think is what you become.

• Art journal in a large sketchbook or scrap book. Draw your own pictures. Paste sayings, quotes, pictures, images, drawings into your journaling book. Healing arts and creative projects move you through the grieving and reinvention process.

• Follow this prescription. Rx: Take a dose of laughter two times each day to start. Increase the dosage size and frequency as it becomes easier to swallow. Fun and laughter are antidotes to anxiety and panic to help your body fight off stress.

• Be selfish. Put yourself first for a while. Selfish is not a bad word at this time. You know what you need. Make yourself the center of your attention. Care for yourself, then care for others.

• Create an abundant varied life for yourself. Just like a salad needs some crisp lettuce, cucumber, peppers, ripe tomato, avocado (if you are from California) and bits of this and that; your full life needs a mix of friends, work, faith, family, arts, adventure and community.

• Change your thought patterns from dark and negative to an uplifting bright perspective. You are the life-script writer and film director who make the movies that play in your head. Write yourself an award winning life story.

• Literally, put your life story on paper. Write the title, create chapter titles, and organize the flow and major themes. By doing this exercise, you can reflect on patterns, fullness and richness of life thus far, and recognize that your life is an ongoing narrative.

• Know that you are the writer, director and producer of this powerful creation you call your life story. You hold the key and are in control of how your story will move forward.

• Write an exciting script for your star role in the movie about your life. Play around with new locations, sets, wardrobe costumes, makeup, leading actors, mystery and adventures.

• Remember that when you change the main character in your life story (you), just like magic the whole story starts to change in order to adapt to the new main character.

Heart

• Recognize the transformation you are going through. See that you are not the same person as before the loss of your loved one. Embrace the change and give up the idea of returning to your old life or being your old self ever again. You can never step into the same river twice say those studying impermanence.

• Don't lose sight of the fact that beneath the surface turmoil, you are whole, good, brave, worthwhile and beautiful.

• Your identity is deeper than that of being a widow. You are so much more than the current suffering part of your life.

• Annie Estland, in *For Widows Only*, advises "Don't be afraid to grieve; but as time goes on, don't be afraid to live." Don't make suffering your new way of life.

• Identify any excuse, story, belief or emotion that is in the way of you making the adjustments or changes needed. What is being resisted? Get in touch with why you want to make certain changes. You will not be helped or changed by mere information, but by inspiration. Find your inspiration.

• Teach yourself to be happy. It has been scientifically proven that individuals can be taught to increase their happiness by an average of 25% through training and affirmations. Love and appreciate yourself.

• Give your dreams all you've got and you'll be amazed at the energy that follows.

• Make your "new normal" day-to-day life one of growth and joy. Remember the saying, "Today is the first day of the rest of my life." How do you plan to use it?

• Choose to become a victor over your tragedy, not a victim of the tragedy. Vow that grief is not going to be the winner; that life is going to be the winner.

• Attitude affects your grief work and the length of your grief journey. Stay positive on your walk toward recovery.

• When the disempowering emotions of fear, guilt, blame, shame, impatience or doubt rear their ugly heads, they tend to damage your self-esteem, destroy hope, keep you stuck in the past and block your view of future opportunities. Use these emotions as guides through change, to point you in the right direction.

• Instead of ignoring the emotions, label them, welcome them and thank them for helping you figure out how you do and do not want to feel during your time of change.

• Find inspirational quotes or poems that express what you are feeling. Look for images in art or magazines that please you and make you feel good, remember good times or project future possibilities.

• Get out and spend time for you. Invest in health and beauty treatments that improve your emotional state, self-image and confidence. It is extremely restorative to pamper yourself, doing things that make you feel better and bring you pleasure.

• To be more motivated, learn to control and positively manipulate your emotions.

• Tell yourself that you are a comeback artist. No matter how low you have felt, you are bouncing back and will be a winner again. Persist until you succeed.

• Don't settle for less. Make a turn around and overcome losses. To use baseball analogy, you only need one big hit to wipe out the strikes. Swing for the fences.

• Take pride in your accomplishments, large or small. Give yourself a pat on the back for a job well done.
• Don't be frustrated if you don't succeed at first. Get back up, try again and learn.
• Realize that your life was not, is not and never will be totally perfect. A balanced life includes both good and bad. You don't have to be perfect to be excellent.
• Don't be surprised by the intensity and unpredictability of your emotions. Uncontrollable tears or laughter at unexpected times may still overcome you.
• Holidays, other's grief, ceremonies, moving music and various conditions may bring back a surge of memories and emotions. Ride the wave. This is a sign of healing and feeling alive again.
• Create new ways of marking events or special dates. Don't throw out all your traditions, but find a new location, include new people, different rituals and unusual menus.

Spirit

• Set aside time for contemplation, prayer and meditation. It is during these quiet reflective periods that you can work on inner healing and draw on strength and wisdom. Meditation is not just another thing to do, it is an invitation to stop doing for a while.
• Teach your mind to pray, meditate and calm down. You may experience a Chicken Little mindset of "the sky is falling" with fear or despair over your personal losses and difficulties. Your chicken mind can be quieted and learn to respond with a "well, maybe it's not falling after all" courage and compassion.
• As you reinvent yourself, your view of life will become deeper and spiritualized, often with more intense insights and connections about what is truly important in your life and future. Positive results come from positive thoughts and actions.
• Read and enjoy books and workbooks that promote spiritual growth and self-improvement. Some fun self-help books include *Life 101, The Wish List, How You Do Anything Is How You Do Everything, Chicken Soup for the Grieving Soul* or the bodacious series of books on empowered living by Sark. Read about others' experiences with grief and faith to recognize the common threads and find hope.
• Make each day count and be rich with spiritual fulfillment and contentment.

• Observe the miracles that happen when you remove any limitations on who you are and what life can and should be.

> There are only two ways to live your life. One is as though nothing is a miracle. The other is as though everything is a miracle.
>
> - Albert Einstein

• Pick a color, other than black, to become your signature color. For example, the color red is the color of courage and joy in the Chinese system of color. Find your most meaningful color to use and wear to remind you of your inner strength, strong spirit and purpose.
• By going through the processes of loss and grief, you will achieve a greater sense of personal strength, spiritual growth, improved relationships, possibilities for yourself and an appreciation for life.
• Experience what the Japanese call *kaizen*, which translates to improvement or change for the better.
• Adopt a symbolic animal or symbol to represent the qualities, beauty and powers you are acquiring. Examples of these might include: phoenix, lion, wise owl, fox, eagle, cardinal, a rock, rose, flower, key, seashell, star or other meaningful items. Some widows wear necklaces, charms, tattoos or shirts, carry objects or totems with them or place figures or paintings around to remind them to remember the spirit and quality or personify that symbol of strength. Each time you see or touch the piece, think of something for which you are grateful.

Connection

• Even though you need to be selfish with your time and energy right now, don't forget to pay attention to children, relatives and friends who are also suffering the same loss. You may have to be part of the support circle for others who are suffering.
• Rely on professionals (accountant, attorney, doctor, counselor, clergy, trainer, decorator, nutritionist, etc.) for necessary or complex dealings and affairs. Go into your appointments prepared with necessary documents, checklists and questions. Don't be afraid to ask lots of questions. Follow the advice you have paid for.
• Attend grief support groups. Although grief is personal, grievers need support. Your presence and having worked through the challenges of the grief process will act as an example and reaffirm

belief in renewal of another widow's life after a great loss. Relating your stories and experiences can help and inspire others.

• Perhaps you are ready to volunteer as a peer sponsor or counselor. Since you have gotten through various phases of this adaptation stuff, it can be additionally healing to put your situation to the side and focus on somebody else. Supporting another widow through change can remind you of your ability to be strong and give back.

• Reintegrate back into work, worship and social organizations. Often you will find compassion and understanding that makes the transition easier than you thought. It can give you a sense of purpose, place and belonging, and provide a support system.

• The state of your work and social relationships can be a significant factor for success or failure in your life changes. Don't waste time on those who won't support you.

• Seek out positive people and experiences. Stay away from people who make you feel apprehensive, who drain your energy or make you doubt yourself. Be surrounded with nurturing folks who support your trial and error experiments as you reinvent yourself.

> Smooth seas do not make skillful sailors.
>
> - African Proverb

• Watch out for romantic rebounds. There is an intimate spot in your life that is feeling empty. Do not try to fill that role with someone new by prematurely rush into a romantic attachment. As wonderful as it might seem, if it fails, you have another layer of loss and grief to deal with.

• Fall in love with yourself before you fall for someone else. Being alone is better than being with the wrong person.

• Know what you had and what you lost, but remain open to future relationships in due time. Dr. Joyce Brothers, *Widowed*, wrote, "I hope I do not spend the rest of my life alone. But if I do, I will not be sorry for myself. Life goes on, and I am ready to join the parade again."

• Consider employment, continuing education, travel, new hobbies, adventures, dating or volunteer opportunities that match your needs and interests.

• Okay, what is it you plan to do with your one wild precious life?

Grief is described as a "terrible gift" because of how you are forced to renew yourself and your life following a devastating loss. Out of the processes of reinventing yourself and rewriting your life script often comes the ability to find and share new found wisdom, compassion and insight as a significant part of your recovery process. You can transform your grief into a meaningful legacy.

> Time is a dress maker specializing in alterations.
> - Faith Baldwin

Yes, you can bring a new perspective into your life and a new gift into the world. Through the grief process, you renew yourself and your surroundings while preserving the meaning of the life of the one you lost. Examples of self-renewal can be seen in the work of Katie Couric, who is bravely raising the country's awareness about colon cancer prevention, and in the efforts of Nancy Brinker who started the Susan E. Komen Breast Cancer Foundation, that sponsors the Race for the Cure. Many others have sought to raise people's consciousness about the illnesses, crimes or conditions that brought their loved ones' lives to a premature end. Others dedicate themselves to carrying on the legacy of the life work of those they have loved and lost.

In continuing to perform work or starting new movements, you can bring a gift to the community, a gift that can lead to the transformation and renewal of your self and the world. You can contribute just by changing your own life, helping your family, or reaching out to your local neighborhoods. You may start scholarships or foundations, help others in similar circumstances, write about your experiences, build memorials, or contribute to your charitable or spiritual communities. Make your renewed life count.

Whatever your project or new image may be, realize that all dreams have an inherent field of imperfection. Don't wait until everything is perfect. Something does not have to be perfect to be excellent. In *The Golden Frog*, author Michael Mamas proposes that folks work within the abstract nature of their dreams. He writes, "Pursuing your dream requires a willingness to get the boat in the water, set your sail and move in a direction that's your best guess at the moment. Life is not a series of perfect conclusions; it's a series of best guesses."

Learn to stop focusing on all the illusionary "what ifs", start working toward overcoming potential or actual obstacles. Stay motivated and follow your dreams. Let your heart be like the sea, ever open, brave and free. Where is your power? Who has your power? Have you given your power away to grief, family, work, religion, internet or addictions? It is time to free yourself from excuses, fear, stories, myths, habits, traditions and other negative outside forces that have power over you. Stop thinking and talking about all the darkness and baggage you carry. The stories you tell perpetuate the old past history and validate your old sad/boring life story. Don't lead from a broken vulnerable victim place. Choose not to be those old stories any more. Remove negative non-loving thoughts. Make space for a new story. Telling your new story from what and how you want things to be creates a different stage of consciousness. This is how you make changes and manifest new beginnings.

> When you have faith in yourself, you follow every instinct that you were born with. You have no doubt about what you are, and you return to common sense. You have all the power of your authenticity; you trust yourself, you trust life.
>
> - Miguel Ruiz

Conclusion of the Transition Phases of Grieving

This finishes the overview of the transition phases of grief and mourning. These transitions included: (1) Acknowledge the reality of your loss; (2) Open yourself to the pain; (3) Revise your world assumptions; (4) Adjust to your loved one's absence; (5) Reconstruct your relationship with the one who has been lost; and (6) Reinvent yourself and rewrite your life story. It included summaries of each phase, what your might be experiencing and feeling, and the suggestions and guidelines through the maze of pain toward healing. It is important to point out that working through the various adaptation phases will not complete or end the grieving process. Grief is not a disease that can be cured; it is a transition. Grieving is a personal introspective process, not a systematic linear program with steps or an end date.

Dr. Robert Neimeyer describes grief like a room we may enter or leave again and again, for years. The character and quality of grief may change across time, but it remains available as a resource we can revisit. The positive word *resource*, was a deliberate choice by Dr. Neimeyer because he feels that being able to revisit earlier losses and their implication for you can enrich your life and make your narrative more coherent about who you are and how you got to be who you are. Every artist has the right to create her own art, her own masterpiece, her own life.

EXCLUSIVE READER ONLINE RESOURCES

A password hidden in *Widow's Key* allows to find your password you to receive extra reader resources. I have put more information for you to access online. There are additional tips, articles, items, checklists and other valuable resources not in the book.

Here are just a few more topics available to *Widow's Key* readers only:

* Inspirational Movies and Books About Widowhood

* How to Find Just the Right Support Group

* Pilgrimages to Sacred Places

* Step-by-Step Legacy Letter Form

Visit the *Widow's Key* companion website at www.widowskey.com. Follow the simple instructions to find your password in the book and get your extra reader-only information.

Chapter Sixteen

COMPLICATED GRIEF

What to Do if You Need Help for Prolonged Grief

While most widows are able to work through the transition phases and meet the adaptive challenges successfully, you may find that you are unable to take on this grief work by yourself or within your support system. Are you feeling stuck or paralyzed with grief and unable to move on? An inability to mentally or emotionally confront your loss is called 'complicated grief'. In some cases, the intensity of grief reaction is so great and lasts so long, that relief can be found only with the help of physicians or professionals experienced in the matters of death, dying, and bereavement. If this type of complicated or prolonged grief happens to you, it is necessary to consult with a therapist, counselor or mental health professional.

> You can't prevent birds of sorrow from flying over your head, but you can prevent them from building nests in your hair.
>
> - Chinese Proverb

Losing a loved one is one of life's most profound and stressful experiences. Grief is the emotional reaction to a loss and typically involves physiological, psychological, social, and behavioral manifestations of distress. Grieving signifies the attempt to come to terms with loss and adapt to it.

Grief work is the emotional, behavioral and mental confrontation with loss, incorporating reflections on events surrounding the death. It is normal for you to experience grief after a loss. Most widows experience and endure a transient period of pain and sorrow, followed by a gradual fading of these bereavement feelings as they come to terms with the loss and move forward with life. If you find that you are like some widows, getting stuck and needing a professional nudge to keep you moving through the grieving process, here is how to deal with your complicated grief.

> All I seem to see are the scattered pieces of my life, like a thousand piece puzzle, cast before me on the card table, waiting for me to pick them up and make the picture.
>
> - Darcie Simms

When You Need Extra Help

If your grief reactions seem to have gone awry and have become much more painful, debilitating and prolonged, you are probably experiencing what is known as complicated grief. Even after taking the traumatic nature or extremity of the particular death, cultural factors, and the duration of the bereavement into account, complicated grief is a deviation from typical grief and grieving reactions.

You can recognize complicated grief responses by their intensity and timing. This prolonged grief is like being in a chronic, heightened state of mourning. A particularly sharp and long-termed grief that lasts for years or worsens and causes persistent difficulties that radically disturb your ability to function at work, in society or to accomplish routine daily tasks is a disorder that needs further attention and treatment. Certain signs may indicate that you need the help of an experienced professional to discover the reasons for this type of unremitting grief.

Types of Complicated Grief

The types of prolonged intense debilitating grief have been recognized in medical, psychological and spiritual manuals for centuries. According to the National Academy of Science, of the approximately 800,000 Americans widowed each year, between ten and twenty percent (10-20%) are thought to suffer a pathological complicated grief. It wasn't until the last few decades that bereavement scientists at renowned research centers like UCLA and the Mayo Clinic have systematically studied complicated grief symptoms, causes and treatments. Complications of grief are halting the natural grief process and can become chronic and deadly unless treated.

Types and variations of grief complications include:

(1) Chronic grief, is an exaggerated, more intense or prolonged emotional experience. Mourning becomes pathological when someone cannot or will not let the loss go;

(2) Absent grief includes an absence of usual symptoms. Mourning is also disordered when someone, in an effort to avoid the pain of the loss, carries on as if nothing disruptive has happened and deceives themselves into thinking they are coping well and don't need to cry or grieve;

(3) Delayed grief, similar to absent grief, is a delayed onset of symptoms. Some deal with a death by failing to deal with the death right away. If and when the barrier drops, especially after another loss, the grief can appear with a vengeance and turn into complicated chronic mourning;

(4) Masked grief, when the bereaved experience physical and/ or psychological symptoms or behaviors that do not seem to be associated with grief. Physical manifestations of grief symptoms can vary greatly ranging from a stabbing chest pain to an unexplained weight loss with no medical basis for the physical symptoms and they go away after the associated loss is dealt with in therapy.

Mary Frances O'Connor, assistant professor in psychiatry and behavioral sciences at UCLA medical center, conducted brain scans on women who had lost family members. When reminded of their deceased loved ones, women with uncomplicated grief showed activation in their brain's memory and emotional centers. In the brains of women with complicated grief, the primary area that activated was the nucleus accumbens, the reward center. Those suffering from complicated grief are still expecting to be rewarded with contact from their loved ones in some way. On a subconscious level they have not yet integrated the loss into their daily reality. Reports suggest that complicated grief activates neurons in the reward centers of the brain, giving these memories addiction-like properties.

The scientific studies and mental health counselors' observations have identified some of the most common symptoms and signs of the prolonged and complicated grief syndrome. You probably experienced some of these symptoms in the first few months after the death of your husband, but if these signs have gone on for years and are still unbearably intense, then you may be suffering an abnormal grief. Don't worry, there is professional help for all these conditions.

Symptoms and Signs of Complicated Grief may include:

- Intense longing or persistent pining for the deceased
- Problems accepting the death or integrating the story of loss
- Detachment and numbness of feelings
- Preoccupation with sorrow or identifying with the grief
- Anger and bitterness about the loss
- Prolonged depression, anxiety and deep sadness
- Extreme feelings of isolation and emptiness
- Severely intrusive thoughts about the lost love one
- Searching for the deceased in crowds
- Unbidden memories or fantasies about the lost relationship
- Keeping every object your spouse possessed how he kept them
- Substantial guilt or self-blame
- Strong spells of severe emotion
- Shattered world-view and feeling overwhelmed and helpless
- Lack of trust in self or others
- Sleep and eating disorders and increased health problems
- Trouble carrying out normal routines
- Withdrawing from social and spiritual activities
- Feeling that life holds no meaning or purpose
- Avoiding doing activities, going places or seeing people that bring back memories of your departed husband
- Difficulty adapting and moving on with life

- Poorer overall quality of life
- Thoughts of suicide or wishing to have died with the loved one
- Extreme hopelessness
- Irritability, agitation or uncontrolled rage
- Substance abuse or reckless behavior
- Extreme focus on the loss and reminders of your loved one

Causes and Risk Factors of Complicated Grief

The causes of complicated grief are not fully known. Like with many mental health disorders, it may involve a complex interaction between someone's personality, genes, body's natural chemical makeup and their environment. While researchers do not know specifically what causes prolonged intense grief symptoms, they are recognizing factors that may increase the risk of developing it.

These risk factors may include:
• Lack of the adaptability to life changes and lack of resiliency
• Unexpected, preventable, violent death or suicide
• Childhood separation anxiety or tramatic childhood experiences of neglect or abuse
• Close or overly dependent relationship to the deceased
• Accumulation of losses and unresolved grief issues
• Misplaced beliefs in high-tech to stop death or prolong life
• Lack of a support system or friendships

If the listed symptoms of complicated grief still apply to you long after the loss of your loved one and you fit into a risk factor category, please seek professional assistance. There is no need for you to suffer anymore.

He who conceals his grief finds no remedy for it.
- Turkish Proverb

Guilt as a Complicating Factor

Sometimes complicated and prolonged grief are caused because a widow is choosing to hold onto guilt, a version of self-blame and judgment. You need to stop blaming yourself for something real or imagined and punishing yourself by holding on to those awful feelings. Guilt and anguish will not go away as long as you harbor certain thoughts and beliefs that are creating and perpetuating the guilt. Once you identify those irrational thoughts, then dispute and replace them, you can let go of whatever distress they are causing, i.e. anger, shame, guilt, anxiety and complicated grief.

You are in control and can do something because it is your own thoughts that are perpetuating this guilt, and you can challenge and change your thoughts, which will in turn address the emotional pain you are harboring. There is a website (www.rebt.org), the Institute for Rational Emotive Behavioral Therapy or REBT that proposes most of our emotional distress is caused by irrational beliefs and thoughts that we hold. It is certainly worth looking into if you are stuck in prolonged or intense grief.

Risks, Prevention and Help for Complicated Grief

All of this information on complicated grief is not to declare that normal grieving is unnatural or unhealthy. Just the opposite is intended. Grief is a necessary process. Complicated prolonged grief reactions, which are so intense and lasting that they cause psychological distress and create substantial disability and health problems. Some risks include heart problems, immunological dysfunction, hypertension, cancer, increased rates of suicide and other adverse health problems and behaviors.

Some widows have a clinical problem of becoming fond of and identifying with their grief. They are reluctant to release the grief because it has been integrated as part of their identity, their new special role of the poor grief stricken woman. A chronic mourner somehow believes that the lost person lives on in the grief. Shakespeare's King Philip chides Constance, "You are as fond of your grief as of your child."

Although they are related, complicated grief is distinct from depression, anxiety, bi-polar disorders, separation anxiety disorders or posttraumatic stress disorder (PTSD). Depression is a condition where a person experiences deep sadness beyond the normal blues everyone feels occasionally, and a diminished interest in nearly all life activities. Almost one third of widows and widowers meet the criteria for depression in the first few months after the death of their spouse, but most are able to emerge and move forward without any medical or psychological interventions. However, if your depression or complicated grief occurs and disrupts your life for a prolonged period, seek help sooner than later. Don't try to diagnosis or treat yourself.

> Waste not fresh tears over old grief.
>
> - Euripides

How to Prevent Complicated Grief

How to prevent complicated grief is not entirely clear either. If you might be at an increased risk of developing complicated grief, you should participate in counseling or psychotherapy soon after a loss. As sages warn, "Dig the well before you are thirsty." Through preparing for death and early counseling and support groups, you can explore emotions and learn coping skills. It is more difficult to overcome negative beliefs and patterns after they become entrenched.

Talking about the loss, how you are feeling, laughing and crying will prevent you from becoming immobilized by sorrow. Empathetic support groups, therapy, spiritual counselors, informed relatives and friends all play a key role in helping a widow avoid the dangers of prolonged complicated grief. If you notice any of the warning signs or risks in yourself, it is your job to seek a mental health professional and join a loss support group.

Professional Help for Complicated Grief

Even though complicated grief treatment is not standardized, psychiatry research studies make a strong case against just medicating the condition. Often when widows believe that depression is just a stage that defines their condition, they wait for the depression to lift and take no actions that might help them. Additionally, when medical or psychological professionals hear a widow diagnose herself as depressed, they often reflexively prescribe psychotropic drugs. Pharmaceutical companies have vested interests in sustaining the idea that grief related depression is clinical. Studies show that depression treatments such as antidepressants do not alleviate acute and prolonged grief. Medications cannot address the root cause. That kind of treatment does not hit on your yearnings. There is no magic pill to make you get over the loss of your loved one.

The treatment that has proven to work most effectively against complicated grief is counseling. Therapists and grief counselors are a great resource when it comes to coping with a loss and the healing process. They offer advice from a well-educated and professional standpoint and can provide you with proven techniques and methods.

Some forms of grief therapy include talk therapy, exposure therapy, trauma therapy, cognitive behavior therapy, interpersonal therapy or psychotherapy. These methods can help you incorporate the death on a deep level, adjust to your loss, explore and process emotions, become less distressed by thoughts and images of your loved one, improve your coping skills, reduce feelings of guilt, redefine life's goals and allow you to return to functioning in healthful ways.

Other successful options, used in combinations are: Exercises for triggering improved mood and tranquility; Hypnosis, Neuro-Linguistic Programming (NLP); Meditation as a form of relaxation and controlling thoughts; Support groups to allow discussions, shared experiences and learn how others cope; Healthy life style and habits; Travel to experience different locales and cultures; Volunteer and mentoring activities; Faith community to gain comfort from rituals and spiritual guidance; Socializing for connection and support; and Professional therapy to guide the bereaved to effective kinds of treatment and support.

Chapter Seventeen

CHILDREN AND THE GRIEF PROCESS

If you are a parent with a child or children, you need information on how a young child or adolescent deals with death and some useful ways to help them grieve. As the widow, you are grieving too, but it is important to gather the strength to satisfy the needs of your grieving children.

Tips to Help Children and Teens Deal With Loss

When death strikes a household, people think of the bereaved survivors as adults like the widow or grown children. Yet, based on current statistics from the U.S. Census Bureau, approximately 1.5 million children are living in a single-family household because of the death of one parent. Among children aged fifteen or younger, one out of every twenty (1 in 20) will have suffered the loss of one or both parents. Children are often refered to as the "forgotten mourners."

You may assume your child is doing all right because they don't seem to understand what is going on and appear unfazed. Everyone feels grief when a loved one dies, including your children. Various reasons young people get lost in the shuffle, include: (1) Adults don't think children can understand death, aren't affected by the loss, or they don't know how to deal with it; (2) During the overall emotional turmoil, the children's psychological needs are overlooked; and beliefs that (3) Exclusion from the details will shield the children from pain and confusion.

Only recently, care providers, social workers and clergy are beginning to recognize the critical need for adequate support and counseling of bereaved children. After a loss, your children need stability, support, honesty and extra reassurance that they will be kept safe and be cared for. A little sensitivity, effort and truth on your part will go a long way toward helping your child process and express their own grief in a healthy way.

Myths about Child and Adolescent Grief

In order for you to address the needs of your grieving children, let's first dispel some of the myths that surround their grief as outlined by Angela Morrow, RN in the Medical Review Board. Specifically, Morrow notes:

Myth 1: "Young children do not grieve is a myth. Children grieve at any age. Their grief manifests in many ways depending on their age, developmental stage, and life experiences. Children often do a very good job of grieving intensely for a time and then just taking a break. The break is usually in the form of play. Don't mistake your child's play as a sign that your child is not grieving, that is not true.

Myth 2: Children should go to funerals. Children should not go to funerals. Both statements are myths. Children, even very young ones should have a choice whether they want to attend the funeral. Each child handles their loss differently and should be allowed to grieve as they wish. For their choice to be a meaningful one, you need to give your children information, options and support.

Myth 3: Children get over loss quickly. You will never completely get over the intense feelings of a significant loss so why should your children? Children may revisit their loss at different stages in their development and as their understanding of the loss changes, their grief may arise again.

Myth 4: Children will be permanently scarred by a significant loss is another myth. Children, like most people, are resilient. Significant loss can affect your child's development, but adequate support and continued care from you help them deal with feelings appropriately.

Myth 5: Encouraging your children to talk about their feelings of grief is the best way to work through their loss. It is important to allow your children to talk through their feelings and to promote open communications. However, other approaches, such as art, play, music and dance allow children to express their feelings. Children and adolescents may use these methods to express their grief and adapt to their loss with a more positive outcome," advises Morrow.

Age and Development Effects How Children Deal with Death

How your children understand and deal with death depends on their age, developmental stage and levels of comprehension. All children of all ages grieve the death of a loved one, often very deeply, but they deal with death in vastly different ways from adults or teens. Your child's grief is multi-layered because it is developmental, linear and circular. It is important to note that your child's comprehension and developmental stage may lag behind his or her chronological age.

General Characteristics of Grief in Five Age Categories

Infants and Toddlers may not understand death but they sense a disruption in the home environment, schedules, feel the focus of attention away from them and react to the emotions of adults, especially their mother. This group especially shows distress if their normal caregiver is suddenly gone or distracted. The best thing to do is to stay physically close to your child and maintain regular schedules, activities and routines.

Children aged three to six may have some concept and understanding about death, but are not capable of abstract thinking and may believe it is reversible. They may ask you about the deceased person's return, believe that they somehow caused the death and act out feelings through play and art. It is best to be honest and explain death as a natural part of life in simple terms and analogies.

Children aged six to nine may realize that death is final and need details about how the person died in order to accept the permanent reality, grieve and find closure. There is a fear that those they love and depend upon will die or abandon them. It is best for you to encourage this age group child to ask questions and honestly answer them. Give your child the needed reassurances that you and others will be there to care for them.

Children aged nine to twelve may have developed a greater understanding of life and death through experience or education. They often will withdraw from you and others because of strong feelings of guilt, angry or aggression. This is when you have to teach them how to talk about the loss and how to appropriately express emotions and feelings. Learning to work through grief can prepare your children to cope better with losses later in life.

Teenagers may act like they don't want to talk about the death or that they don't need any help. Teens try to hide their feelings of fear, anger or guilt. Adolescents and teens may react by trying to take care of you or others. Even if the teen resists personal closeness, you need to continue to provide extra support, love, guidance and structure while still respecting their privacy. Working daily through grief, sorrow and adapting to loss is very important for your children and especially important for teens to process the loss.

Psychological research and various studies done on children have proven that young children, adolescents and teens who experience unrecognized or unresolved grief are at a much higher risk for developing severe anxieties, physical and mental ailments, hostility, acting out, behavior problems, regressions, depression, and sadly, more suicidal tendencies.

Expressions and Symptoms of Grief in Children

Children and teens are not miniature adults. They do not express and process grief in quite the same ways that you or another adult would grieve. Although there is a natural progression of grief from disorganization to transition to reorganization, it can be complicated by the circular and regressive nature of a young person's grief. Young people may not be equipped to verbalize their feelings about a death. Or, they appear to be unaffected because they are holding back feelings due to being so overwhelmed. Your children will sometimes defer their own grief in an effort to protect you and allow you to grieve first. Children will wait until you are strong enough to console them before they feel safe enough to express grief and anger.

Remember that your child suffers a double loss. They have lost the parent who died and additionally lost a little of you, because you are still around but you may have been swept away by the process.

It is common for your children to express themselves through behavior and play. Regardless of your children's inability to express themselves like an adult would, your child does experience intense grieve. While each adult or child's reactions and expressions of grief are unique and individual in nature, there are some common reactions to death that children have.

Specific symptoms and common expressions of children's grief include some of the following:

(1) **Shock** – Since the thought of death is too so overwhelming, your child may deny that the death actually happened and act as though it did not occur. Children's minds have a way of protecting them from what is too powerful to handle all at once.

(2) **Physical symptoms** – Children express their grief through complaints of headaches, stomach aches, refusing to eat, overeating, waning energy, sleeplessness or nightmares.

(3) **Mental anxiety and fear** – Your child may fear that she may die or some other person she loves, like you, will die. They worry about who will take care of them and cling to you and ask for reassurances of love. There may be a preoccupation with the loss and related worries, exaggerated fears, hopelessness, despair, daydreaming and

trouble paying attention. School and learning problems may occur. Your child may demonstrate sadness or depression by temporary quietness and decrease in activity.

(4) **Anger and guilt** – Anger is the most common way that your children will express sadness. Your child may be angry with the deceased for leaving them alone and not caring for the child's needs. Additionally, your child can express anger at you, others or God because they didn't make the person well and keep them alive. Sometimes children feel guilty and think they are somehow responsible for the death because they were upset with the deceased or were not good or did not behave in the proper way. Children express feelings of guilt and anger by throwing temper tantrums, fighting or acting out hostile feelings. Your older children may experience mood swings and detachment.

(5) **Regression** – Children often revert to behaviors they had previously outgrown, such as thumb-sucking, bed-wetting, wanting a bottle or experience other developmental delays. These are common grief symptoms and should pass soon.

All of the reactions and symptoms are normal expressions of grief you may observe in your children. Your love, support of family and time are important factors in the grief process. Within six months after the death of a significant person, child psychologists say that normal routine should be returning. If your child's symptoms and reactions seem to be prolonged and overly intense or extreme behaviors occur, it is best to seek professional advice from those familiar with children's grief, like a pediatrician, teacher, clergy or mental health provider.

Positive Ways to Help Your Grieving Children

When someone dies, your children mostly need support, acceptance, demonstrations of love, stability, consistency, and honesty. You may inadvertently or purposefully exclude your child from the adult bereavement process and rituals. Some adults feel it is best to shield children from details of the death or from seeing people cry. In a misguided effort to avoid pain and confusion, many parents pretend that nothing is wrong. Secrecy, whispered exchanges or exclusion from the family grief will not protect your child. Children sense the family anguish and they become confused and frightened. Children need to reach an age-appropriate level of understanding about the death, feel the loss, remember the loved one, integrate the loss into their lives and then grow from the experience.

Children of all ages are affected by a death and grieve, often very deeply. Depending upon your child's level of comprehension, development and age, they should be able to participate in services and encouraged to discuss the death and their feelings frankly. Trust that no one is ever too young to deal with the difficult parts of life. This is an opportunity for you to share this time and all its lessons with your child.

At News of the Death

• **Tell the truth**. Speak openly to your child about what has happened. Explain in an accurate, but simple, manner why and how the death occurred. Your child needs some honest basic details so that their active imagination doesn't create gruesome images that may be more frightening than the truth. For example, you can say "Dad was in a bad car accident. He hit his head so hard that it killed him" or "He was very sick from an illness called cancer and he died." It is important to use the words "death" "died" or "killed" no matter what age the child is.

• **Honesty is the best policy** even when the cause of death was stigmatic such as crime, drug abuse, AIDS or a suicide. Explain the facts at an age appropriate level. If you attempt to hide the truth from your child, when they hear it later from another they will resent your dishonesty. It also adds a complicated new layer to their grief. If the death was due to substance abuse or suicide, explain that self-destructive acts or habits are caused by mental illness and never cool or glamorous. Young adults and teens, who might romanticize the suicide of a peer, absolutely must be told that suicide is not acceptable. Remind your children that there are always other options and the deceased totally irreversibly gave up any second chance they would have had at a happy life.

• **Answer your child's questions and satisfy their curiosity** about death. Give short, direct honest answers to the questions your child actually asks. Be age appropriate and speak in a language they can understand. When answering questions about what happens to a body after a person dies, answer honestly that once a person is dead, their body, mind and heart no longer work. Say that the body does not work anymore and that it cannot be fixed. Do not burden a child with unsolicited information or more than asked for or needed.

• **Tell your children they can ask you about anything.** This way you become the safe person they turn to with serious questions about life and death or other issues in the future. It is all right to answer some of the "why" questions with "I wish I knew, but I don't know." A hug is acceptable when words fail you.

• **Listen carefully** to what your child is saying, and just as important, to what he is not saying. Encourage your child to ask questions. Be patient because they may need to ask the same things repetitively to come to terms with the meanings and reality. Answers should be in response, not to the exact words used, but based on the needs your child is expressing. At the same time, your child's anxieties and questions are not always put into words. Looking at their art, watching your child play or any acting out behaviors may provide insights on how they are dealing with the loss. Books help your children project feelings onto story characters. Provide avenues of expression and pay attention.

• **Willingness to discuss difficult topics like death** teaches your child that there are no taboo subjects between you. Let them express all their thoughts and questions as they arise. Your honesty and openness lets your children know "we can talk about anything" and that will go a long way for building communications and trust during the crisis and in the future.

• **Point out examples in nature to help you explain the concept of death** for your younger children. You can take them for a walk and for instance show them the flower that wilts and dies, leaves falling from the branch, a dead lizard, an egg that has fallen from the nest or such parallels. There are numerous children's books or movies that discuss loss of a loved one.

Home Life

• **Explain to younger children that their father will not be in their daily life,** but they can still remember and talk about him. At the death of your loved one, it may be the time to explain your religious values and beliefs about the spiritual hereafter or pray with your child. Clearly explain that the spirit is no longer inside the body; that it leaves the body behind to go to heaven. Otherwise, your children will think they can go with them or go visit.

• **Provide a structured home environment** that is consistent and predictable. Keep the daily routines as normal as possible. It is the disruption in their surroundings that frightens your child the most and causes your child to worry about basic needs and who will take care of him or her. Maintain usual activities and schedules as much as possible. Keep tasks simple.

• **Assure your children that people still love them, that they are safe** and that you are here for them and will be for a long time. Your child's first experience with death shatters their illusion of being immortal. Your child may become very fearful that they will die too or they will lose you or someone else they love. Say that if people are sad that does not mean that they are sick or going away.

• **Show affection and allow your child to express caring for you.** Loving is receiving as well as giving. Physical touch calms your children, reassures them of your presence and helps them to feel secure enough to talk and express emotions. Hugs do indeed heal.

Emotions

• **Reassure your child that that they are not at fault** and that nothing they did caused the person to die. These feelings of guilt over the death are not farfetched to your child. Explain the true cause of death and explain that any naughty behavior or thoughts he had about the person who died did not cause the death. Allow your child to express their thoughts so that later they will not have a difficult time resolving feelings of blame or guilt.

• **Let your children know that it is okay to cry.** Don't stifle your tears. By crying in front of your child or crying together it sends a message that it is all right for them to express sorrow and feelings too. Your child will see that feeling bad and experiencing grief is a normal reaction to a tragic loss. It may upset your child initially, but they will not be harmed by seeing an elder react normally at a time of grief by crying or losing a little control during bereavement. Sharing grief with your child creates a connecting bridge with them.

• **Encourage your child and teenager to express sadness and emotions freely.**
At times a better approach to getting your child to open up is not a question like "How do you feel?" It is better to express your feelings first and talk openly about your sorrow. Your child sees that it is okay to speak from the heart about all sorts of feelings.

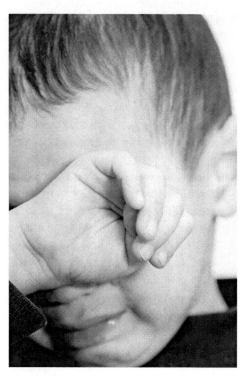

As painful as it is to watch, it is a valuable lesson for your child to cry, grieve and learn to cope with loss. Unexpressed deep feelings and incomplete mourning can create emotional problems later in life.

• **Invite your child to reminisce, recall incidents and tell stories** about both the good and bad times they spent with the lost loved parent. Look at photographs and objects to trigger memories and conversations. Talk often by name about the father who has died. Laughter and tears over remembrances are remarkably medicinal.

• **Include your child in the family's experience of loss and mourning.** A funeral serves as affirmation of the death, some closure, and needed support of family and friends. Let your children contribute ideas and suggestions for services and if they want to, even take part in the ceremonies. Some tasks make your child feel useful and important during an emotional and overwhelming time.

Funeral Services

• **Prepare your child** on what will happen and what to expect beforehand at a funeral or other service. Explain the ceremonies and rituals to your children and let them decide if and how they will participate. For their choice to be a meaningful one, your children need information, options and support. Do not force anything on your children that they are not comfortable doing.

• **Explain ahead of time what your child will see and what will be happening** around them if the child is attending a wake, viewing, funeral, memorial gathering or burial. Tell your children what the body will look like if there is an open casket. Give them the choice of whether or not they want to view it. If not thoroughly prepared about what to expect, a funeral can be very traumatic for children. Have a supporting adult with your children and a backup to take them away if the situation becomes too difficult.

Adjusting to Daily Life

• **Meet regularly as a family** to comfort, share and evaluate how everyone is coping with the death and if they need help in any way. This sends the message that loved ones still remember the departed and will be there to care for each other.

• **Sometimes your child will have unresolved feelings** of grief that cause him or her to get angry or upset over unrelated matters, become unduly frustrated over a task, become disrespectful, ignore rules, withdraw or act out in other ways. Give your child an opportunity to explore these feelings by acknowledging the real source of the stress.

• **Contain manifestations of acting out behaviors.** Insist that your children make the effort to express their feelings, needs and wants with words, not by acting out. Encourage them to talk to you whenever they are worried or having a difficult time. Tell them "I'm always here to listen and help."

• **Realize that some children become over-achievers**, rather than responding with delinquency. Additionally, you may observe repetitive actions like computer games, sewing, hitting a ball, raking or washing a car repeatedly. These actions are manifested efforts to stay above the grief. Help your child deal with the suppressed grief so that they do not have serious problems in the future.

• **Help your children find ways to symbolize and memorialize** the lost loved one. Some things you can do together to say goodbye or remember the deceased: Plant a tree or bush; Light a candle on special days; Make a memory box, scrapbook or computer album; Write a story, letter or draw a picture of the loved one to keep; Recite poetry or a prayer; Hold a special memorial ceremony that your child helps plan; or Visit the grave or other special places. Simple small acts can give great comfort and mean a lot to a child in grief.

• **Provide appropriate support and therapy for adolescents.** The death of a loved one presents significant challenges for teens because it reinforces their feelings of lost control; a task they seek to accomplish every day. There are adolescent-specific support groups (to connect socially with others in their age group who are feeling the same emotions), counselors and grief techniques available. Innovative poetry and music therapies provide options to help teens acknowledge and express their sorrow and fears. You can encourage your teenager to create poetry, writings, music or lyrics for unique songs dedicated to the lost individual or thoughts about life.

• **Provide items or gifts that might offer soothing comfort** or emotional support for your grieving child. Supportive items may include things like: Keepsakes that belonged to the deceased person; Cozy guardian angel blanket; Symbols like keys, flowers or animal totems; Memorial engraved jewelry or charms; Grief resource books like Pat Schweibert's *Tear Soup* or E.B. White's *Charlotte's Web* or *Sad Isn't Bad* by Michaelene Mundy; Cuddly stuffed teddy bears or other animals; Framed photograph of your child with the loved one; and other such remembrances.

• **Being consistent, loving, truthful, sensitive, available and accepting** will help your child understand and cope with death. A little effort will go a long way helping your child process feelings and grieving in a healthy and positive way.

There are no great things, only small things with great love.
We shall never know all the good that a simple smile can do.
- Mother Teresa

What to Avoid With Grieving Children

Outlined below are some attitudes, behaviors and explanations that parents and other adults may give children to explain death and grief. Unfortunately, many of these dishonest answers and distractions can lead to misunderstanding, increased fear, anger and mistrust, acting out, withdrawal, suicide and other destructive paths.

On News of the Death:

• **Don't try to protect or shield your child from the death of a loved one**. You can help them heal, adapt and learn to deal with traumatic or significant losses now and in the future by confronting the issue directly and including your child in the grieving process and services.

• **Don't think that your young child doesn't understand death** and is therefore not affected deeply by it. Even a very young child is aware of the absence of a person or confusion and anguish in their surroundings. Recognize that your children of all ages grieve the loss of a loved one. They need to ask you questions about death and be given the chance to work through their own childlike grief with parent and adults who are responsible for their wellbeing.

• **Don't use phrases or euphemisms** like: "Grandpa went to sleep" "The angels took her" "He is no longer with us" "Sam died because he was old and tired" "It was God's will" "Daddy went away" "They are much happier and better off in glorious heaven" or "He was sick and went to the hospital where he died." Young children take what you say very literally. They don't understand that these explanations were given in a way meant to soften the reality that the person is dead.

• **Dishonest or misleading answers only serve to multiple uncertainty and fear.** These euphemism terms, seen from your child's point of view, may result in your child being afraid to go to sleep, wondering why the person left without saying goodbye, mad at God for taking father away, want to die too because going to live in heaven sounds so wonderful, live in terror that angels may snatch them or another loved one or be afraid when they get tired or sick.

• **It is best to use the accurate meaning words** like "death" "died" or "dead" to stop the misunderstanding, confusion and fear. Follow that with simple truthful concrete explanations of how the person died, patiently answer questions and listen. Listen to more than just their words.

• Additionally, if your children are to attend or be part of the funeral services, make sure they are fully informed and prepared beforehand about what they will see and what to expect. Give them support, behavior standards, information and options.

Emotions:

• **Don't assume your child knows appropriate behavior for the situation.** You and other adults are the models for how to act and express feelings. Allow your child to see you cry, grieve, express emotions, perform ceremonies and receiving support and comforting assistance from others. Don't tell someone how they should or should not feel or to "get over it." Don't force or suppress expressions of grief. Each person, whatever the age, will grieve in unique individual ways on their own timeline.

• **Don't hesitate to cry in front of your child.** It lets them know that it is okay to cry and express feelings of sadness as a normal and natural reaction to loss. Being the strong silent type for your children is nonsense and sends incorrect signals to them about healthy bereavement. However, don't pressure your child to publically mourn or express feelings on cue.

• **Don't tell your child to stop crying or not to feel bad.** A child needs to experience and express the full constellation of emotions and grief in order to heal. Don't suppress your child's spontaneous expression of grief or distress.

• **Don't overwhelm your children with your own grief** and turn them into your personal confidants. Don't expect your child to act like an adult. "You are the man of the house now. You need to take care of your mother" will not help your child deal with the death of a father. Don't place that much responsibility or confusion on the shoulders of your child. If you need help, call upon a support group, clergy or a competent adult.

• **Don't think that your moods or timing of grief will coincide** with your child's grief timelines or expressions. You may be at opposite stages at different moments. When you are having a difficult day coping with the loss, your child may appear indifferent, disinterested or unsympathetic to your expressions of sorrow. On other days, when you are feeling relatively calm, your child may begin acting out or burst into tears at the expense of your hard won peace of mind. Allow individual moments of grief and moments of peace in order to promote recovery.

• **Never discredit or ignore a child's grief.** Talk to them. Listen carefully. Answer all questions truthfully. Observe their actions and play for insights. Let them vent their anger and guilt. Allow a child to cry all they need to express the sorrow that a grievous loss merits. Unreleased grief can cause serious emotional problems later in life.

• **Don't lightly dismiss your child's strong sense of guilt.** Of course, the child's feelings of guilt or self-blame for the death are misconstrued but you need to let them express those thoughts in order to resolve their guilt. Once the facts are explained, your child will see they didn't cause the demise and stop blaming themselves.

Definitely, do not be someone who takes advantage of your child's possible feelings of guilt by saying things like, "If you had been a better son" "Your behavior killed your poor father" or "You were so naughty he went away." Avoid comments that assign fault for the bad thing that happened. Unresolved guilt over your child's alleged thoughts or actions can cause severe psychological problems.

Home Life:

• **Don't send your children away** by themselves to their room or off to find an activity to keep them busy or distracted. Busyness or denial just delays grief work that needs to be done. Children need to learn hope to cope with loss in a direct and healthy manner.

• **Don't let your child grieve alone.** Sometimes when you as a parent don't know how to deal with it, you might leave your child alone…alone in the bedroom crying. Shutting your child out of your grieving or avoiding theirs can create a large gulf between you.

• **It is helpful to do everyday activities together, reminisce and retell stories** about the deceased, plan and participate in memorial services, have long walks and talks about death, life and the meanings of it all, cry and laugh together, perform rituals and ceremonies, and motivate each other to move into the new normal.

• **Don't overreact when your child ignores rules, expresses anger and becomes brooding or disrespectful**; it is natural for them to respond this way. Explain that they are not bad for feeling anger towards God, you, medical persons, other survivors or their loved one who has left them by dying. Assure your children that it is okay to feel angry and sad and help them make sense of the loss.

• **Talk to your child** and assure them that these feelings will pass. However, do not condone any behavior that is destructive to property or themselves. Insist that your child uses words to express hurt, wants and needs.

• **Don't forget to take care of yourself.** Ask for and accept offers of help. When you are having difficult days, arrange for other responsible adults to be with your children.

It is very important for your children to work through grief and adapt to loss with a more positive outcome. Young children and adolescents require you and others around them to recognize and respond appropriately to their symptoms and normal expressions of grief.

You must provide support, reassurance, affection and access to the necessary resources. A little honesty, sensitivity and effort on your part will go a long way to help your children process their own grief in a healthy way. You are grieving too, but it is important to gather the strength to satisfy the current and future needs of your grieving children. This caring strength enables all concerned to heal and grow through the experience.

Chapter Eighteen

TAKING CARE OF BUSINESS

The time right after the death of a loved one is an exceptionally emotional period. As a new widow, you are probably overwhelmed by all that has happened. You may be feeling that life has spun out of control and feeling extremely low on energy. When your emotions are on a roller coaster, making even simple decisions seem more than you can handle. First, give yourself time to be with your family, stabilize and grieve.

Organizing Financial and Legal Matters

After the funeral, you still face day-to-day realities such as running a household, working, caring for children and perhaps maintaining a business. In all the busyness of this business, treat yourself gently and acknowledge your grief. Grief is a journey that never completely ends. Life goes on in spite of your grief.

After suffering an emotionally devastating event, the last thing you probably want to deal with is money and legal matters. But, they really do matter, now and for your future, so try to do the best you can. Even while you are still somewhat in shock, doing grief work and adapting to a new life experience, there are practical matters that cannot be ignored or put on a back burner until you feel stronger and ready.

The process of organizing documents and dealing with government, legal and monetary matters can indeed be addressed in a manageable step-by-step manner. Organizing your financial and legal affairs doesn't have to start immediately following the death. As they say, you don't need to run from the funeral home to the attorney's office. There are timeframes with a few things that have to be done right away, some that can wait a month or so and others like taxes you start that may ultimately take a year or more. But you must start.

Where do you begin to organize all the legal and financial matters? First, know that there are professionals ready and capable of helping you. Additionally, you can call on trusted family members or friends to assist in some of the tasks. To get started, you just need to find as much of the necessary paperwork and documents as you can. Sadly, many deaths are unexpected and most folks do not have their estate plan or financial affairs in order. Whether your late husband's documents and affairs were in order or not, this section will outline what needs to be done in each time period. There are checklists, explanations and often contact information for each task. Follow these guidelines and systems for structuring your records and you will regain control and not feel so overwhelmed. Break your immediate organization tasks into manageable sections and take one at a time.

Immediate Obligations and Actions

Simply by getting things in order, you can avoid costly and unnecessary losses that result from a failure to organize personal and estate affairs. Millions of dollars of bank accounts, investments, stocks, real estate holdings and policy benefits go unclaimed and are turned over to the state government treasuries each year because the rightful property owners did not process the paperwork or it couldn't be found.

On a more personal level, invaluable pieces of family history, heirlooms may get lost and friends and family members may not get notice of the death in a timely manner. You can avoid losses like these by some advance planning, organizing and getting paperwork in order. Documents and personal information are not always easy to find after the fact. It may be time-consuming and frustrating to sort it all out, but it really is worth every effort made. The sooner you get started, the sooner you are finished.

After you do your executor's job and at the same time get your own personal, legal and financial affairs in order, you can relax in the knowledge that everything is simplified and organized for the future. Your attorney, accountant and financial advisor can help you understand and complete all the necessary forms and processes. How do you get started?

Gather Information and Documents

There are immediate obligations and actions that depend on you gathering your essential records, information and paperwork. The first thing you should focus on is gathering, organizing and making an inventory of the assets and liabilities.

Documents and paperwork you may need to complete tasks:

- Funeral Arrangement Contract
- Death Certificates
- Estate Plan Will or Trust
- Letter of Instruction or Last Wishes Binder
- Social Security Cards
- Marriage Certificate
- Birth Certificate
- Military Discharge Papers
- Birth Certificates for Minor Children
- Passport and/or Citizenship Papers
- Divorce Decrees
- Medical Insurance Policy
- Bank Account Books or Statements
- Safe Deposit Box Key, Location and Code
- Pension or Profit Sharing Plans
- IRA Retirements Account Statements
- Workers Compensation Benefit Plan
- Partnership or LLC Agreements
- Unpaid Salary and Bonus Agreements
- Royalty Contracts
- Annuities
- Savings Bonds
- Tax Returns
- Life Insurance Policies
- Stock Certificates
- Investment Brokerage Account Statements
- Real Estate Deed or Mortgage Data and Insurance
- Credit Cards and Account Statements
- Vehicle Titles and Loans
- Art and Jewelry Appraisals
- Digital and Computer Accounts and Passwords
- Legacy Letter

Unfortunately, few people have the foresight to prepare estate plans, letters of instructions or a binder with the necessary documentation for their widow or estate administrator. Most people prefer to avoid the subject of death altogether. A Martindale-Hubbell conducted research study found that 55% of all adult Americans do not have a will. Only one in three African American adults (32 percent) and one in four Hispanic American adults (26 percent) has a will or trust.

A big part of financial freedom is having your heart and mind free from worry about the what-ifs of life.

- Suze Orman

It is hardly surprising that widows are typically unprepared deal with a death and all that it involves. Without estate plans and organized documentation, it can become a big task to oversee the legal, financial and personal affairs of your deceased spouse. Organization is not an option at this point of the game; it is a fundamental survival skill and distinct competitive advantage. Something has to be done by you to organize and settle the financial matters and estate, so the following chapters cover your detailed action plan.

Chapter Nineteen

FINANCIAL AND LEGAL AFFAIRS ACTION PLAN

Statistics show that the plight of dealing with estate administration is largely a woman's ordeal since only one in four widowed Americans are male. Women are at an immediate disadvantage on several fronts when their husbands die because:

- Women have statistically earned cents on the dollar compared to men with the gap widening with age
- Women spend more on family and save less of their income
- Women start investing late and lose on compounded interest
- Women have smaller retirement and pension accounts and less Social Security payouts
- Women have less experience managing family finances, investments or insurance
- Women have not been included in decisions or made aware of the family's complete financial portfolio

Traditionally, you may have paid the monthly household bills, but never dealt with the big picture stuff before. What is frightening is that you may not even know who the life insurance agent is or where the family investments are held. Often we attorneys hear, "He did it all. I never asked any questions. Then he died suddenly. I don't know where anything is or who to call." Don't worry, because this section will be your key to getting all the rest pulled together and dealt with for the estate and for your future.

> Don't agonize. Organize.
>
>   - Florynce Kennedy

Dealing with the immediate practical concerns and then getting the financial and legal affairs in order will be your objective in this first stage. During this period, you should focus on gathering, organizing and making an inventory of all assets and liabilities. Here you will find systematic guidelines of how to proceed through the maze of documents and contacts after the death of your spouse. This section is divided into organization systems, contacts, checklists and timeframes of what needs to be done first, second and over the long term. The following serves as the preliminary guide for getting your financial and legal affairs in order.

By gathering the applicable documents listed and preparing an inventory, you will be prepared to be a competent executor or trustee and able to make informed decisions about the administration of your loved one's estate. The advance work of gathering and organizing documents will save you time, confusion, frustration and money.

Now is the time to be deliberate. Do not be hasty with decisions or pressured into making any distributions. Don't be in a hurry to start or try to take on administration of an estate before you consult with your attorney for guidance. It is smart to hire a professional who understands the estate administration process and can give you good advice. A trained estate attorney can walk you through the maze of will probate and trust administration. Especially helpful is the fact that professionals can act as a buffer between you and the clamoring world.

Organizing Techniques and Tools

Conduct a thorough search of your home, files, autos, bank and the workplace to locate any financial and legal documents. The latest tax return will often tell you what investments you have and give you information about who the tax advisor may have been. If there was an attorney, accountant or financial planner, that would also be a good place to get updated information and compare notes with them. As you work through the process and meet with advisors, you might consider taking a family member or trusted friend with you. If you forget to take notes or can't remember some details, your relative or friend is likely to remember.

With the checklists and guidance of this section, you can gather the necessary pieces to complete your inventory and tasks. Once you have a grasp on the financial situation, it will be time to start notifications, transfers, estate administration and whatever else necessary.

Sort Paperwork And Set Up Payments

A financial filing system, for many, has meant a drawer full or box of papers under the desk in the den or a pile of unopened bills on the dining room table. If this is similar to your situation, it is time to tackle the whole bunch and get documents in some kind of order.

Start by dividing paper mounds into categories.

1. Separate the current statements and bills from other documents you need to keep for your records.

2. Set up accessible marked baskets or an organizer in which to keep outstanding bills you need to keep on hand. In attending to immediate practical concerns, you should quickly get control of the regular household bills and pay them in a timely manner.

3. Get a calendar and mark in a bright color when bills are due. An officer at your bank can help you set up automatic or online checking account withdrawals for most monthly or periodic payments. It is easy to set up and less for you to think about or let accidentally slip between the cracks. Timely payments prevent costly problems.

4. Get in the habit of setting aside time twice a month to go through financial documents to pay bills and file or discard the paperwork. As you look through the statements, make sure that your financial institutions and other accounts have your current address.

5. Any advertisements, documents or things you planned to get to eventually that are wasting space or your time are to be pulled out and tossed. Throw away old bills, bank statements, bills, receipts and cancelled checks with no long-term significance for tax or other purposes. Consult with an accountant if you are not sure.

6. Checks or receipts that have to do with major purchases, investments, home improvement, charity, warranties or support your tax returns should be retained, clearly marked and filed.

7. For the benefit of your heirs or for your own memory's sake, take precautions with old accounts by either disposing of proof of void life insurance policies, brokerage accounts, bank account and other asset paperwork that you no longer own or clearly mark them as closed, sold or cashed in. This will save a lot of time and effort in researching mystery accounts where there is nothing to claim.

8. To avoid becoming a victim of identity theft, as you dispose of papers shred any documents that contain a Social Security number, bank account number or other personal or financial information.

Categorize and Label

Documents you decide to keep need to be sorted in categories, labeled and filed. As significant a role as the computer has assumed, digital technology still has not been able to eliminate the vital importance of having hard copies of primary documents. You can use a large three ring binder with tabs, an accordion file, storage box or a filing cabinet with marked hanging folders to keep documents at your fingertips. Establish a permanent place for your financial and legal records.

Develop your own record keeping system. Whatever you choose, it must be clearly labeled so that you, or in the event of disability or death, anyone else can find records easily and quickly. All your categories can be expanded or divided later as needed. Aim for consistency and predictability in your filing system as you label each folder.

Broad categories for your files, folders and labels may include:

- Bank, money market, mutual funds accounts;
- Insurance policies life, medical, mortgage, car or homeowner
- Employment contract, benefit package, profit sharing plan and employer contact data
- Retirement, 401(k), IRA, annuity and pension accounts
- Investment accounts, stocks and bonds
- Credit cards and statements
- Tax returns and receipts by dates
- Deeds or leases for real estate holdings
- Vehicle titles and drivers license copies
- Trust, wills, powers of attorney, medical directives
- Funeral arrangements, cemetery plot deed, or pre-paid plans
- Letter of Instruction and Legacy Letter
- Buy-sell agreements, royalty contracts or business ownership
- Birth, marriage certificate, divorce decrees, education degrees, military, social security copies and/or locations of the originals
- Contact information for family, friends, employer, social or religious organizations, attorney, accountant or other advisors
- Digital computer accounts, assets identification and passwords
- Pending or ongoing transactions, IOUs, notes receivable debts
- Lists of files, safe deposit box inventory, location and access codes
- Warranties and guarantees
- Family history, with location of heirlooms, photos and genealogy

Inventory Spreadsheet

It is advisable to create a spreadsheet, list or chart of some kind that notes pertinent details of all assets and liabilities. This at a glance summary of the finances will be of great assistance in managing your affairs and making decisions. Establish a permanent place for financial and legal records. With up-to-date documents, spreadsheets, inventory lists and an organized filing system, you will not feel like such a novice or feel so intimidated when you work with officials, attorneys, accountants or financial planners.

You may also keep scanned copies of important documents on your computer. Prepare a set of instructions for your family so they will be able to get into your computer financial and estate files. The important thing is that you create a clear, easily accessible system that will make it simpler for you to manage financial and legal matters and one that will light the way for your family and friends if anything happens to you.

Be sure to keep all statements and receipts for expenditures that you have used or are going to use on your tax returns. These keepers may include purchases related to home improvements, home business, medical and dental expenses, prescriptions, charitable contributions and warranted items. You should keep supporting documents for tax returns for at least four years. Hold on to your tax returns indefinitely. Other non-government documents to hang on to indefinitely are the records of large ticket items like the deed for your home or other real estate, vehicle titles, investments, pension or retirement plans and major household or business purchases.

Saving and Storing Documents

It is imperative that you store your important documents in a safe place. Place vital documents like birth or marriage certificates, wills and trusts, powers of attorney, insurance policies, social security cards or military records in a fire-resistant and waterproof container or safe deposit box. The key to the safe deposit box, files and lock-box can be put on the ring of your trust or last wishes binder or another obvious known location.

Print out a master list of where things are filed, stored and how to access them. Give copies of your master asset and contacts list to your lawyer, a trusted family member, estate executor or accountant. Keep any lists and instructions up-to-date. Leave a clear and accurate paper trail. Make sure that the person who will settle your estate and business affairs is on the safe deposit box signature card so that they will have access when the time comes. Label all keys and be sure people have duplicates or know where to find the ones in your possession.

These organizational hints will help you get the paperwork in order. It is never too late to organize and simplify your late spouse's and your own financial and legal affairs. I know that you may not feel like doing all this overwhelming detailed hard stuff. You'd probably rather let someone else do the work and make all the decisions for you, but this is the worse time to do that. Think of this winding up of the affairs after a death as an indication of the person's trust in your capabilities. If you don't do it, who else can or who will? The obligations and problems will not go away and must be faced.

You really can take care of these organizational and administrative parts little by little, by focusing on one thing at a time. There is a much-needed sense of accomplishment, pride and control when you have finished. Follow the checklists to guide your first baby steps of dealing with the various obligations and actions. Remember the Chinese saying that even the greatest journey starts with a single step.

Chapter Twenty

SETTLING THE ESTATE – PART ONE

Death Certificates

The funeral home director typically handles the task of ordering the death certificates for you. The hospital and doctors will provide the date, time, place and cause of death to the funeral home. The number of death certificates needed depends on the complexity of the deceased person's finances and estate planning done beforehand. Generally, you should order around a dozen (12) death certificates to start with. The cost is usually about $10-$15 for an official copy of a single death certificate. You can always get more certificates later, if you need them by contacting the county clerk's office, health department in the county where the deceased lived or the state's vital records department. Death certificates are legal documents that will be required for administrative purposes to obtain certain information and benefits such as insurance or investment accounts.

You, as next of kin, will need to provide accurate personal information when you apply for a death certificate. Generally, you must supply the following vital statistics:

- Full name, address and telephone number of the deceased
- Social Security number
- Date and place of birth
- Marital status and spouse's name
- Father's name and birthplace
- Mother's maiden name and birthplace
- Length of time deceased resided in the state

- Occupation, title, business address and telephone number
- Ethnicity
- Citizenship status
- Veteran rank, serial number, service branch and discharge date
- Sometimes you will asked to provide level of education, religious affiliation, clubs or noteworthy achievements
- List of close relatives for the death notice or obituary

Social Security

Legally, the Social Security Administration (SSA) must be promptly notified of the death. If your husband was receiving Social Security payments, other government benefits or health services, such as Medicaid or hospice care, these agencies need notification as well. The mortuary or funeral home director will often inform the government and help you with paperwork.

You can report the death to a service representative at the Social Security Administration by calling the toll-free number 1-800-772-1213 or the TTY hard of hearing toll-free number 1-800-325-0778. An alternative way is to visit the website (www.ssa.gov) to set up a local appointment or (www.socialsecurity.gov/survivorcharted.htm) to view a chart showing survivors benefits and act on that information. Be prepared to identify the deceased's relationship to you, Social Security number, date of birth, date and place of death, surviving spouse or next of kin social security numbers, and medical history on whether the death is service related or not.

Your notice of your husband's death to the Social Security Administration will stop monthly payments. Do not cash checks received for the month in which your spouse died. The Social Security Administration is very wary of fraud. It is a real hassle if they are not informed immediately or you accept money after the death. You must return any Social Security benefits to the SSA that you are no longer entitled to have. If you received Social Security benefits via direct deposit, you need to notify the receiving bank to stop future incoming payments from being deposited. Overpayments will result in a complex process of repayment.

Immediate benefits include a one-time lump sum death payment of $255 to the spouse or minor children. If you are a surviving spouse, ask your local Social Security agent about your eligibility for increased survivor benefits or benefits that any minor or disabled children may be entitled to receive. Eligible family members may receive monthly payments as much as the full retirement amount. Benefits are not automatically paid out after a death. You must apply for them. Ask for a copy or go online and print the Social Security Survivors brochure.

Practical Estate Administration Tips: The telephone conversations, meetings and types of notification are the first of several you will conduct over the next several months. The processes of notification and restructuring can be repetitive, arduous and sometimes frustrating. A good plan is to keep time and dated notes every time you speak with a government or company representative. Be sure to write down the complete name and employee identification number of the person with whom you spoke, your list of tasks and the results of the conversation. Saying "I talked to someone named Jim a few weeks ago" will not cut it in the complex paper world of corporations or government agencies. Don't get sent back to square one for lack of a paper trail.

The tasks facing you after a death are multi-layered and tend to run together, so making reference notes in a notebook about your talks or meetings with people will prove very helpful. Put everything in writing and retain copies of all correspondences. Keeping careful records will ease your mind and in the long-run save you much time and duplication of efforts. Additionally, it is advisable to take a trusted family member or friend to appointments sometimes to listen with an extra set of ears, so no important details get missed or misunderstood.

Estate Will or Trust Administration

If your husband had a trust or will, locate his and/or your estate plan documents. Original versions, not copies, are required for probate and many other transactions. Often the original documents are in the safe deposit box, strongbox, filed in a cabinet at home or sometimes the attorney who drew up the documents will have the original or a file copy.

The will or trust establishes the appointed personal representative or trustee with the tasks of settling the estate. If there is no will, a court hearing will be held to appoint someone. Whoever is in charge, usually you as the surviving spouse or an adult child or parent, needs to make an appointment with the trust and estates attorney in the state in which the deceased resided at the time of death. If the will names you as the personal representative or executor, prior to appointment by the court, you only have the power to carry out written instructions regarding the funeral and burial arrangements. It is also your fiduciary duty to protect the deceased's property. Do not remove, sell or distribute any property before the opening of the estate and court probate proceedings. Having an attorney at your side will help you stay on the correct estate settlement road and help buffer all the forms, questions and assaults from lienholders, contract holders and even family members.

You can prevent the state and others from taking your money and property. Tell anxious relatives, creditors and others that you need to consult with your attorney first. It is highly advised to use an attorney for the probate and any trust administration. It will save you time, prevent costly errors and keep others out of your hair through the process.

If there is no will or trust, all states have a set of laws relating to intestate succession (transfer of property after dying without a will) and the state decides who gets which assets. The probate court will appoint an administrator (usually the surviving wife) to maintain or distribute the assets of the deceased according to state law.

Practical Settlement Tips:
Seek professional help from the beginning. You should establish an early relationship with an attorney who specializes in will, trusts and estates to assure that all matters are addressed properly in a timely manner. The majority of folks would never think of ripping apart a computer or their car engine to fix it by themselves. They are wise to hire a person who specializes in electrical or mechanical matters. The same thing goes for settling estates.

Wrapping up your loved one's affairs can be tedious and stressful. Find guidance you can trust. Hire a licensed professional who knows what they are doing and work with them. Each State Bar Association has a list of licensed lawyers who specialize in estate planning and administration. Call your state professional association of attorneys and they will help you find someone you are comfortable with and feel you can trust.

Seeking an attorney's advice before you act may avoid costly mistakes and court, administrative, taxes and legal fees later. While your family and friends may have good intentions and want to help you fix things quickly, they may be misinformed and offer advice that is not objective and unprofessional. Never act in haste or before you are fully informed.

It is best to work with trained professionals and fulfill your obligations properly the first time rather than pay to fix the mistakes later. Some actions can't be undone or fixed after the fact. Always check with an attorney, accountant, insurance agent or financial tax advisor before making any legal or large decisions regarding an estate.

Not only will the professionals who work with estates regularly guide you through the process, they are usually caring counselors and great hand-holders. In my law practice, I was known as the "kitchen table lawyer" because I went to the homes of my widowed clients as a caring friend to help them. Many estate plans I worked on were designed, signed and settled over a cup of tea at someone's kitchen table.

Attorneys do these sorts of administrative tasks all the time and can really save you time, frustration and money. It is smart to contact someone knowledgeable for help with pulling it all together. This section outlines how you can prepare documents to assist your professional advisors. Please put the call to your attorney at the top of your list.

Step-By-Step Estate Settlement Processes:

> Organizing is what you do before you do something, so that when you do it, it is not all mixed up.
> - A.A. Milne

Veterans

When a military retiree or veteran passes away, you as the spouse or next of kin should make a timely call to the Department of Veterans Affairs (VA) at the toll-free number 1-800-827-1000. If you are the widow of a man who served in the military, a range of veteran's benefits may be available. Benefits may include: lump sum death benefit, if death was connected to service; continuing monthly payments; Aid and Attendance pension funds to pay the costs of in-home or assisted living care; financial assistance with funeral expenses; cemetery plot or burial in a national cemetery; headstone or memorial marker; U.S. Flag; or White House Certificate commemorating the veteran's time of service.

Additionally, the last wishes or will may contain a military funeral honors request. This can be arranged through the VA. Ask for the Federal Benefits for Veterans and Dependents publication or go to the VA website (www. va.gov) for more information. You will need to know your deceased husband's Veteran Administration service number, dates of active service and have copies of the military discharge papers.

Marriage, Birth Certificates, Divorce Decrees, Passport and Citizenship Papers

Any or all of these certificate and status documents may be required to complete, authenticate and process various notices, applications and benefit packages. Gather as many of these as possible and make copies in advance. You may have to write to government agencies and state or county vital records departments to obtain certified copies.

Employment

If your spouse was working, contact the employer immediately with news of the death. It is advisable to write a formal letter to the employer, union, publisher, investment partner or any other professional organization or group with which he may have had an association. Many companies and organizations have insurance policies of which you or your children may have been the beneficiary.

Ask employers or business partners about your deceased husband's employment savings, any 401(k), pension, profit sharing plans, credit unions, company stock options, corporate benefits, buy-sell agreements, salary or bonus due, including vacation or sick leave, disability income, workman's compensation, life insurance and other such benefits. Have them send you any forms needed to apply for entitled benefits.

If your spouse received pension payments, write to the retirement or pension provider about death benefits, obtain claim forms and/or information on how to collect one-time sums or continue payments to the survivor.

Medical Insurance Policy

Contact the medical insurance company or employer regarding termination of coverage for your late spouse while continuing health coverage for others covered through the policy. In making payment claims for the final illness or accident, it is usually okay to hold off on paying medical bills until they are all in and you see what insurance covers. Do not settle the claim or sign releases until you receive all the billings and expenditures. This could take months, so organize them and process them as necessary.

Inquire whether you can continue the health insurance for a certain period under the employer's group plan. Find out whether the family health insurance falls under federal or state jurisdiction. Under federal law, you would be eligible to continue the family's current health care coverage up to 36 months under the Consolidated Omnibus Budget Reconciliation Act (COBRA). They may charge more, but it is a transitional option. COBRA only applies to companies that have 20 or more employees. Similar programs exist under some state laws, so look on your state Insurance Commissioner website for information.

In many cases, you and your children have to find other health insurance, often at escalated prices. Another federal law that provides access to health insurance is the Health Insurance Portability and Accountability Act (HIPPA). This law allows you access to health insurance if you have been denied insurance, as long as you file within 62 days. It provides access, but not necessarily affordable insurance.

Credit Cards and Account Statements

Once you receive certified copies of the death certificate, you should notify the three major credit-reporting agencies:

- Experian P.O. Box 9595, Allen, TX 75013-9595,
  Telephone: 888-397-3742
- Equifax, P.O. Box 740241, Atlanta, GA 30374-0241
  Telephone: 800-685-1111
- Trans Union, P.O. Box 1000, Chester, PA 19022
  Telephone: 800-888-4213

Notify all credit card companies in writing that the cardholder has died and cancel the credit card. The companies may ask you to return the card with a copy of the death certificate. Inquire about card company policies for life insurance or debt balance insurance attached to the account. If you, as surviving spouse, wish to retain the use of the card, get a new one issued in your own name or open a new account. Credit card company phone numbers are on the card or on the most recent statement. If you notice any unusual activities or unknown charges on the credit card statements, report and dispute them immediately to stop identity theft or fraud.

Some questions I often get from widowed clients include: What happens to credit card debt after someone dies? Does that debt die with the person? There is no one-size-fits-all answer. A number of factors, including who applied for the card and where they lived, can radically alter the situation. Here is the simple answer: If the card belonged to your deceased spouse alone, with no joint account holders, the debts are his alone. However, if your spouse, family member, or business partner signed the card application as a co-signer (joint account holder), then that person could be liable for the balance on that card, with or instead of the estate. If that second cardholder is merely an authorized user (didn't sign the application, isn't liable for bills, and merely has charging privileges), then she isn't responsible.

When someone dies, the estate is responsible for paying off the credit card balances. If the estate goes through probate, the administrator or executor will look at the assets and debts and, guided by law, determine in what order bills should be paid. If the decedent spouse was indebted, the creditor needs to be paid from the estate. If there is enough money, the Credit Card Act of 2009, part of which went into effect in February 2010, requires the executor of an estate to be informed of the amount owned to the credit card company quickly, and requires credit card issuers to stop tacking on fees and penalties during the time the estate is being settled.

If a creditor makes a valid timely claim against the estate and the personal representative has distributed all the assets, the representative may be held personally liable for the debt. Again, when handling the estate, do not be hasty or pressured into making distributions. Important choices are to be in accordance to statutes, the will, other instructions and any applicable tax laws. Remaining assets, after the debts are settled, are distributed to heirs by following the will if there is one, or state law if there is none.

If the estate is insolvent and there isn't enough money, credit card companies have to write off the bills and often that's the end of it. Children, friends, or relatives cannot inherit debt. A card company can't legally force someone else not on the account to pay. Be warned that some creditors will try to guilt, trick or cajole spouses or relatives into assuming the debts while on recorded telephone calls or in correspondence.

> Any informed borrower is simply less vulnerable to fraud and abuse.
>
> - Alan Greenspan

Fraud and Predators

Sadly, identity theft after death is a common problem. Identity thieves sometimes impersonate dead people, using personal information obtained from death notices, obituaries, gravestones and other sources to exploit delays between the death and the closure of the person's accounts. Thieves rely on the inattention of grieving families and weaknesses in the processes for credit checking. Such identity theft crimes may continue until you or the authorities notice and react to anomalies.

There are also unscrupulous people who prey upon you and your family after the death of your loved one. First, some may try to burglarize your home during the funeral service or in the weeks following. Alert your local police department and request extra patrols the day of and after the memorial service. Ask neighbors to help you be vigilant about any suspicious activity in the neighborhood or to stay at your house that day if they are not attending the services.

Criminals also follow death notices and may make unfounded claims against the deceased. Do not easily accept the claims, bills, invoices or notes of unknown companies or individuals that lack documentation or arouse your innate suspicions. In my practice, I have even heard of neighbors or caregivers charging the heirs for fake debts or damages. Check claimants and solicitations out with licensing authorities, on the legitimate charities Guide Star web site, or with Better Business Bureau. The fraud problem is growing in depth and width.

Be aware that numerous bogus charitable organizations may aggressively approach you. Even during times of vulnerability and stress, it is your choice of which legitimate non-profit charities you may want to support; not those that target cold call you on the phone. Many fraudulent appeal letterheads or email sites are similar in name to valid organizations, so be cautious about such matters.

Cancel Appointments, Memberships and Retrieve Items

As a courtesy, cancel any medical, dental, haircut, therapy or salon appointments your loved one may have scheduled. Cancel unwanted subscriptions, redundant cell phones, email services, classes, travel reservations, health or social club memberships, book or movie memberships, reunions, periodic charitable donations, church duties and such. Retrieve any mid-transaction funds held to secure a future purchase like a car, home, boat, trip, large purchase or other down payment. Collect any items that are on lay away, being repaired or on loan located somewhere other than in the home.

Create an Inventory of Assets

Take a financial inventory of real estate, major purchases, personal property, accounts and investments as of the date of the death. A price history can be reconstructed in the future, but sometimes at great difficulty and expense, so the inventory of assets is easier if captured as close to the death as possible. This type survey charts and records the value of assets at a precise time. Additionally, an inventory and photographs of the home, household goods, personal belongings, contents of the safe deposit box and other valuables is recommended. Sometimes art, jewelry, collections, vehicle and real estate appraisals are required. This financial picture accounts for all property and prepares for the transfers of ownership, title, deeds or distributions.

When conducting an inventory of the safe deposit box, it is advisable to have a non-bias third person witness and to take video or photographs of the contents upon first opening. This careful behavior is especially important if there is even the slightest possibility of challenges to the will or trust. Any person whose is a signer on the safe deposit box and has a key can enter it at any time. Additionally, a spouse, heir or beneficiary can ask a bank to open the box in their presence to search for a will, burial instructions or a deed to a burial plot. In some jurisdictions, the bank retains possession of the will and forwards it to the court. After the will is filed with the court, the named personal representative can petition the court for appointment in order to begin the probate process. It is the fiduciary duty of a personal representative or trustee to gather, inventory, protect, maintain and distribute estate property as instructed by the deceased.

Chapter Twenty-One

SETTLING THE ESTATE - PART TWO

Much of this administrative phase is not as immediate as the first part of organizing and processing, but title changes and collection of benefits are part of the process still required to settle estate affairs. Once you have organized the estate, legal and financial documents and have an informed overview of your financial situation, it is time to notify all concerned parties of the death and to begin transferring accounts and titles into your own name or your trust name wherever possible. Wait until you have a certified copy of the death certificate before advising financial institutions of the loss to avoid complications in accessing accounts.

It is best to seek the counsel and assistance of an attorney to advise you on the sequence and shortcuts to administering the estate. There are so many changes each year in the federal tax codes and state statutes that you need an appropriate professional to guide you through the steps. The following information will give you a list of the key documents you need and basic outlines of what is required to transfer assets.

Life Insurance Policies

Contact the insurance company and agent in writing for claims on all life insurance policies. You need to complete a statement of claim form and provide an original or certified copy of the death certificate and the policy number. The insurance agent can order or supply the forms and perhaps assist in completing them. Ask lots of questions and be clear about your policy coverage, benefits and options. Remember to ask about payment options. You may have a choice between receiving a lump sum or having the insurance company put the money in an interest-bearing account from which you can write checks. Some annuities continue for the widow or family members. Avoid making claims or accepting lump sums as a beneficiary until you have consulted with an attorney or financial advisor to consider whether either a tax or a non-tax reason exists for refusing to receive an asset.

When life insurance settlements are not taxed, financial advisors may suggest using the insurance money to pay down or pay off high interest credit card or other debts to become more solvent. Depending on the financial circumstances, some widows find it appropriate to pay education bills, make down payment on homes, invest in business starts or make other loans to their children or grandchildren. Most place the funds in interest bearing money market funds or treasury bills and make decisions later.

You don't have to make investment decisions right away. Sometimes the insurance agent will try to sell you other policies or annuity. You don't have to decide anything then and there. Get other financial advisor guidance before any major decisions. There are many options, so find the ones most suitable for your unique situation. When you eventually have all the financial facts, you then develop a customized long-term plan. It is important not to immediately make any major life changes or put funds where there is little or no liquidity. Do not get involved in any schemes. This is a time to go slowly and act deliberately.

A thorough search for death benefits can be time well spent. Look through your deceased husband's paperwork, checkbook, mortgage or credit card statements, tax returns and other places for any indications of premiums paid on annuities or life insurance. In addition to life insurance policies, many people have accidental or death benefits attached to bank accounts, loans, mortgages or credit cards, with previous and current employers' group term-life coverage, memberships in organizations or unions and even death benefits on auto, home, travel or health insurance policies. Often the insurance agent can help you with their claim forms.

Determine if your own life insurance and retirement beneficiary designations have the proper coverage and are updated to prevent your benefits going to the wrong person or persons. I had a client whose forty year old life insurance was payable to her mother, who had passed away thirty years prior. What a probate mess that was. If your late husband is the beneficiary on any policy you own, this is a good time to change the designated beneficiary to others while you are dealing with the insurance company. Keep a copy of all correspondence and dated notes on all conversations with the insurance companies and agents.

Bank Accounts and Safe Deposit Box

Collect the bankbooks, bank statements, online accounts and inventory the contents of the safe deposit box. Depending on how the account was set up, you may be able access the bank account to conduct business as usual. Some bank accounts are 'pay on death' (POD) to a named survivor or joint account holder. The assets in the bank account or safe deposit box are distributed in accordance with the written bank contractual instructions and wishes of the decedent. Watch out; in some states, banks automatically freeze the assets when notified of the death.

Normally only the will's personal representative, executor or trust administrator can access the account after providing the certified copy of the death certificate and required paperwork to the bank. Call or visit the bank to inquire about what is required to access accounts. Arrange to release joint bank account funds to you and change any accounts into your name only or into your trust. If the bank account is in your deceased husband's trust, work with a bank officer to put the account and safety deposit box into your trust or your name.

Be sure you keep the safe deposit box key, its location and codes in a readily available spot. In the three ring binder of your trust or letter in instruction is a good place where those who need it can find it, but unauthorized others would not think to look. Often widows open a new bank account and safe deposit box right away just for the estate of the decedent. This way there are records of all the receipt and disbursement of funds in that account statement. The assets and estate administration expenses are in order in one place.

Make sure to continually make automatic payments such as mortgage, insurances, car and other important bills through the proper account or manually. Delays in paying your bills can have serious financial repercussions. Unpaid bills could end up in collections, interest rates go double digit and be devastating to your credit scores. Bounced checks can result in banks closing accounts. Neglected investment accounts could suffer unecessary losses. Unpaid insurance coverage could lapse. The list goes on. Avoid financial distress by staying current with the bills.

Learn from the estate mistakes of comedic actor W.C. Fields. Because of his secretiveness, and his desire to have cash available wherever he was in the world, Fields opened some 200 bank accounts under fictitious names and he kept no record of the deposits or the banks. His safe-deposit box in a Berlin bank contained $50,000, deposited under another name, but this was lost when Berlin was bombed in WW II. His executors were able to find 45 of these bank accounts, but the remaining deposits estimated at $600,000 were never located.

Retirement Accounts

Individual Retirement Account (IRA), 401(k), pension and retirement accounts must be retrieved or retitled carefully. Hopefully, at a minimum your deceased husband listed every retirement plan that he had, whether or not it pays benefits now or in the future. Retirement plans may include: pensions, employer-sponsored plans, IRAs (traditional, Roth, SIMPLE or SEP-IRAs, Keogh, profit-sharing plans, or 401(k)s. If you do not have such a list, contact the employer or financial planner and search through paperwork to find these possible benefits.

Each retirement account and pension plan should name a specific beneficiary. Most 401(k)s and pension plans are required by law to name the spouse as beneficiary unless she signs a form giving up that right. Annuities, pension and profit sharing plans may provide for joint payment to a surviving spouse or others. For IRAs and other employer profit sharing retirement plans, the earner may name any beneficiary of their choice. Community property state spouses have a legal right to half of the money earned during the marriage.

Under recent IRS regulations, beneficiaries of IRAs and 401(k) plans have to make some important choices. If you are the beneficiary on an IRA or a 401(k) plan, remember that this will be taxed once you claim it and use it for income. If you roll the IRA or 401(k) over into your own IRA, taxes may continue to be deferred. It is essential that you get professional legal and financial advice and understand tax consequences before claiming it.

Estate Taxes

Not all estates are subject to taxes. However, there are two types of taxes assessed against someone's property after their death: estate taxes and inheritance taxes, both commonly referred to as "death taxes." The phrase death tax includes estate tax, inheritance tax, or any tax imposed on the transfer of property after death. Taxes are based on the total value of the decedent's property or who is inheriting the property.

The United States enacted an estate tax in 1916. When John D. Rockefeller, America's first billionaire, died in 1937, his estate paid 70 percent. Since then the rates have fluctuated, but 2010 was the first year the estate tax was repealed altogether. In 2010, Texan pipeline tycoon, Dan Duncan and the NY Yankees owner, George Steinbrenner both died with multi-billion dollar estates that they passed to their heirs tax-free. The year before, an estate valued more than $3.5 million, like theirs, were heavily taxed.

Estate tax is a tax imposed by a state or federal government on the right to transfer property to your heirs after your death. The federal estate tax affects only about 5,500 estates a years. Congress failed to reach an agreement beforehand so the federal estate tax disappeared for 2010. Federal estate tax rules reinstated the tax for 2011, preserving the levy for two years at the 35% rate, with an exemption of up to $5 million for individuals and $10 million for couples. That means you can transfer five million dollars of assets to your beneficiaries tax free; but any amount over that is subject to federal estate taxes and possibly additional state estate taxes.

Ask your attorney for the latest federal and state specific tax rules applicable to your estate. Be sure that the rewrites of the estate tax law changes have not become retroactive and applied to those who died in 2010.

As of 2011, the District of Columbia and the following states impose a separate state estate tax in addition to federal estate tax: Connecticut, Delaware, Maine, Maryland, Massachusetts, Minnesota, New Jersey, New York, North Carolina, Ohio, Oregon, Rhode Island, Tennessee, Vermont, and Washington. Inheritance or succession tax is a tax imposed by a state government on the privilege of an heir to receive a deceased person's assets. Seven states collect an inheritance tax - Indiana, Iowa, Kentucky, Maryland, Nebraska, New Jersey and Pennsylvania.

Assets left to a surviving spouse are exempt from the inheritance tax in the seven states, but only four states exempt transfers to descendants. Two states, Oregon and Tennessee, collect what is referred to in state statutes as an inheritance tax. The inheritance tax is based, not on who receives the property, but on the value of the decedent's property. State inheritence taxes are usually less than federal estate taxes and vary by state.

Tax Returns and Forms

You do not have to worry about taxes immediately after the death. It is important to seek expert tax advice to file an income tax return for the year of the death and determine your full tax liability. Federal law requires that an estate tax return be filed, within nine months of the death in many cases. A surviving spouse and decedent can file a joint return for the year of death, as long as he or she has not remarried before the end of the tax year. You will need to provide monthly bank statements, investment records on all individual and joint accounts, real estate appraisals and the like that show the account balances and values on the day of death, since this information is needed for estate tax returns.

If there is a revocable living trust, a separate tax return, Form 1041 will have to be file for the estate. Since the deceased can no longer use his Social Security number, the trustee applies to the IRS for a new EIN number for the deceased for the tax filing and other trust accounts. Estate taxes file on Form 706 and are marked final return for the individual. Publication 950, found on the Internal Revenue Service website (www.irs.gov), provides information about filing out the tax forms.

It can take up to six months for an estate tax return to be processed. Make sure that you receive your closing letter from the IRS to prove that all matters concerning taxes after death are settled. The attorney and tax advisor can help with these matters during the administration of the estate. Taxes after death do not have to be stressful or complicated. If you understand what your tax responsibilities are after a death, the process can be relatively hassle-free. Please consult your own tax, legal or accounting professionals before you make any decisions. Never ignore taxes. Uncle Sam knows you and the estate are there and the IRS won't go away.

Real Estate

Assemble the deeds of your late husband to see what real estate is owned by him or by you both. If your husband owned real estate in more than one state, special proceedings called ancillary administrations may be required in each state not the residence state. If there is real estate or a business property, you as the executor, trustee or personal representative should be sure to maintain the mortgage or lease payments, taxes and insurances on the properties. It is your task to re-title real estate deeds or loans.

One of the biggest mistakes you can make is putting the real estate or other large assets into your children's names. There are possibly devastating financial, legal and tax ramifications that you must consider. Detailed information about the dangers of will substitutes or joint tenancy with children and others is found in chapter twenty-five of this book.

Vehicle Titles and Loans

In most circumstances, a surviving spouse can transfer the ownership of a motor vehicle without going through the probate process. There is a Department of Motor Vehicles form or affidavit for you to fill out requesting each vehicle titled in your name. Your insurance agent may have the necessary form, and if not, it is generally available on-line at the state DMV internet webpage. Also, inform the DMV of the death of your husband if he had a state issued driver's license.

Investment Brokerage Account

Look for investment account statements to see if you or your husband owned any securities, stocks, bonds, mutual funds or other financial investment ventures. Have the stockbroker, investment company or bank help you with the forms to change the stocks and bonds into your name or the account into the trust name. Transfer savings bonds and certificates of deposit to your name or jointly with your heirs. The banks, attorneys and investment advisers can help you with this task.

Partnership or LLC Agreements

If your late husband was a principal person or controlled a business, check to see if there are Buy-Sell Agreements under which the business entity or other business owners would purchase his interests. There may be additional key man insurance benefits.

Legacy Letter

Trusts and wills or probate take care of the tangible real and personal properties of an individual. There is an old custom of writing an ethical will or legacy letter to the family and friends that pass on your history, memories, values, blessings and advice to generations to come. If your deceased loved one left a legacy letter, set up an occasion to read and share it with others. Chapter twenty-eight of this book teaches you how to prepare and present this type of precious legacy gift.

Secure Storage and Passwords

A great deal of your legal and financial information is confidential and sensitive, so you will want to store it in secure locations like a locked file cabinet, fire-proof safe or a safe deposit box. Without a doubt, online banking, emails, electronic bill paying, brokerage trading, paperless accounts, EBay, PayPal and personal finance software make modern lives easier. If you die or are lying in a coma, you have to make sure that someone you trust can find and access the all the accounts and files. Concerns about security and identity theft shouldn't go so far that a family member is tangled in a digital mess and can't get access to the needed information. When it is time to prepare for your funeral or start administration of your estate, your family or executor has to know where your documents are and how to get to them. Make sure that the necessary information is not hidden away or protected by unknown codes or passwords.

Here are some ways to provide essential directions for your executor for each secured place. Make a list of each service and product for which you have a user name, personal identification number (PIN), key, code, password and brief description of what the box or account contains. For each item prepare a spreadsheet, chart or list with notes of the account name and number, semi-current amounts, contact information for agents, account managers or advisors, password, combination, password, PIN, storage unit locations and numbers, safe deposit box number, location and keys of all sorts. You might also write down the answers to common security questions, such as your elementary school, your mother's maiden name and the name of your first pet.

Common items that have codes, keys and passwords:

1. Cell phones, pagers and voice mail
2. Personal Digital Assistants (PDA) or Droids
3. Computer security systems
4. Bank ATM card and credit cards
5. Online bill pay systems
6. Online banking and stock trading accounts
7. Internet service providers or hosting services
8. Email accounts
9. EBay, Amazon and PayPal accounts
10. Online services
11. Blogs or web hosting sites
12. Social networking sites
13. Web site domain names
14. Digital photograph and music files
15. Software applications
16. Home security and vehicle alarm systems
17. Home safe and locked boxes, drawers or file cabinets
18. Mailboxes or entry gates
19. Safe deposit box
20. Storage facility and unit
21. Valuable items locations/hiding spots
22. Map to buried treasure

Survivors have enough to contend with when you die, so take steps to ensure that accessing your locked boxes, secured accounts and digital files doesn't become a trauma, totally loss or get overlooked. Don't take your passwords and codes to the grave. Communicate verbally and in detailed writing to your most trusted people who have an absolute need to know the whereabouts of the documents and codes. You can put these lists in envelopes and dramatically label them "Open only upon my disability or death." As part of your estate planning and settlement game plan, good repositories for copies of such sensitive information include several locations such as your lawyer's office, in a water and fire resistant safe in your home, secure off-site locations such as a safe deposit box and at a different location with a trusted relative or estate executor.

Inability to access a person's vast online life and records after their death has become such a problem that several new web-based services have created a plan for recovering digital virtual accounts and assets. Companies like LegacyLocker.com or AssetLock.net allow tech-savvy users to set up a kind of online will, with beneficiaries that would receive the customer's account information, passwords and instructions after they die. Plans currently range from $10 a year to a one-time fee of $300.

You can specify who gets access to their posthumous online information, along with messages to be conveyed to loved ones. Upon death, for example, if someone contacts Legacy Locker to report a client's death, the service will send the customer four emails in 48 hours. If there is no response, Legacy will then contact the people the client has listed as verifiers in the event of death. After examining a copy of the death certificate, only then are digital assets information released to the designated beneficiary. Additionally, it is still necessary to have all the information about documents, accounts and access codes in hard copy placed in safekeeping with those who will need it after you log off for the final time.

Letter of Instruction and Last Wishes Binder

Estate planning is not just about legal issues; there are practical ones as well. Many of the tasks and decisions spouses will have to handle usually are not covered by basic estate planning documents. A letter of instruction is not a substitute for a complete estate plan will or trust. Your will or trust legally directs how your major property is to be distributed, protected and who will serve as your estate executor. The letter of instruction or last wishes binder is an informal supplement to your estate documents. It is like a cover letter that addresses your more personal wishes and guides those left behind to the location of information and paperwork needed to administer your estate.

A letter of instruction does not have the legal effect of a proper trust or will. Think of it as a personal guidance letter that you can easily change as your circumstances or wishes change. You don't need a lawyer to prepare your letter of instruction or to organize a last wishes binder.

A detailed letter of instruction or last wishes binder can help your family and make the executor's job easier. It is a wonderful parting gift. Those left to manage your affairs will thank you for your foresight and thoughtfulness in preparing a set of instructions. It will make sure that your wishes are known, see that nothing important is overlooked or lost, and ease the stress of loved ones at a most difficult time. Additionally, a detailed letter or binder will save your administrator a great deal of trouble and time. This will simplify the closing of the estate and reduce the fees charged by an attorney or accountant. A little pre-planned instruction means less hassle and more resources for your family.

When you aren't able to tell them, the letter of instruction and last wishes binder can help your family know what to do and where to find important information. These flexible personal documents or information usually includes parts that do different things such as conveying your funeral wishes, charting financial and legal details, useful contacts and information for locating documents, how to access records, bequests of some sentimental personal effects and other personal messages.

Letters of Instruction or Last Wishes Binder Key Categories:

1. **Funeral Wishes**: This first section of your last wishes letter lets your family know if you have pre-arranged plans, contracts, insurance or have pre-paid a particular funeral home for any of your funeral, memorial or burial arrangements. Describe and provide information and locations of the burial plot or crypt deeds. If you want to be cremated, where you want your ashes to be placed or scattered. You can include special instructions about the type of funeral or memorial service you want, whom you choose as pallbearers, who should officiate, locations, flowers, and if you have any favorite scriptures, verses or music to be performed.

Compile the personal data needed for the death certificate, such as social security, family history. You could write a first draft your own obituary in advance. Include a list of the names, relationships, addresses, telephone numbers and emails of special people, co-workers, religious group, service organizations, beneficiaries and others that you wish to be told that you have died. The email list can be stored on your computer with a message ready for sending out. Be sure someone has all the access codes and passwords.

If you are a designated organ or tissue donor, identify the receiving organization and all their current contact information so that your representative can make prompt arrangements. You should note any religious or personal objections to autopsy or embalming in advance in case the question should arise. If you want a favorite cause or charity to receive donations in your honor or in lieu of flowers, list the organizations' names and locations.

2. **Legal and Financial Data**: All the detailed facts about your estate plan and finances will need to known by your family or estate administrator. Inform your family or administrator exactly where your original trust and/or will can be located and which law firm created it for you.

Prepare a list of essential documents. For example, list social security, birth and marriage certificates, military discharge, income tax returns and insurance policies for the survivor to gather right away. Describe where to find all this important paperwork and any other information needed. You can copy, organize, file and label all these essential records. Many originals need to be protected and stored in airtight waterproof fireproof containers and secured locations. Make note of where to find your records and be sure that they are readily accessible to your administrator.

The instructional letter or last wishes binder is where you can include a list, worksheet, chart or spreadsheet of all your financial assets, liabilities and debts. Make a detailed list of bank and brokerage accounts, pension plans, retirement accounts, stock portfolios, real estate and all other assets. Create a list with the names and all the contact information like addresses, emails and telephone numbers of your employer, attorney, accountant, insurance agent, stockbroker, financial planner, banker, publisher or others who have assisted you in legal or financial matters. Include instructions on how to get in touch with any beneficiaries to your estate or accounts.

Write your instructions to the person most likely to take over your accounts if you become unable to manage your financial affairs or after you die. This might be your spouse, adult child or other relative, your attorney or the person you have selected to administer your estate.

Make copies and place your letter of instruction or last wishes binder in an appropriate place. Keep one copy with your trust and will and another copy in a place your family would look first. Don't keep the document a secret. The location must be known and accessible to the trusted family member and administrator. Finding your instructions in a safe deposit box long after the funeral won't serve its purpose. Don't be overly concerned that some thief might find or use it. How many crooks would look through books and letters? They go for the low hanging fruit and things they can quickly sell, pawn or use.

3. **Personal Effects and Legacy Letter**: The third portion of your letter of instruction should be the personal messages that you want to convey to your survivors. This is where you tell those you loved what you never got around to saying. It might include special memories, hopes or values you want to pass on. Chapter twenty-eight in this book, complete with a detailed outline on writing an Ethical Will or Legacy Letter. Your will and trust will take care of the physical possession distributions, but it is highly recommended that you also write a legacy letter (also called an ethical will) to those left behind and future generations.

The letter of instruction and binder should include instructions about the care of your pets or your list of who gets what special personal effects. Many families, who start out with the best of intentions, are torn apart after a death, not over the larger assets, but over how to divide sentimental items that may have little or no monetary value. Yet, the simple emotional personal items are the things that most families and estate plan documents fail to talk about beforehand. Eliminate potential divisive feuds by listing specific gifts to relatives and friends you want to have your personal possessions.

Getting these special remembrances to the right person can make a big difference to you and to them. You need to put your specific wishes in writing, if you want your life-long best friend to have your diamond earrings, your granddaughter to have your mother's china; your son to have his great-grandfather's watch, the church to have your piano, the women's shelter to have your clothes, or the nieces and nephews to have their pick of your books.

Reviewing Your Letter of Instruction

Once you have created a letter of instruction and last wishes binder, they are flexible and it is easy to revise them over time as your circumstances, assets and wishes change. Every few years, you should revisit your letter of instructions and binder to update the worksheets, contacts and financial data in order to make the necessary adjustments. There is no legal format. However, if you don't entirely replace the old instructions, be sure to sign and date each revision to eliminate confusion or challenges over which might be your most current statements and wishes. Just make sure that your family knows about your letter of instructions, last wishes binder and estate planning documents and where to find these important papers.

Chapter Twenty-Two

ESTATE PLANNING BASICS

Sometimes death occurs before your loved one or you have a chance to put estate plans in place. Nevertheless, when you lose your loved one you are the one left with the responsibility of settling his affairs and estate. This blueprint section will assist you in understanding what is encompassed in estate planning. You need to know what your role is and what you are required to set up and later manage the estate settlement.

The goal of this section is to prepare you for the task by providing you with simplified terminology, questions to ask, problems to stay away from, practical advice and resources for further information and assistance. By learning the system and available options to you as the administrator of an estate, you can avoid taking wrong actions or missing opportunities that could have maximized the estate for you and other beneficiaries.

Planning Ahead

If the very thought of legal matters or estate plans causes your eyes to glaze over, you are not alone. However, you need to be aware of at least the basic concepts in order to be an informed participant in the settling of your late husband's estate, as well as the necessary planning of your own last will and testament for the future well-being of yourself and your family.

This chapter is Estate Planning 101 in plain understandable language, examples and real stories. Following texts offer peeks inside the wills of famous people and fun projects like writing your legacy letter or deciding on surprise gifting.

An estate plan is a systematic plan for the accumulation, conservation and distribution of a person's assets and estate. A proper plan will accomplish your goals efficiently, expedite administration with minimum costs and eliminate or minimize taxes. This section of *Widow's Key* is to acquaint you with the basics of estate planning, wills, trusts, health care directives, powers of attorney and other relevant documents. You are provided ways to understand what you are dealing with in the administration of your deceased husband's estate or how to plan for your own demise or incapacity. This guidance, while not to be taken as legal advice, will make you a more informed consumer so that you can make decisions and choices regarding your own estate plan and acquire enough information to see you through the basic administration of your husband's estate.

Widow's Key text is narrative, definition glossaries and occasionally in the format of commonly asked questions and answers. By becoming more knowledgeable, you will get better service, save time and money, and gain the confidence to handle one of life's greatest challenges, that of being a widow and settling your late husband's estate. You really do hold the key.

> Always plan ahead. It wasn't raining when Noah built the ark.
> - Richard C. Cushing

Necessity of an Estate Plan

Starting or going through the settlement of your late husband's estate will certainly convinced you of the necessity of at least a basic workable estate plan. Having your own estate plan in place is critical. Hopefully, your own death occurs after a long, healthy and productive life. You do not want to be in a position where you still had to organize your life, put your affairs in order and rush into estate planning decisions filled with the emotions that come from an imminent death. You need to plan for it today, while you are well and competent.

Since you care about your loved ones, you want to see to their provision. Rather than have a difficult time administering your estate, it is essential that you develop and implement a plan that accomplishes your objectives and reflects your last wishes. An effective estate plan with all the proper documents will be your blueprint for managing your estate during your lifetime, dealing with potential incapacity, and providing instructions for the distribution of your estate after you pass away. A proper plan can protect you and your loved ones from financial and emotional turmoil.

There are many parts to a complete estate plan, including wills, trusts, directives, powers of attorney, right of survivorship, joint ownership, partnerships, payable on death, contracts, gifts and other will substitutes as ways to distribute property after death. Good estate planning is simply making sure that the financial assets, no matter how great or small, gets to the intended recipients as quickly, economically and easily as possible.

Common Reasons for Making an Estate Plan

The common reasons a person has for estate planning typically include:
   • Providing property and assets for the immediate family;
   • Nominating guardians and conservators for minor children;
   • Selecting trusted and competent executors and trustees to carry out your directions;
   • Providing for family members who might have special needs or protection or guidance;
   • Providing for friends, pets, partners or charities;
   • Reliving the emotional strain and burden from family members;
   • Avoiding probate court process expenses, frustrations and delays;
   • Minimizing expenses of estate administration and taxes;
   • Reducing or eliminating state and federal estate taxes;
   • Simplifying the administrative procedures;
   • Providing for orderly succession and continuance of a business;
   • Planning for incapacity by preparing health care powers of attorney, directives to physicians and nomination of a guardian.

Not Just for the Rich and Famous

I really wish I had a dollar for every time I have heard a person or client say, "I'm young and don't have a lot of money or possessions, so do I really need a will or other estate plan documents?" I cannot emphasize enough that estate plans are not just for the elderly and wealthy. The false myth is that one has to be rich, like Bill Gates, Donald Trump or Warren Buffet, or have lots of properties or worldly possessions to develop an estate plan.

Every adult, especially parents of minor children, needs an estate plan, regardless of wealth. Estate plans arranges for the care of children and distribute property and personal assets. Estate plans are about the process used to distribute your worldly possessions, not how much they are worth. If you are incapacitated later, proper documents make your wishes known.

Personal Guardians for Children

Parents should create wills regardless of the size of their estate. Too many young and middle-aged people die without a will, trust or any directions for their families, or written instructions about the children who need personal guardians and provisions to care for them. If you don't name a guardian for your children, anyone can volunteer for the job. Then a judge, whom you don't know, decides who raises your children and how their inheritance will be spent. The amount and size of your estate does not determine whether you need a will. I have seen too many horror stories about what happens when there is no plan. Leaving guidelines for those left behind is a matter of a simple plan and some basic documents.

Statistics - Estate planning should be factored into every financial and health care plan. The American Bar Association states that only two of every five Americans have a will. A study by Prudential Life Insurance reports that only fourteen percent (14%) of women have wills. Persons of all ages and socio-economical levels, especially women, have to get over the reluctance to arrange beforehand how they are to be cared for and their property managed and distributed if incapacity or death strikes.

Getting Started on Your Estate Plan

How do you get started with your own estate plan? The estate planning process can begin with a checklist, inventory of assets and questionnaire to help you organize personal and financial information. See the confidential Estate Planning Questionnaire in Chapter 27. In order to evaluate, analyze and assist you with the best plan to fit your personal objectives, you must provide the attorney with complete and accurate information. The whole process can be quick and painless. Additionally, you will sleep better at night knowing that there is a plan in place when your time comes.

Your estate plan can be tailored to take care of special family issues or concerns. During the preliminary planning stages, there may be family or health concerns that need to be addressed specifically in various documents or planning alternatives to explore. Issues such as family members with mental or physical special needs, government assistance and eligiblilty requirements, addictions, substance abuse, illegitimate children, unequal distributions, specific gifts, former spouses, estranged family members or conflict challenges that may arise, all need to be discussed and arrangements made to accommodate them legally.

Believe me, other attorneys and I have heard thousands of sorrowful, tragic, strange and shocking family stories. You can be assured and perhaps comforted that every family has sad situations, family secrets and concerns or an odd duck or two in the flock. Your information stays confidential.

In preparation, organize your paperwork and family data beforehand, so that you can discuss the details of your financial situation, family, and your personal goals with the lawyer. Bring records, including financial statements and deeds, for your attorney to review. Attorneys are bound by strict confidentiality rules. Any information that you share with your attorney will be kept secret unless you authorize or request its release.

In the creation and implementation of a solid estate plan, your attorney will assist you in working with your insurance adviser, financial planner, investment consultant, CPA/accountant, banker, charitable foundations, real estate broker, as well as family and friends as needed. After you inform the attorney of what you have in assets and how you want to preserve and then distribute them, you have options to accomplish your goals and objectives. This way you receive a plan tailor-made for your unique circumstances and needs.

An estate plan is not a static, one time transaction. Like cars that need tune-ups periodically, you should review your estate plan occasionally, especially if there are significant changes in your family, career, property, intentions or life.

Chapter Twenty-Three

MINIMUM ESTATE PLAN
Legal Papers You Should Not Live or Die Without

By default, everyone has an estate plan, because your state legislature has written statutes with a basic plan for somehow distributing your possessions when you pass away. If it wasn't important enough for you to bother with a will while you were alive to direct who gets your stuff like the motorcycle, apartment furniture, your dog, cameras or music collection, it probably won't matter to you when you are gone.

If you die without a will, "intestate," the state laws of intestate succession will write your will for you and decide to whom and how all the properties owned by you will be divided up. In many cases, this plan requires distributions that you would never have wanted and involves long drawn-out and costly court proceedings. Do you want to leave this mess to those you leave behind?

Most people want more control over who gets their possessions after their death. The wealthy can use estate planning to reduce taxes and challenges. The last thing you want to think about as a widow is that something may happen to you and leave your children orphans. As a conscientious mother, you must deal in possibilities and not probabilities and make setting up a will that names guardians for your children a first priority. A parent of minor children should absolutely have a will to designate who will take care of the children in case of their demise. You owe it to your young family to spare everyone the anguish of a potentially ugly custody battle or unsuitable guardian placements.

More importantly, what the state does not have in law is an efficient way to take care of you if you are in a coma or have an incapacitating illness. If you get killed in a car accident and die, your estate will be settled under state laws or your will. Get in the same accident and end up in a coma, unable to make your own health care or financial decisions, you and your family could be in for a nightmare if you don't have a few simple legal papers in force. A court-appointed stranger will make life and death decisions for you just when you are most vulnerable.

It is typical to think of estate planning solely in terms of planning for death. What happens to your family and finances if you become physically incapacitated? Whom do you want to pay your bills, argue with the insurance company about your care, to sue the driver that hit you, shut off the respirator or remove the feeding tube that is keeping you alive? If you don't have certain current written documents in place in advance, the person authorized to make critical decisions for you could end up being an appointed neutral stranger, or a distant, estranged or greedy relative.

You minimally need to have the following three documents:

1. **Durable Power of Attorney for Financial,** designates who handles your assets and decisions if you become incompetent
2. **Advanced Directive for Health Care or Power of Attorney for Health Care** (called Living Will), appoints someone you trust to make decisions about your medical care and life sustaining treatment if you are unable to participate in those decisions yourself
3. **Up-to-date Will or Trust** with the necessary paperwork and funding designed for your circumstances.

It is time to stop being superstitious and avoiding facing your own mortality or incapacity. Review your documents to make sure you are still comfortable with your choices or draw up new documents to cover the possibility of you being disabled or incapacitated. You don't have to look far to find cases that should convince you to act right away. The news headlines are full of gut-wrenching legal battles, like Terri Schiavo or Robert Wendland situations in which the lack of living wills made it difficult to honor their end-of-life care wishes. While you may not need an elaborate trust, at least have an attorney draw up a basic will and powers of attorney for financial and health care for you. These are three documents that you should not live or die without. A small investment of time and money could save you and your loved ones a lot of heartache and grief.

Powers of Attorney for Financials

A Power of Attorney (POA) is an appointment and authorization for an individual or an entity to act on someone else's behalf in a business, financial or legal matter. A power of attorney must be in writing, witnessed and notarized. This avoids having your document declared invalid because of mental competency, fraud or undue influence. The person (you) authorizing the other to act is the principal or donor of the power, and the one authorized to act is the agent. The agent can be a spouse, family member or friend whom you trust to manage financial affairs with the same diligence as you would yourself.

As an agent, the person named by you in your power of attorney is a trusted fiduciary for the principal. Law requires your agent to be completely honest and loyal in their dealings and have the duty to protect your interests. The agent is required to act in your best interests, maintain accurate records and avoid conflicts of interests. You control how much power to give your agent and under what circumstances the power may be used. The power of attorney does not remove your power to act for yourself until a trigger event like your incompetency as certified by a physician.

The durable power of attorney is a legal document tool that can be used to carry out your wishes and provide for your needs if you become incapacitated, such as in a coma and unable to make decisions or act for yourself. You, as the principle who signs it, are naming an agent to conduct business on your behalf. You can choose any trusted adult to be your agent. Talk to that person beforehand to be sure they are willing to be your legally designated agent. It is wise to name an alternate agent so that if your first choice is deceased or unable to act, you have appointed a back up.

The power of attorney is 'durable' because it continues even after you as the principal becomes incapacitated or disabled. You must specify or check the box for 'durable' so that it does not automatically end, as it does in most states, if you become incapacitated. However, your durable power of attorney will end at your death. If you want your agent to have authority to wind up your affairs after your death, use a will or trust naming that person as your executor or trustee.

There are different types of powers of attorney for different purposes. A general durable power of attorney gives broad authority to the agent, while a limited nondurable power of attorney gives limited authority for a specific single transaction, such as selling a vehicle. Use nondurable or special powers of attorney if you are away and can't conduct business from home. You can change or cancel a durable power of attorney at any time or for any reason, as long as you are mentally competent. The power of attorney allows someone to act on your behalf until it is either revoked, terminated by divorce or upon your death. For individuals who become incapacitated or are facing a potentially debilitating illness, a durable power of attorney for financials could fit the situation. The durable power of attorney is written for use in the future when disability or incapacity strikes. Usually a physician or other recognized authority is the one to certify the condition and time when an individual is no longer competent to manage their own legal or financial affairs. You may see reference to 'springing' power of attorney. In the event that you are unable to manage your financial obligations or make personal decisions, this will cause the power of attorney to 'spring' into effect for the agent to begin handling your financial matters. You are in control until you are incapacitated.

If you have not prepared a power of attorney for financials, a court proceeding is probably inescapable. Your family will have to ask the court for authority over at least part of your financial affairs. When an owner has sole or joint tenancy on property and then becomes incapacitated, the property is in legal limbo. This is because the owner is incapable of signing legally binding documents or conveying legal title. This can prevent the property from being sold or even leased. An expensive and time-consuming court conservatorship process is often the only answer. Having a durable power of attorney would have taken care of the problem.

Your durable power of attorney agent can be given general powers to do things like: pay your bills, conduct financial transactions, file and pay taxes, operate a small business, claim inheritances, transfer property to your trust, handle investments, apply for benefits for you, do Medicaid planning, hire care givers, make housing decisions, sell or lease property, continue patterns of charitable or family gifts, exercise your legal rights, or conduct lawsuits on your behalf. An agent cannot create, revoke or change your will, trust or living will. Health care decisions are not part of the financial power of attorney. Your health care decisions and wishes are in separate documents Advance Directive or Durable Power of Attorney for Health Care.

Once you have a power of attorney for financial matters, be sure to talk to your appointed agent about what you want and how you want help. Keep the original for your self in a safe place, give a copy to the agent and copies to your bank and any institutions the agent is likely to do business with under the set conditions. Some brokerage firms, banks and organizations provide their own forms for clients, customers, patients, employees, or members. If you want your agent to have an easier time, you may need to prepare company forms in addition to your own durable power of attorney document. Many banks or other institutes will not even allow your chosen representative to use funds for your care if your power of attorney is not relatively current. Review and update your forms periodically, because some documents are considered too old or stale after a few years.

Health Care Power of Attorney

The Health Care Power of Attorney is also called a Living Will or Advance Directive. Similar to the Power of Attorney for Financials, a Health Care Power of Attorney allows you to plan ahead and select an agent to make your health care decisions in case you are unable to speak for yourself. Generally, Advance Directives have two main parts, one dealing with health care instructions and the other appointing the health care representative. Even after signing, you remain in control of your medical decisions as long as you are mentally and physically able to communicate. You can accept or refuse any medical treatment. If you cannot participate in decisions due to being in a coma, unconscious or unable to convey your desires, the doctors need someone to turn to for vital treatments or end-of-life instructions.

Should you have an incurable and irreversible injury, illness or disease that your attending physician believes to be a terminal condition, with your death being imminent except for death delaying procedures or machines, your health care power of attorney can direct that you are permitted to die naturally. The agent can make sure that only the administration of procedures deemed necessary by the physician to provide you with palliative comfort care are given, so there is death with dignity.

Both state and federal laws govern the use of advance directive or health care power of attorneys. The federal law, the Patient Self-Determination Act, requires health care facilities to inform patients of their rights to execute health care advance directives. All fifty states have laws recognizing the use of advance directives.

As you prepare the health care power of attorney, think about what makes your life worth living. If you were disabled, unconscious or supported by tubes or machines, at what point would you want to let go. What is appropriate for one person may not be for others. Put your decisions about health care treatments you would want in various situations in writing.

The typical heath care living will contains a section for signing the document and having it witnessed by persons who are not a relative or entitled to any portion of the estate. Some states require notarization on the page with the signatures. You, as the principal, should give a copy of the signed advance directive and accompanying documents to your treating physician, long-term care facility, hospital, hospice, close family, friends and your attorney. Make it part of your medical and pharmacy records. Another idea is to prepare a card to carry in your purse or wallet that states that you have advance health care documents along with the names and telephone numbers of your physician and appointed representatives.

Health Care Living Will Coverage

Popularly called a Living Will, the health care directive or power of attorney, is a written statement of a person's health care and medical wishes. It appoints another person to make health care decisions when the principal is unable. If you become terminally ill, permanently unconscious or if you enter a "persistent vegetative state" your health care directive can inform caregivers whether you want life-sustaining treatment and at what level. You choose future health care that assures your comfort, cleanliness and dignity. This power of attorney for health care becomes effective only in the event when death is imminent and if you are incapable of making known your own health care decisions.

In some jurisdictions, a Health Care Power of Attorney, Advance Directive or Living Will, which records your wishes and empowers your agent, health care proxy, or attorney-in-fact to stand in your shoes. They can make health-care decisions, up to and including terminating care and life-sustaining machines keeping you, as a terminally ill patient, alive. Health care decisions include the power to consent, refuse consent or withdraw consent to certain types of medical care, treatment, service or procedure. Specific living wills include information regarding an individual's desire for such services as hydration, feeding, analgesia (pain relief), antibiotics, and use of a ventilator or cardiopulmonary resuscitation. If you choose to have life-support stopped, you will still receive care to assure your dignity and comfort. Some health care directives even speak to personal matters such as last rites, whether they want to die at home, if they want prayers, music, or chants at the bedside. Your representative must act in the way you specify in the documents and follow your known wishes. If they do not know what you want, they must act in your best interest. Health care representatives may not decide about mental health treatment, abortion, sterilization, shock treatment, psychosurgery or mercy killing. Your health care power of attorney lapses if, and when, you regain your ability to make your own decisions.

Studies have shown that adults are more likely to complete documents that are simple and written in everyday language. An example statement in a simple living will is: "Being of sound mind, I willfully and voluntarily make known my desire that if I suffer from an incurable, irreversible illness, disease or condition and my attending physician determines that my condition is terminal, I direct that life sustaining measures that would only prolong my imminent dying be withheld or discontinued."

Additionally, over the last few years many states have combined the directive to physicians of instructions for courses of treatment with the separate health care power of attorney forms. State laws also sometimes set document expiration dates after seven years or so. Even if you signed something years before, your documents may be expired or have out-of-date information on your wishes or representatives. Be sure to update your health care powers of attorney if there is a death of appointee or a divorce. Health care and financial powers of attorney are of little use if they are out-of-date or the appointed agent cannot be readily located.

Selection of Your Health Care Representatives

Many people find that the people they trust to handle their finances are different from the ones they want to make health care decisions. You don't have to name the same person or persons for both powers of attorney. Although most people choose their spouse or an adult child as the health care proxy, these may not be the best choices. These same folks may be reluctant to acknowledge the reality that death is imminent and not be willing to let you go when your time has come. Sometimes there are contentious family members who argue with your end-of-life instructions. This can cause spending lots of money on pointless medical care, attorneys and court challenges. While doctors are not at liberty to depart from instructions made by a principal or by a validly appointed health care representative, in reality lawsuit-wary physicians might temporarily placate the dissenter and prolong the inevitable. So, choose your health care decision maker carefully. You need a strong advocate who will follow your wishes, deal with the medical system, as well as unite and comfort the family. Also, consider naming one or two alternates if your first choice can't serve or is not immediately available. Signing a health care directive does not affect insurance and does not make the representative responsible for your medical bills.

Communication is the key. Continue to talk about what you want if you become terminally ill and your death is imminent. Make sure your family, your decision maker and your doctor know where you stand on these issues. By sharing your values and wishes with your family, close friends and physician, you can guide your future health care while lifting the burden of deciding from your loved ones.

Physician's Order for Life Sustaining Treatment (POLST) and Health Insurance Portability and Accountability Act (HIPAA)

Additionally, unless there is a doctor's order to the contrary, paramedics and emergency technicians are required to provide emergency treatment to a patient who is unable to convey his or her desires, including life-sustaining procedures. Your advance directive is not controlling in an emergency because it is not a doctor's order. If a person is seriously ill and does not want resuscitation procedures, request that the treating physician sign a Physician's Order for Life Sustaining Treatment (POLST). The POLST can be given to paramedics to serve as a physician's order to withhold treatment. Place the 'pink sheet' on a refrigerator door in plain sight.

Older Health Care Directives and Powers of Attorney signed within five years may be rejected by your health care providers if the document lacks the Health Insurance Portability and Accountability Act (HIPAA) privacy waivers. One of the primary purposes of HIPAA is to ensure the privacy of an individual's health information unless there is a signed authorization. Some have carried it to the extreme, not even allowing a spouse to pick up the other's prescription from the pharmacy or discuss the other's medical conditions with the doctor. Attorneys will draft a HIPAA amendment to your Advance Directive with a waiver and release information addendum so the appointed health care representatives can act on your behalf without question, have discussions with physicians, receive prescriptions and be allowed access to medical records and information required for a determination of your incapacity and treatment. Future health care may depend upon having the necessary documents in place.

Chapter Twenty-Four

WILLS

If you are settling your late husband's estate or preparing your own estate plan, this chapter's detailed information on wills, followed by probate should prove helpful.

History of Wills

Historically, wills have been around for thousands of years as evidenced in archaeological records. For example, there are Biblical references, like Jacob leaving Joseph an inheritance and Egyptian hieroglyphics found in ancient tombs directing who gets what property. The law of wills, as we know them today, has its foundation in the English feudal system. Under this land ownership system, the father was required to pass on real property to his oldest son and him to his oldest son, and so on.

Personal property distributed to others could only be done by using a document called a testament, under the jurisdiction of the church. Landowners soon found ways to get around the government rules and dispose of property without paying distribution taxes. Stricter inheritance rules were enacted under the 1536 Statute of Uses, followed by the Statute of Wills, which finally allowed real property distribution by written will. By the late 1600s only one document was needed to distribute both real and personal property, hence the term 'last will and testament.'

It is interesting and insightful to look up the wills of historical and famous persons on Internet sites. Examples of the wills and trusts of the rich and famous are included on the www.widowskey.com website because they provide a glimpse into history and give some insight into the lives and types of wills that famous people have created over the years. Have you ever wondered how Marilyn Monroe, Elvis Presley, Jackie Kennedy Onassis, Princess Diana or Michael Jackson distributed their goods and to whom?

Among those famous wills, it is surprising to see that Warren Burger, a Chief Justice of the U.S. Supreme Court, who should have know better, only left a brief incomplete will, 176 handwritten words to be exact, that resulted in a long drawn out probate to settle his estate.

Elements of Wills

A will is a written document, instrument or legal declaration by which a person gives instructions to explain how they want the particular disposition of property to take effect after death. A will generally includes the following elements and technical requirements:

• Publication clause to identify you as the testator or maker of the will; To state your domicile or place of residence; To specifically state that this is your last will and testament to show your intent to make a will; and Revocation of any prior wills or codicils.

• Identification of Family with data such as full names, birthdates, marital status and other named beneficiaries.

• Appointment of Personal Representative, Guardian of minor children and Conservator, with fiduciary powers, responsibilities, duties, obligations and bond requirements.

• Instructions to pay debts, expenses and taxes.

• Dispositive Provisions giving personal property to beneficiaries.

• Residual Clause, instructions to cover the administering and distribution of any and all assets or property not covered otherwise.

• Simultaneous death and predeceased information.

• Last Clauses to establish the end of the will by presenting the testator's signature and date of signing.

• Witnesses declaration that the will was signed in their presences.

• Self-Proving Affidavit is a separate page declaration by the witnesses, signed and sealed by a Notary after watching the testator and witnesses sign the will and affidavit.

Signing of a Will

A will must be 'executed' with the formalities required by each state's statutes or laws in order to be valid. The term 'execution' does not mean to put before a firing squad. It is legalese talk that means completed, carried into full effect, done or performed.

Your will must be properly executed, which requires that it contains a statement at the end attesting that it is your will, the date and place of signing, and the fact that you signed it in the presence of witnesses who then also sign it in your presence and watched each other sign. It is important to make sure that you strictly observe and follow all the legal requirements.

The proper execution requirements to make your will effective include:

1. The will being signed in the presence of at least two neutral third party witnesses over a certain age;

2. Signed affidavits that you appeared to the witnesses to be of sound mind, competent and signing of your own free will;

3. Appearance of competence, knowledge of family and wishes;

4. The will is to be notarized. You have heard the term "signed, sealed and delivered" and this especially applies to your will.

Who Can Make a Will?

In most state laws, to qualify as one who can make a valid will: (1) You must be of legal age, that is at least eighteen years old or live in a state that permits those under eighteen to make a will if they are married, in the military or otherwise considered legally emancipated; and (2) You must be competent in order to create a valid will.

Legal requirements to prove mental competency hold that you must:

(a) Understand the relationship between yourself and those people, like a spouse or child, who would be named in the will and to any people you may disinherit;

(b) Be aware that you are creating a will, that it is your intent to create a will, what it is and accomplishes in regard to your property and possessions;

(c) Understand the general nature and extent of your property;

(d) Have a provision that disposes of said property; and

(e) Be capable of the transaction of simple business affairs and able to decide how you want your property distributed and to whom.

The presence of these characteristics and the absence of any incompetency render a person legally fit and qualified to create a will. Anyone who is impaired to the extent that they lack sufficient understanding or capacity to make or communicate responsible decisions concerning one's estate or person is called incapacitated and unable to make a valid will.

Purposes and Benefits of Having a Will

The purpose of your will is to:

• Make a deliberate legal expression or declaration of last wishes

• Identify your family and named beneficiaries

• Appoint a Personal Representative, Executor of the Estate and Guardian (if your children are minors)

• Give specific instructions and directions regarding the distribution of your personal and real property

• Define the fiduciary duty and responsibilities of your chosen Personal Representative.

A will lets you decide who will manage your money and how it to distribute it upon your death. It is an important legal document that has significant impact on your family. Letting your wishes be clearly known can prevent disputes among your family members.

You sign a will with the objective of protecting your family and hard-earned assets. You specify which of your assets and precious possessions go to whom you want, when you want and how you want. You desire the process to go quickly, smoothly, inexpensively and hope that specific appointments, written instructions and clear directions on distributions of tangible and intangible property will avoid fighting among family members and other named beneficiaries. Having a profession prepare and oversee the signing of your documents gives you assurances that your voice will be heard.

Estate planning apathy anecdotes and excuses range from "My estate is not large enough" to "I don't like thinking about dying" to "It's too expensive." The process is not as complicated or expensive as many seem to believe. The wise know that wills and trusts are not documents of death, but roadmaps for the living. Creating a will is beneficial regardless of the size of the estate. Probate, administration and guardianship hearings for an estate that does not have any guiding documents are far more expensive and emotional. Having a will or trust helps avoid problems and costs.

When there are minor children involved a will is an absolute necessity. Parents will make sure their children eat properly, buckle into their car safety seats, wear bicycle helmets, exercise and rest adequately and have medical checkups. They invest in orthodontics and education, yet many leave their children vulnerable to the whims of a court by not having a will or trust. If you are a parent, you need a will regardless of your estate size.

A positive aspect of having a will or trust which is often overlooked is, that by leaving estate planning documents, it empowers the survivors with a sense of purpose in completing the decedent's unfinished business and carrying out the final wishes. There is a feeling of being useful and in control of something by having an active role in settling an estate. Since the will is the last communication from the deceased, the will and estate settlement process fulfill a role in emotional healing and the mourning process. By leaving concise estate documents to follow, the family generally appreciates the efforts put into advance planning and can reflect favorably on the actions taken and meaning of the decedent's life.

> Though no one can go back and make a brand new start,
> anyone can start from now and make a brand new ending.
>   - Anonymous

Essential Elements that Make Your Will Valid

While there are differing forms in differing states, to be valid a will must to have certain elements present. There are surprisingly few requirements and restrictions on the will making process. However, there are some common necessary factors and conditions that all wills must include:

(A) Competency and Capacity: To make a will you need to be of legal age, of sound mind and memory and have the capacity to execute a document. The person making the will should know: (1) the nature and extent of their property; (2) know the object of their bounty, that is, the people and your relationship between yourself and children, family members and others who would normally expect to receive a share of your estate; (3) be able to decide how to distribute their belongings.

The standard for proving in a court of law that the person making the will was incompetent is very high. Any challenger must rebut the court's presumption of competency with more than evidence of mere forgetfulness, illness or reduced mental capacity. When there is a possibility of a lawsuit to invalidate a will, some people prepare and put in safekeeping, a videotape or tape recording as a form of evidence to prove competence or testamentary capacity and intent.

(B) Intent: There must be a provision that indicates that you fully intended to make the will document your last instructions on what happens to your worldly goods upon your death. Intent means that you acted with design, resolve and with the specific intention the document you signed was to be your last will and testament to dispose of your property or name a guardian for minor children.

(C) Form and Provisions of Disposition: All states have standard forms and provisions. While a will doesn't have to follow a specific formula, the will must contain a substantive provision and language that makes it clear how you want to give away some or all of your property and/or naming a guardian for minor children. There needs to be a residuary clause to cover the disposition of the property not expressly disposed of in other sections of the will. Old English Common Law language like "I hereby bequeath and devise…" is not necessary.

(D) Valid Signature: All wills must be signed voluntarily and dated by the person making the will. To sign a will is also called subscribe. A subscribing witness to a will is one who sees the will maker/testator execute or sign the will. The witnesses attest to the validity of the will execution and observed intent and capacity of the will maker.

Often you initial each page in the same place to assure that no pages are ever added or taken out. If incapacity or illiteracy prevents you from signing the document yourself, you can direct a witness or the attorney to sign for you. Having someone sign for you requires legal guidance under the state law and proof of directions and intent. Not signing for oneself invites challenges and an invalid signature could void the entire will.

(E) Witnesses: In most states, a will must be witnessed by at least two disinterested adults who are not receiving property under the will. These witnesses must understand that they are witnessing a will signing and be competent to testify in court if the need arises. The witnesses should be in your and each other's presence when you sign your will. The witnesses do not need to read your will. They are only verifying that it was you that signed it and that you appeared competent to do so.

Usually there is a separate notarized affidavit statement attached to the will in which the witnesses attest to the validity of the will's execution. This may include statements that the person whose name is on the will is the same person who signed it and that the signature was a voluntary and knowing act, and that the will was not signed under undue influence, duress, malice, menace or coercion. The self-proving affidavits are generally enough to eliminate the necessity of witnesses having to appear in court to testify that they did indeed witness the signing. A properly witnessed will and notarized affidavit is less vulnerable to claims of forgery or incompetence or to will contests.

Will validity requirements vary from state to state. If the key elements and technical requirements of your residence state are contained in your will, it is legally valid and can accomplish what you want. Please note that a will valid in the state where it was created and executed, is valid in other states. You can move to another state or live overseas in another country and your original will is still a valid will from the state where you had residence and ties. If you relocate permanently, ask an attorney if you need to prepare a new will, powers of attorney and health care directives.

Personal Representative

The personal representative, or executor (male) or executrix (female), as he or she is called under some state laws, is the person or institution you appoint in your will to carry out the terms of the will and administer your estate after you are gone. Pick a person or professional who is familiar with your family, affairs and property. Many banks and trust companies have experienced people, who, for a fee or a percentage, will manage the estate after you are gone. It is the duty and responsibility of your personal representative to gather all the assets, pays the debts, taxes and expenses and then distribute the property as the will instructs.

Selecting Your Personal Representative

When selecting a personal representative, psychological qualities like personal integrity, devotion to duty, objectivity and compassion are attributes as valuable as knowledge of financial matters or all the intricacy of your family or business affairs. Individuals who are inexperienced, but willing to obtain the necessary information and secure professional help whenever needed, can do an outstanding job of administering your estate. You may give financial or medical powers of attorney to others.

Working on the behalf of your estate's beneficiaries, the representative's ultimate responsibility is to preserve and manage the estate and until the assets can be transferred in the most timely and efficient manner possible. The fiduciary level of duty for the person in that position of trust is usually higher than that of a reasonable person. The status of being an executor or personal representative gives rise to certain legal obligations, including the prohibition of making speculative or imprudent money or property investments. Personal representatives must use the standard of care of a prudent investor. Many states have adopted uniform fiduciary acts to govern management of estates.

You may choose a personal representative who is physically near the assets of your estate and the beneficiaries. With the advent of internet, faxes and far-reaching communication, attorneys often work with distant representatives and heirs. However, logistics are easier when there is proximity of the proposed executor to an estate. Distance and travel can cause delays, expenses and hardships. Don't underestimate the amount of time, access, face-to-face work and effort it takes to settle an estate. Proximity of your representative can reduce expenses and expedite the administrative process.

Additionally, working with a local attorney who specializes in estate matters can make handling the estate go smoother and help the personal representative with the business end and family members. It is especially helpful if your representative establishes a good work relationship with the attorney who drew up the will or trust and is knowledgeable about you, your family and financial matters.

You can appoint more than one individual or professional to serve as personal representative or executor of your estate. In many instances, a person may appoint two or more surviving children to act as co-representatives, co-executors. You may have your spouse or child act as co-representative with a professional trust administrator or attorney. This of course, requires temperament and personalities that allow joint decision-making and co-operation.

If someone or one of the co-executors decides for any reason that they are unwilling or unable to serve in that capacity, they have the right to resign, decline or renounce the position. This is done by filing a renunciation form with the probate office. Generally, a sole executor makes administration matters simpler and more efficient.

Guardians for Minor Children

A guardian is someone named by you in your will whose role is to protect the interests of your minor children if you should die or become incapacitated. Naming the right people to carry out your final wishes is essential to any estate plan, especially when it comes to naming a guardian for your children. Choose someone who is willing and able to raise your child, someone who has the same values and beliefs as you and someone who your child respects and is comfortable being around. Often a parent forgets to consider guardianship from their child's perspective, but that should be a factor. Choose wisely. If you leave your child to a guardian who is self-serving or incapable of raising them, it can result in judicial intervention and litigation. If you don't have a will or don't name a guardian, anyone may step up for the position. At that point, a judge, who doesn't know the child or others involved, will decide who raises your children. Regardless of the size of your estate, if you have minor children, you have the moral duty to create a will.

Will Instructions

Does my appointed Personal Representative have to follow my will instructions? The word 'will', as used in your last will and testament documents, is comprehensive, mandatory and dispositive in nature. 'Will' has a sense of 'shall' or 'must', unlike the word 'may', which is uncertain and speculative. The law requires the executor or personal representative named by you to follow your instructions to the letter if feasible.

Lawyers often talk about the 'four corners rule,' referring to the face of the written instrument on the four cornered pages. Under a four corners rule, the intention is known from the document as a whole and not from isolated parts or any information left out of the document. So, be sure that your will is deliberate, complete and there are no assumptions made regarding your intentions or last wishes. The more communication you have, through written statements or discussions, with family and representatives, the less chance there will be for a misunderstanding of your last wishes and instructions.

What Not To Include in Your Will

Be aware that while, for the most part, instructions in your will are your call, there are state restrictions on what conditions or provisions you can include in your will. A probate court would throw out any conditions that are illegal, bizarre or against public policy. For example, if you wanted to use your estate assets to fund the set up of an illegal drug cult, terrorist society, or order beneficiaries to commit illegal or immoral crimes, the court could void the bequest or instructions. Don't invite a will contest.

Sometimes people try to control their family members from the grave by attaching special conditions in their wills and trusts. For instance, you cannot require a named beneficiary to marry or divorce someone, give up having children, enter the nunnery, or perform some weird act in order to claim their inheritance from you. Nor can a spouse make an inheritance contingent on a promise that the survivor will never re-marry.

There is an occasional limited use of 'incentives' designed to motivate children to achieve by passing out the inheritance funds upon completions of goals such as finishing college or receiving matching funds based on annual earnings from a job. Unfortunately, some parents, trying to be puppet masters, go overboard, trying to control adult children, some already in their 50s or older. Other will conditions fail to make the language flexible enough to accommodate emergencies or changes in circumstances.

It is best to curb your enthusiasm for 'dead hand' tactics, revenge, scolding, nagging, belittling or other negative contents that can leave lifelong scars and resentment. Most attorneys will not allow personal vendettas to be part of the will or trust texts. You can include language or personal instructions if they are purely advisory or to clarify your intent, but this is better in your Legacy Letter, as outlined later in Chapter twenty-eight of this book.

Beneficiaries - Who Gets What, How Much and When

As the creator of your estate documents, you can decide who gets what, how much and when they get it. You, as the author of the will or trust, name beneficiaries who are the natural object of your bounty, such as a child, family members, friends, new spouse, charities or pets. You are not required to leave anything to anyone, except your spouse if you are married. You cannot completely disinherit a spouse. A surviving spouse may have the right to a fixed share of the estate regardless of the will's designations. Some states limit how much you can give to charity if you have surviving children or a spouse. Under most state laws, a spouse has a right to claim twenty-five percent (25%) or more of your estate.

In every state except Louisiana, children can be cut loose. Otherwise, you can select any beneficiary you want, as long as they are clearly identified by specific name or class, i.e. "to all my grandchildren" or "to my dear friend, Robert J. Newton" or "to the living 1965 graduating class members of Jacksonville High School."

If you decide to disinherit a family member, it is best to express it specifically in writing. Get the professional assistance of an attorney to protect your estate from challenge or a will contest. There is 'cut/love' language that states your intent to disinherit that reads similar to, "Although I express my love and affection for my son, Guy Jr., it is my specific intent that he take nothing under the terms of this will or trust, and that he and his lineal descendents be deemed to have predeceased me." This may appear harsh, but it leaves no doubt of your intentions, which may be for very valid or preservation reasons. The will or trust document is not the place to record all the reasons or hard feelings behind the disinheritance. If done at all, that explanation is better said in a separate confidential letter, so you don't let your rationale or venting make you appear unstable or incompetent.

There is a myth that you have to leave at least one dollar ($1) to all your heirs. There is no requirement to leave anything to your children or to leave their inheritances in equal shares. You can dictate the specific amounts or percentage of the net estate anyone will receive and whether it will distributed outright at a certain age, held in trust for health, education, maintenance and support until a certain age or held in trust for your beneficiary's nature life. Wills and trust also have sections for specific gifts of personal property, such as jewelry, household goods or heirlooms. Most personal property is distributed after the death of the surviving spouse, so it remains for the enjoyment and practical use after the first death.

Sample Preamble to a Will

A Christian or other faith preamble to your will provides an opportunity to share a personal statement of your faith and beliefs with your family and friends. At the time of their loss, this preamble may comfort and encourage them. Here is a sample Christian Preamble: *First, I commit myself to God's care, secure in His love for me and trusting in the salvation purchased for me through Christ's suffering and death. I leave those who survive me the comfort of knowing that I have died in this faith and have now joined my Lord in eternal glory. Second, I commend my loved ones to the protecting arms of God, knowing that He will continue to provide for them despite my absence; and I encourage them to place their faith and trust in Him alone.* The body of a will follows.

Words of Caution about Will Kits or Online Forms

The differing state statutes, regulations and specific legal requirements regarding wills are the reason why many generic online or fill-in-the-blank forms found in books and kits don't hold up in court or when challenged. The one-size-fits-all type will and trust kits often create more problems than they solve. Lawyers will tell you that these do-it-yourself jobs have created more work for lawyers and bills for clients than they have avoided.

The American Bar Association *Guide to Wills and Estates* includes a famous case about a fellow who tried to get two wills for the price of one from one kit. He produced a will for himself, then took that and substituted his wife's name for his own in the introductory and signature clause. Sadly, he failed to change the name of the beneficiary, resulting in his wife leaving all her property to herself when she died. This case, of course, ended up in court at a substantial cost to the surviving husband.

Complicated Family Trees and Mixed Families

It does not matter that your family tree is complicated and there are unusual internal dynamics. Often estates are larger than you may think and family relationships are often more complicated. There are not adequate spaces on generic forms to describe the 'his, hers and ours' family tree situations, or the out-of-wedlock or adopted grandchildren, for example.

If you have a child or grandchild with special developmental, mental, physical needs or one with a substance abuse situation, do-it-yourself forms are generally not prepared to deal with those cases. If not worded correctly, the family member on state or federal assistance programs can be disqualified and lose all their financial or medical assistance help because of an inheritance, even a very small one. You must write clearly that the person who has serious issues with addictions is not to receive all their distributive share directly or your documents fail to set up a testamentary trust to hold their funds for their entire life and distributerd as needed or until proven cured. If it is not properly prepared, those disabled people often get a lump sum that is soon misspent or used to destroy their life.

Don't hesitate or be embarrassed to tell the attorney in all confidentiality what concerns you have about family members so that your will or trust can protect your estate and distribution to your loved ones in the future.

Use of Attorney to Write a Will

Most self-help will kits and forms do not get the job done because they are out-of-date, not state-specific and not properly signed under state regulations. These shortcuts often end up costing your surviving family members more grief and money in the long-run than a valid will professionally prepared in the first place would have. Make sure any alternative wills are complete, especially since probate laws vary so much from state to state. The average person just doesn't know all the hocus-pocus words, conditions, procedures, formalities and legal requirements to correctly draft and execute such important testamentary documents. A few states have statutory will forms created by state law. It is a fill-in-the-blank form that when witnessed can be a valid will. But, these type wills are very limited because they assume everything goes to your spouse and children, and don't allow for special needs, specific bequests, codicils or changes to the boilerplate form.

Legally, you don't have to use an attorney to write your will, but what you end up with on your own had better satisfy all the conditions, elements, technicalities and requirements in your state, or it is worthless invalid paper. If you have any question about your ability to fulfill the legal requirements, have special family situations or you believe that your will could be contested by another person for any reason, it is best to consult an attorney. There are good reasons why more than eighty-five percent (85%) of Americans who have wills used a lawyer in preparing them.

Costs of Will Preparation

The cost of having an attorney professionally prepare your estate plan, trust or will depends on the complexity, size of your estate, where you live and the lawyer's experience and rate structure. Often first consultations are free to determine what is required according to your circumstances. For basic wills, trusts and the related document packages, your attorney will probably charge a flat quoted fee that covers the drafting, production and execution of the documents. Additional charges may include filing or recording fees for property titles.

Generally, the expense and trouble of not having a will far outweighs the cost of the will. It is cost effective to do it right originally. If your estate is more complex, contains multiple properties, contracts, business entities and the combined assets exceed the state and federal estate tax limits, your attorney may charge by the hour for additional professional services to help prepare a package that will minimize the taxes and facilitate the administration of your estate. You, as a client with a complicated estate, can save time and money by providing complete documentation and putting your wishes in writing for the attorney preparing your plan.

If your estate is over the state or federal inheritance limits, if you own a business, if someone in your family has special medical, mental or developmental needs, or if you can foresee a challenge to the will from a disgruntled relative or creditor, then you should definitely use a lawyer.

A will or trust is a wise investment that inevitably saves time, money and heartache for those left behind. Additionally, having a law firm team in place to guide and assist the surviving spouse or children through the maze of settling an estate, is a welcome wise friend at the time of need.

How to Make Changes to Your Will

As long as you are of sound mind, you can change your will at any time. Major events such as marriage, divorce, second marriage, relocation, new baby arrival, death of a family member, changes in tax law or a change of circumstances are valid reasons to consider changing your will. If the changes you want to make are minor, you can have your attorney prepare a document to attach to your will called a codicil. Drawing up a codicil requires the same formalities as a will, so it is wise to have your attorney create and execute the change documents.

Can a person make changes to a will by themselves? The simple answer is 'no.' The importance of legislatively required elements and proper execution (signing and witnessing) is why you should never ever write on, scratch though or add names and or items to your will after the signing event. Changing material elements of the document could make your will invalid or open to challenge. Writing on your will could possibly make your will null and void because there is no proof or witnesses to attest to the fact that it was done voluntarily and not under undue influence, fraud, menace, malice or coercion. This goes for adding pages or notes on separate sheets of paper that change pertinent details such as appointment of different personal representatives/executors, named beneficiaries or distribution of your estate possessions. Once officially signed according to state law, leave your will alone. Change or revoke your will properly with a codicil or new will all together.

Alternative Drafting Sources

Millions of Americans belong to their union, military, AARP, legal clinics or group legal service plans which provide basic estate planning services at reduced rates, modest or no fee. Be aware that the more complex work, special needs, assignments, deeds or seeing a will through probate may not be covered. If you have a small, simple estate, the use of legal services groups may be a low-cost alternative.

Use caution, because the alternative drafting source work often is an adaptation of computerized templates, prepared by legal assistants, who come and go in the labor market and have little or no loyalty or liability for their mistakes. The overseeing attorney can see that your will meets the basic standards for validity in your state, but too often there is no personal concern, responsibility or continuity in generic group policy plans. You get what you pay for.

Other Kinds of Wills

A few alternatives to the simple will that exist in less than half the states and are rarely used include: Oral wills; Holographic, handwritten, un-witnessed wills; Joint wills, one document covering two people; Living wills for health care directives; and Soldier and Seaman's wills. These types of wills are used under very limited circumstances, such as when they are jotted down, spoken at the deathbed or written by the service person during wartime in a hostile zone.

In Canada, there was a famous case where a farmer trapped under his tractor scratched a will into the fender. The probate court accepted that fender and it is currently on display at the University of Saskatchewan law library.

Although under certain situations alternative types of wills are permitted, they are not recommended because they cause tremendous problems of proof, rarely follow legal formalities, don't cover all the decedent's assets and are vulnerable to fraud. In about twenty of the fifty states, un-witnessed handwritten holographic wills are invalid. There is a type will used in addition to a Living Trust to name guardians for minor children and to dispose of property that was not in the trust. This type 'pour-over will' takes property through probate or a mini-probate, called a small estate affidavit, and pours it over into the trust for distribution according to the trust instructions.

Chapter Twenty-Five

CAUTIONS ABOUT WILLS AND WILL SUBSTITUTES

Dying Without a Will

Dying without any will or trust to provide instructions for passing your estate on to your heirs or appointing guardians for your children is called dying *intestate*. Dying intestate can be as bad as it sounds both emotionally and financially. Dying without some type of estate plan documents leaves your family and assets vulnerable to probate, death taxes, creditors, con-artists, lawsuits, judgments, social services and lawyers. Much of the value of your estate ends up damaged or destroyed by the process.

Thorough planning and proper documents can insure that your family members or children are aware of your preferences and avoid potential legal battles or losses. A will is among the most important documents you may ever write. A will is the last statement of your ideals and values, which reflect the concern and love that you hold in your heart.

Without a will, your life-long investments, personal property and hard-earned money ends up going to federal and state governments, not to family, friends or favorite charities. The court and their appointed administrators are expensive, and the estate will pay for it, not the state. Having state laws distribute or keep your estate is not an acceptable substitute.

When a person dies without a will or intestate, the state inheritance laws of intestate succession will decide to whom and how all the properties owned are distributed. By not leaving a valid will or transferring the property in some other way, in effect, the state legislature is free to write your will for you. Individuals who fail to plan will have their assets administered pursuant to state statutes and under court supervision. State statutes make certain assumptions and decide who among your next-of-kin will receive the property and in what proportion each takes the property. The state rules for moving assets may not be what you would have done if you had written your own will. If you do not want to have others making personal decisions for you, both during life and after death, you must plan for those events and put your wishes in writing.

In general, intestate succession laws are based on the belief that a decedent's assets should pass to a few close blood relatives, according to a set formula. There is an exception to the blood relationship rule for a surviving spouse, provided for first with an elective share. Yet, if you have no children, the laws may require your spouse to share your property with your parents. Sometimes the spouse's share is as little as one half.

If there are minor children involved, having no will leaves them with no named personal guardian to care for them or trustee to manage your property on their behalf. If both parents die or are unavailable, intestate laws leave it up to the courts and social service agencies to appoint a guardian and conservator for your children. If you are married and have children from a prior marriage, half of your property will go to your current wife and the other half will go to all your children.

State intestate laws often exclude other relatives, friends, pets and charities. No state's intestate succession law gives an unmarried partner any property. In reality, while laws protect the conventional family, they often do not reflect the true wishes of the decedent. A person's estate can be distributed to people that the decedent would never have wanted to inherit their property. For example, when Howard Hughes' multimillion-dollar estate was finally distributed, the majority of it went to estranged distant cousins (referred to as 'laughing heirs;), not at all where he intended.

The laws of your domicile state, where your primary home is located, will determine what happens to your personal property, while distribution of your real property (real estate) is governed by the laws of the state where the property is located. Dying intestate does not mean your assets will escheat, revert or go to the state itself, unless there is no individual surviving relative, even a very remote one in existence, who is competent to make claim and inherit. If you have no heirs that fit the state's formula or no heirs can be located, all your assets will be taken by the state.

Dirty Dozen Mistakes to Avoid When Writing Your Will

1. Not having a will is the worst mistake. Procrastination and inaction all but guarantees that you will leave your survivors vulnerable to the court system, confusion, and the heartache. Wills do more than distribute your assets after you pass away. They clarify your intensions and leave a final impression with your loved ones.

Dawdling and not having a will can compound the grief experienced by your survivors. If you die intestate (without a will), going through probate is a necessity. The executor, appraiser, attorney and court costs can chip away a significant percentage of the estate. Having a will minimizes the financial and emotional exposure.

2. Trying to do all the estate planning and documents yourself without professional help is a sure way to leave a mess for your heirs. Mistakes practically make themselves when you don't know what you are doing. On one hand, educate yourself about the estate planning process so that you are a knowledgeable consumer, but don't think that scanning a book or two on wills prepares you to create and execute a complete package by yourself.

Avoid the do-it-yourself route. Hiring a good estate planning attorney who knows the inheritance and tax laws is highly recommended and not that expensive, especially if you go in prepared. Generally, the expense and trouble of fixing a homemade will far outweighs the cost of having your will drawn up professionally in the first place.

3. Failing to update a will can cause unintended consequences like accidental disinheritance, uncoordinated documents, contentious lawsuits, additional taxes and administrative costs, just to name a few. Reviews and revisions are appropriate at least every few years, especially after one of life's big three: marriage, divorce or the birth or adoption of a child. The state legislature and Congress are constantly fiddling with inheritance and tax laws, while IRS and court cases alter how those laws get interpreted.

It is impossible to anticipate all the potential future scenarios and to draft around them, so use review and amendments to keep your will up-to-date. What worked in your estate planning documents drawn up when you were 40 may be all wrong, very costly and hurtful if you die at 70 without updating your will. You have to assume some responsibility for updating your will to accommodate every change and contingency.

4. Failing to have a complete package of estate planning documents and failing to coordinate your documents can leave a mess. In addition to a will and/or trust, you need to have the Power of Attorney for Financials, Health Care Power of Attorney Directive to Physician, Letter of Instructions and Legacy Letter. The ownership arrangements for everything from stock holdings to property deeds need to correspond to your will. When you name beneficiaries on retirement accounts or life insurance policies or hold property in joint tenancy, contractually those assets will automatically go the people named. If you try to leave those assets to a different person in your will, you could set off a legal battle.

Accounts, such as brokerage and bank accounts, will pass payable upon death directly to heirs. Be sure that the beneficiary information on all such accounts is current and the named heirs can be located. Too many ex-wives or estranged family members have collected on accounts and wills that were not updated or coordinated. If your properties are sold or accounts closed, revise your will to make sure distributions are made in portions you wished among the heirs.

5. Naming the wrong executors or guardians can be a disaster. Being the designated executor of your estate is a responsible position. This job requires someone who is organized, honest, stable and calm. Be sure to discuss the job requirements with your chosen candidate and get his or her consent to serve in that capacity. The job demands a trustworthy person who will protect your estate and follow your instructions for distribution.

Additionally, it is advisable to name alternates, backup executors in case your first choices predecease you or are unable to serve for some reason. Likewise, in naming skillful guardians for your children, you must take time to consider the best interests and comfort preferences of your children. If your first choice guardian happens to be deceased, unable or unwilling to take on the responsibility of raising your children, plan for other trustworthy alternates.

6. Naming the same person to serve as guardian for your children and trustee of their inheritance is not always the best formula. A loving caring person capable of raising your children may not be the best money manager. You can put in place a good check and balance by naming separate people as guardian of your kids and trustee of their inheritance funds. This helps eliminate conflict of interest and allows reviews of expenditures.

7. Consider the worst case scenarios, such as **when the named beneficiaries (spouse, child, family members) die before, when or shortly after you do.** Name alternate beneficiaries so that your estate won't be distributed according to state law to people you didn't anticipate or wish to receive your assets.

8. Don't get too detailed in the will when it comes to specific gifts under $5,000 or so. You may be tempted to use your will to list everything you own and designate who receives what items. What happens when you sell, break, close or give away one of the items or accounts? You do not want to rewrite your will that often. Don't go to the other extreme and not leave any instructions for sentimental or valuable items.

All attorneys have horror stories about heirs who are to receive mega-bucks, but they fight over who gets grandma's yellow mixing bowl or daddy's camera. It is best to bequeath personal assets or valuable collections in groups or types like "My daughter Kathleen Laval is gifted all my jewelry." "My neice Lauren is to inherit the automobile that I own at the time of my death." or "I leave all the books in my library to the Sravasti Abbey of Newport, Washington."

A side letter or specific gifts list is the best way to supplement your will. Except for the prohibitions about writing on your will, you can change only this separate addendum personal specific gifts list by signing and dating it yourself. Others often begin giving away special gifts while they are alive, name tag items, set up a system with the executor for the family to draw straws or choose what they want in a 'round robin' fashion or have a sale or auction with proceeds going to heirs in cash. Have fun with your list of gifts and surprise old friends or organizations with sentimental or meaningful bequests.

9. Not organizing records or telling your heirs where to find things creates delays and downright chaos. Even if you don't want to divulge what is in your will or trust to your family, they should at least know where to find all your original estate planning documents. The stress of rummaging through someone else's messy paperwork to unearth a will, funeral instructions or other important records is not leaving a good final impression. A letter or binder of last wishes and instructions can really make the final processes simpler and accomplish what you wanted without adding to the confusion.

It is vital to organize and keep track of all your legal and financial information in a recognizable way. There should be copies and contact lists readily available, this includes the digital computer accounts and codes. It is a mistake to entrust your information exclusively to your executor. Don't put the only will in a safe deposit box that may be unknown or sealed and inaccessible upon your death.

10. Leaving too little or too much to a spouse is a common will error. You can't totally disinherit a spouse. Depending on the state laws, the surviving spouse can elect against the estate plan and demand a larger share of one-quarter to one-half of your estate. It is especially important to make a share equitable and/or have a strong prenuptial in a secondary marriage where you intend to take care of your recent spouse, but want the remainder of your estate to go to your children from a prior marriage or specific charities. In community property states, your spouse has certain rights to all community property, as well as a share of the deceased spouse's separate property if the will was before marriage and not updated.

On the other hand, leaving too much to a spouse could cost you in estate taxes. Putting some of your wealth into trusts could minimize taxes, allow assets to support the spouse but grow and eventually go to your heirs without triggering a second round of estate taxes on your spouse's death.

Additionally, if you bequeath everything outright to a spouse, you lose control over what happens to the assets. He or she could leave everything to their next spouse, spend or gamble it all away, be conned out of it by the latest pyramid scheme or televangelist or in a subsequent marriage, give it all to others and exclude your intended heirs or designated charities.

11. Relocating without checking local laws can call some documents into questions. There are different estate-planning laws in each state. For example, every state has its own form of the health care power of attorney and directive to physician and these generally need revisions if you move so they are acceptable at the new location hospital. If you permanently relocate and don't update your legal documents there may be confusion about your residency and which state can or can not demand inheritance taxes or which courts have jurisdiction. Failing to update your residency status can cause delays in the distribution of the estate.

12. Overlooking the tax burden on your heirs can create gross inequities if you don't specify what assets will be used to pay taxes on the estate. If you leave accounts that pass tax free, such as IRAs, life insurance and 401(k)s to certain heirs and the remainder to others named as beneficiaries in the will, those named in the will could foot the entire tax bill, while the others who inherit retirement accounts pay absolutely nothing. To assure that taxes and other expense shares are divided fairly among the heirs and are paid, work with an estate attorney to structure the estate expense payments.

How to Handle Will Contests

A will contest begins if someone produces another will or files an objection to the will presented to the probate court. Will contests are common and around one third of the challengers actually win one. Some wills and trusts have "no contest" sections saying, if people challenge the will, even if they win the challenge, they are totally disinherited. Never the less, challenges to a will can take a lot of time, necessitate hiring an attorney for litigation, and cost a lot of money.

Only a person with 'standing' can contest a will. This means the person must have a personal financial stake in the outcome. Examples of people with standing to contest a will include: (1) a child or spouse who was cut out of the will; (2) a child who receives one third of the estate if a sibling receives two thirds; (3) children who feel that the local charity should not get all the parent's assets; or (4) anyone who was treated more favorably in an earlier will.

Often will contests happen because someone wants a different person, bank, or trust company to serve as personal representative for the estate, or as a trustee of trusts. Most will challenges are from potential beneficiaries or heirs left little or nothing. Will contest filings are required in probate court within a certain number of days after receiving notice of the death, or petition to admit the will to probate, or issuance of Letters Testamentary to a personal representative.

Reasons to challenge a will:

- There is a later dated will which would replace an earlier will
- The decedent was not mentally competent to make a will at the time the will was drawn up
- The will was not properly signed by the decedent or witnessed
- The will was the result of fraud, mistake or undue influence
- The so-called will is believed to be a forgery
- The will is invalid for a reason such as a pre-existing contract

If there is a will contest, you should hire an experienced probate lawyer. The probate court may rule to invalidate all of the will or only the challenged portion. Unless there is a prior, revoked will revived and admitted to probate and the entire challenged will found invalid, the proceeds probably get distributed according to the state laws of intestacy.

Jointly Owned Property and Accounts

Property and accounts owned jointly are not a substitute for a will. Joint accounts and beneficiary designations are only supplemental estate planning techniques. They are in conjunction with a will or trust. Many married couples own real estate, investment accounts, certificates of deposit, bank accounts and other types of property held jointly with right of survivorship and payable on death. That means that if one spouse dies, the jointly owned property passes automatically to the other spouse as co-owner, regardless of what the will or trust may say.

Likewise, life insurances and retirement accounts are contractual accounts that have named beneficiaries. By operation of law, when the owner of the account dies, the company pays the death benefit directly to the named beneficiary without probate. The will directs how and by whom you want your debts and taxes paid and how you want your personal property distributed. Joint account instructions and designations cannot answer all the questions that the survivors will have at the time of your death.

There are times when the payable on death or beneficiary space on a policy or account paperwork says "payable to the estate of…" This type designation will throw those assets into probate. If, like my own aunt and uncle, the husband and wife die simultaneously in an accident or too soon after the first spouse for the surviving spouse to change the beneficiary on the accounts, then a probate is necessary to release funds to their estates.

If you use joint accounts, be sure that there are backup, secondary, contingent beneficiaries named to receive the assets. In the case of Individual Retirement Accounts (IRAs), some annuities and tax-deferred accounts, these policies rollover to the surviving spouse without incurring a tax consequence, but when they pay out to the secondary beneficiaries, such as children, the taxes will be collected at the time of distribution.

Will Substitutes and Joint Ownerships Cause Problems

Whenever you see a list of the ten most common estate-planning mistakes, it inevitably contains a very strong warning against having your children on your financial accounts or real estate titles as co-owners or joint tenants. Many think that this type of substitution method of transferring property without a will or probate works, but it can turn out to be a costly mistake.

In operation of law, the joint account assets transfer automatically to someone without regard to the desires of the decedent or the terms of the will. For example, if you put your child on your main bank checking or savings account so that he or she can help with shopping or bill paying, your child becomes a co-owner and the legal owner of all the assets. If a joint owner child has a falling out with you, they could take all the money out of your account. There isn't anything you can do to reclaim those funds, because you made them a co-owner on the account.

Additionally, if during your lifetime your adult child is ever pursued by creditors, sued, declares bankruptcy, gets divorced, has tax liens, court judgments or has wages and accounts garnished; whatever is in jointly held accounts is vulnerable and can be taken as belonging to your child. Any judgment to garnish a bank account that has another person's name on it could freeze the account and you would not have access to your money to pay bills. Any outstanding checks may bounce and add bank charges.

The whole amount of an estate held in joint tenancy is subject to all of the liabilities of the joint owners. What may have been created as a convenience, can turn into a nightmare. Placing someone else on your bank account or titles is not the safest approach and can have unexpected and undesirable consequences.

Uniform Probate Code creates a presumption that joint property is owned by the surviving owner. Upon your death, your child has the right to possession and is under no legal obligation to put the jointly held account funds into the estate total to be divided with your other named beneficiaries, nor is there a requirement that he or she use the assets for last expenses, debt or taxes as you intended. The co-owner's sense of entitlement and temptation is often too great to keep the money, not pay estate bills, and not share with other heirs; ending up in long-term family rifts.

It sometimes happens that joint owners, even spouses, can't access the accounts or funds because some states automatically freeze jointly owned accounts upon the death of one of the owners until the tax collector can examine it. As a side consequence of putting your child on titles or accounts, depending on the value of the asset, the transfer may be subject to a gift tax imposed on the person making the transfer. Often a surviving widowed spouse doesn't do any formal estate planning, so the probate that may have been avoided on the death of the first spouse is not avoided on the death of the second.

You lose control of real estate such as a house if you give someone co-ownership. You cannot sell, mortgage or refinance it unless he or she agrees. If your child is married, their spouse may also have to agree. If you do sell, the child is going paid a share of the proceeds at the close of escrow. On top of all of this, the transfer of property setting up a joint ownership could result in adverse income and capital gains tax consequences when the surviving beneficiary sells the appreciated property.

One of my saddest law practice examples of this mistaken planning error was when an elderly widow client put her son's name on her house, reasoning that he would eventually get it anyway. When junior got a bitter divorce, the ex-daughter-in-law enforced a sale of the family home to get her part of his joint half interest. After all, mother had made the son a legal owner of the property. The eighty- year-old mother was forced to sell and leave her family home that she had lived in over sixty years.

Don't put your children's names in joint tenancy on your accounts or property as a self-help estate plan. It creates a liability for them and makes your resources and property very vulnerable. Having other estate planning documents such as Durable Powers of Attorney for Financial and trust appointments are more than sufficient to deal with the situations where you need help or someone to sign if you cannot sign.

In the case of second marriages, the new spouse often moves into the other's original family home. If hubby puts his new wife's name in joint tenancy ownership with right of survivorship on the title of the family home, the entire house passes to her at new hubby's death. Even if his will or trust says that his children by the first marriage are to receive the house upon his demise, it does not happen. The will or trust cannot change the legal effect of the joint ownership right of survivorship titling. The surviving spouse has outright control of the assets. The danger is that the surviving spouse may give some or all of the assets away to her own children, a new spouse, lover or con artist, leaving the original heirs cut out of the father's estate.

Review Your Estate Plan

In law practice, attorneys ask clients to take the estate plan "snapshot test". It is a visualization of the future when you are sitting up in the clouds and looking down on your family while they prepare for your funeral and the estate settlement process. How would the funeral and transition look if you were to die right now? Do the people left in charge of your affairs know the attorney who prepared your estate plan, where all the documents are located, or how to proceed? Would there be chaos, confusion and frustration because your family has no idea where to start?

If you follow the steps provided and work with an estate-planning attorney, your snapshot is a clear picture and the funeral and administration proceeds smoothly. Knowledge is not only power, it is a great relief for your survivors when your estate plans and decisions have been made in advance.

EXCLUSIVE READER ONLINE RESOURCES

A password hidden in *Widow's Key* allows you to receive extra reader resources. There are more items, links and other valuable resources not in the book that you can use. Here are topics available to *Widow's Key* readers only:

* Sample Will and Trust Questionnaire

* Easy to Understand Glossary of Wills and Trusts Terms

* Heritage Trusts for Wayward Heirs

* Websites Featuring Wills of Famous People

Visit the *Widow's Key* companion website at www.widowskey.com. Follow the simple instructions to find your password. A password hidden in the book gives you access to your extra reader-only information.

Chapter Twenty-Six

PROBATE

If you have to probate all or a portion of your late husband's estate, the following is a descriptive outline of the probate purpose, process and steps. Here is the information you will need and the guidelines to help you understand probate and save you time and money. Additionally, this chapter gives you methods for preparing your own plan so that you can avoid or simplify probate of your own real and personal property.

What is Probate?

Probate is a legal process for transferring your property when you die. Some of the most common misperceptions about probate include that probate is caused by: anyone's death; not having a will; having a will; having a large estate; involving attorneys; having a poorly written will; or if there is a will contest. What really causes a probate is simply the need for the decedent's signature before any title changes or distributions can take place.

Probate is necessary in order to transfer deeds, banking accounts, stock certificates and distribution to the intended beneficiaries. The problem is the need for the signature; the solution is probate. The probate court supervises administration of the estate of a person who dies.

In probate proceedings, the court validates the will, appoints a personal or court representative, identifies the deceased person's property, oversees payment of debts, determines the proper heirs, identifies who receives the property and asset and approves the final distributions. The court will reach an estate settlement, oversee distribution and close the probate case.

Since a deceased person cannot retain property or sign documents, probate is the process that determines who gets the estate property. The primary function of probate is to transfer title of the decedent's property to the heirs and beneficiaries. The personal representative named in the will (usually a spouse, relative or friend of the deceased person) does some of the actual work, with assistance of an attorney and often an accountant.

Probate involves several steps that are generally overseen by the personal representative or executor if there is a will or by a court-appointed representative if there is not. The typical probate includes:

- Validation of the will
- Notice to creditors
- Identifying and inventorying the deceased person's property
- Appraisal and accounting of the property
- Payment of taxes, expenses and creditors
- Formal distribution of the remaining assets as the will directs or by state laws of intestate succession.

The legal profession refers to a will as "an engraved invitation to the probate court." Whether your property needs to go through probate is determined by how the property is titled, not whether someone has a will. Having a will does not keep you out of probate court, but it can reduce the cost of probate and reduce the burden to your family and representatives. The probate court has general powers over the probate of wills, administration of estates and sometimes they are empowered to appoint guardians or approve the adoption of minors.

By the way, you cannot avoid probate by not having a will. Probate will take place, but it invariably takes more time and costs more money because you didn't appoint a representative or leave any instructions. If your objective is to avoid probate, then perhaps you should consider a Living Trust as discussed in other sections. Trust packages even include 'pour-over wills' as a safety net for any assets left out of the trust, to name guardians and trustees for minors and to protect the inheritances of special needs beneficiaries. Sometimes an account or property omitted from the trust can be put into trust with a special affidavit shortcut.

Probate is not always necessary. Property held in a living trust avoids probate and passes seamlessly to the trustee or your named beneficiaries. If the deceased had life insurance, retirement accounts, bank accounts payable upon death and joint tenancy with right of survivorship property, these all contractually pass directly to the appropriate beneficiary automatically. A common error in life insurance or investment accounts is naming the insured's estate as the beneficiary rather than designated persons and contingent beneficiaries. Naming the estate will place the proceeds from that insurance policy or investment account into probate.

If a person dies with very few possessions, these can be distributed among the heirs without the supervision of the court. However, even in small estate situations a probate is sometimes needed to: clear title to land; transfer stocks, bonds, large bank accounts held in the deceased person name only; settle disputes between alleged heirs; collect debts owed to the deceased; and resolve disputes about the validity of a will. To gain the protections of probate and to simplify the probate process for comparatively small estates, you may qualify for a Small Estate Affidavit of Claiming Successor.

Probate Court Process Step-By-Step

If your late husband's estate or a portion of his estate needs to go through the probate process, you should be familiar with the players and the steps involved. The probate court is a court having jurisdiction and supervision over an estate in order to ensure that the decedent's property is distributed according to the will and/or the laws of the state. Probate court may be called by other names in different states.

For example, in California it is the Probate Division of the Superior Court, while in New York the Probate Court is the Surrogate's Court. These courts have statutory authority to deal with probate, conservatorship and guardianship matters.

Typical Probate Process Steps

(1) **Selection of a personal representative.** A family member or friend, banking institute, lawyer or trust company is selected by the deceased person in his will or by the court. If the deceased died without a will, the court can appoint a spouse, close family member or choose a professional administrator.

(2) **The court examines the will** and statements of the witnesses to make sure the will is valid. The will is to be delivered within thirty days to the personal representative or to a court. The will is proved by the written statements or affidavits made under oath by the witnesses to the will. Each witness must be able to testify that the person was of sound mind and knew what he was doing at the time of the signing of the will.

(3) **An inventory of assets compiled** and given to the court. The personal representative gathers information and documentation about the deceased person's property and assets and presents an inventory to the court. If not forbidden by the will, expenses are covered by the sale of some assets. The court makes sure that there are proper receipts collected by the personal representative for all expenses taken from the estate during probate.

(4) **A notice to creditors published** in a local newspaper three times. The public notices to creditors informs the creditors and lien holders that they have four months to bring any claims against the estate for debts the deceased person owes them. The personal representative must also give written notice to all known creditors and possible creditors. The probate court requires debts to be paid.

(5) **Heirs and persons named in the will are given written notice** of the probate proceedings.

(6) **Debts owed to the deceased are collected** by the personal representative.

(7) **All required federal or state tax returns and any inheritance, gift or estate tax returns to be prepared by the personal representative and paid**. The court will not close probate until all taxes are paid. You can hire professionals for this.

(8) **The court reviews and approves the inventory of assets and final accounting** submitted by the personal representative.

(9) **After approval by the court, the estate assets are distributed** to the entities and people named in the will or to the statutory heirs of the deceased.

Probate involves a lot of record keeping and official paperwork, which must be filed in a timely manner. Probate should be handled by professionals with an understanding of the legal principles, strict timelines, inventory management, estate administration and the processes involved. An attorney is especially needed in the preparation and filing of the court required legal documents. The lawyers and court fees are paid from estate property.

Keep in mind that the probate attorney works for the personal representative, not for the heirs. Hearings, estate management problems, challenges, family disputes, litigation and tax traps can be avoided by having an experienced estate attorney on your side.

Small Estate Affidavit

In most states, smaller estates may fall within a probate exemption allowing a certain amount of property to pass free of probate through a simplified procedure. Many states allow an abbreviated procedure for handling small estates which may otherwise require a probate proceeding. This process done by filing an Affidavit of Claiming Successor or a similar document, is sometimes referred to as a small estate affidavit.

As a small estate example, in the state of Oregon, an Affidavit of Claiming Successor may qualify and be filed if the estate has personal property that has fair market value of $50,000 or less and the estate has real property that has fair market value of $90,000 or less. A small estate affidavit must be filed by a claiming successors. A claiming successor can be an heir or devisee of the decedent (depending on whether a will exists) or the person nominated as personal representative in the will or a creditor of the estate who has not been paid within 60 days after the decedent's death.

If the decedent died without a will or heirs, the creditor must have the written authorization from the Division of State Lands or the Director of the Division of State Lands, if there is no will and no heirs. See your own state or county websites or ask your attorney for the proper small estate qualifications and forms. There is also an Affidavit in Lieu of Probate used by a surviving widow to remove the name of her deceased spouse from ownership of the property without having to go through probate. If your late husband's estate was not required to go through probate or if it has been three or more years since the death of your spouse, the Assessor's Office will generally accept a death certificate and notarized Affidavit in Lieu of Probate to change the ownership title of the property.

Benefits of Probate

There are actually some real benefits to probate. Most importantly, probate court supervision assures that a deceased person's property be accounted for and distributed as intended. There is legitimate closure and finality for the family and other claimants. Having a will can reduce the burden to your family and reduce the cost of probate. Making sure that creditors are notified and their claims settled is an important part of court supervision. Probate limits the time that creditors and others can make claims against the estate. Once the probate creditor's claim period has passed, it stops the creditors from pursing payment. Additionally, for professionals such as accountants, doctors or attorneys, probate can bar later lawsuits that otherwise would be difficult to defend without the help of the deceased.

Drawbacks of Probate

Many people try to avoid probate because of certain drawbacks. Probate can be very time consuming and expensive. Formal probate takes, at a minimum, six months to a year to complete. Probates have been known to drag on for years and in extraordinary situations, for decades. Throughout the probate process, anyone may challenge the will and make a claim on the estate, either by petitioning the court or the executor. If the claim is rejected, the claimant may file a lawsuit to prove the claim and collect money. Any dispute generally causes the court to treat the probate more formally and delay the distributions.

Whether or not your late spouse or you have a will, unless there was a living trust, your estate will likely be subject to probate. The process can be an expensive proposition, no matter the size of the estate. The expenses of the probate process come from court fees, publishing legal notices, challengers or claimants' lawsuits, and administrative fees paid to the personal representative and the professionals (appraisers, accountants, attorneys and such). No doubt, probate is expensive. Attorney and court fees can average five percent (5%) or more of an estate's value. Additionally, the personal representative or executor's fee of two to five percent (2-5%) based on the gross estate are considered reasonable to the court.

Remember that your gross estate, not your net estate, is used in probate calculations. For example, if a person owns a home valued at $250,000 mortgaged at $200,000, they may pay around 8% of $250,000 (not the $50,000 equity) or $20,000 just for the home to go through probate. Looking at a typical probate fees chart, with personal representative and attorney fees at 5.5%, if your estate gross market value is $1 million, the fees alone would total $55,000. There would be additional court, real estate broker, apppraiser and other fees on top of that.

If you own real estate in other states, you will be required to go through probate in each state. This ancillary probate multiples the costs substantially since an attorney for that state must be employed and fees paid in another probate court. When you are deciding between doing no advance estate planning, a will or trust, compare the emotional and monetary costs. An average living trust package can be prepared for around $2000. When you consider that the cost to probate a $1million dollar estate is over $55,000, the amount saved is obvious and dramatic.

Most of what happens during probate is essentially clerical. In the majority of cases, there is no conflict, no contesting parties, none of the usual reasons for court proceedings. Probate rarely calls for legal research, drafting, or a lawyer's adversarial skills. However, probate attorneys and their paralegals complete and draft a small mountain of forms and keep track of filing deadlines and other procedural technicalities. The attorney may have to make a few routine court appearances. The court may approve extra costs if the estate is complicated. Probate will order all estate taxes paid, so the heirs have no options to minimize or avoid taxes as is done with the use of a living trust. What most people really dislike about probate is that the probate process is public and anyone can access the court records to see your estate worth and distributions. The contents of your will and information regarding your finances become part of a permanent public record. Probate has the disadvantage of invading not only the deceased's privacy, but also the privacy of the heirs.

Tips for Keeping Probate Fees Down

(1) Choose a family member or close friend to be your executor who is willing to perform this job without charging a fee. This will be a substantial savings, as the executor may charge up to 2-5% of the value of the estate for services. You can also shop around for a bank or corporate executor, find and negotiate the best rate.

(2) Include a special clause in your will that waives the personal representative's bond requirement. If the court has an insurance policy like bond, it might be $500 or more. Bonds are to insure that if the value of the probate property declines as a result of the executor's or administrator's misconduct, the bond will make the estate whole again.

(3) The personal representative should get estimates for completing the inheritance tax documents from certified public accountants (CPAs) if an estate is large enough to owe federal or state estate taxes. Using the deceased's accountant, who may already be familiar with the deceased's assets, may be prudent. To a certain extent, you can negotiate lower charges because they already have some of the information on file.

(4) If appraisals are necessary for real and/or personal property, the statutory amount is a maximum and may be negotiable. However, the fee for the appraiser, also sometimes referred to as a probate referee, may be set by custom in the area or statutory.

(5) The attorney's fees are a large portion of probate fees but may be negotiable. The amounts may be set by state law or by practice and custom in the community. However, it is worth asking for the best price. Being organized, prepared and by doing some of the legwork yourself, you may be able to reduce the billable hours. Like with the accountant, using a lawyer who drew up the estate documents and is familiar with the deceased's affairs may prove prudent. Many times part of the estate administration may have been prepaid.

Some fees are not negotiable, such as court's filing fee and the newspaper's fee for publication of a legal notice. Other fees, even if statutory in your state, are negotiable to a certain extent or may be avoided altogether. Don't make assumptions or be shy; Ask.

Chapter Twenty-Seven

TRUSTS AND TRUST ADMINISTRATION

If you are overseeing your late husband's estate and he had a trust or you are getting your own trust prepared or amended, you should be familiar with the basic aspects of trusts and trust administration processes. Following are trust and trust administration introductory outlines to help you.

Revocable and Irrevocable Living Trusts

A trust is a legal device that you can use to own and manage your property during your lifetime and directs distribution of your real and personal property after your demise. A living trust is a legal agreement between you as the trust maker and you as the trustee. The trust entity holds your estate assets during your life, with you in complete control as trustee. Upon your death, the trust seamlessly distributes the assets to your named beneficiaries. The administration of the estate is not interrupted by conservatorship or probate, because the trust does not die or become incompetent.

As an alternative to having just a will, growing numbers of people are using revocable trusts to manage estates and dispose of their properties afterward. Commonly referred to as a 'Living Trust' or a 'Family Trust,' a revocable trust is part of an overall estate planning strategy that is customizable and flexible. A living trust is also known as an 'inter vivos' trust because it is in operation during the lifetime (vivos) of the creator or grantor of the trust, as well as following the death.

Your trust can be set up to be revocable or irrevocable. You can revise or even dissolve a revocable trust at any time. But, an irrevocable trust can never be changed. The assets placed in the irrevocable trust must stay there and beneficiaries are never added or deleted. People with significant estates often chose to have an additional irrevocable trust because when they die, that trust property is not considered part of the estate and is therefore not subject to estate taxes.

Benjamin Franklin was wrong. He said "Nothing is certain but death and taxes." If you have a living trust, you will be able to reduce or eliminate the estate taxes your heirs may be required to pay on the inheritance you leave them. The main motivations for making estate plans include wanting to avoid or save on taxes and have property pass smoothly to the people or charities, institutions or causes that you name.

Additionally, a living trust is set up to help during a disability, if you have children or grandchildren with special needs, if you own real estate in more than one state, desire privacy about your financial matters after death, or as a way to avoid going through probate. A living trust is not expensive when compared to the costs of court interference and oversight at your incapacity and death. A living trust is a solid financial decision.

Trust Versus Will

You need this basic background to understand the differences between a will and a trust. After death, assets pass by legal methods such as:
1. Joint ownership
2. Heir or beneficiary designation
3. Probate (by will or by state law if there is no will)
4. Living trust

A will only goes into effect after you die, while a trust is recognized life-long estate management tool. The primary difference between the trust and the will is that a trust, if properly funded in the name of your trust, avoids probate. All wills and lack of will (intestate) estates must go through probate court. If you have only a will, any asset titled in your name must pass through the probate process. People using wills and joint tenancy as their estate plan are subject to probate costs, problems, heartaches and agony that they might have been spared by having a living trust.

Other than avoiding probate, people create trusts for other reasons: like privacy; the reduction or elimination of estate taxes; as safeguards for guardianship and distributions to minor children; to protect benefits received by disabled children or adults; to name alternate trustees in case of your incapacity; and to allow the seamless transfer of assets to named multigenerational beneficiaries upon death. The trust holds and manages your assets during your lifetime, with you as the controlling trustee and then distributes the estate to your beneficiaries at your demise.

Establishing a Trust Package

A living trust is a legal document that, like a will, contains what you want to happen to your property and assets when you pass away. Unlike a will, the trust also covers you and your property if you are still alive but incapacitated. People of all ages, marital status and wealth are good candidates for living trusts. Proper estate planning takes careful and professional oversight. When you have an estate planning attorney draw up a revocable living trust, you legally bring all your assets together under one plan. An estate professional should prepare a living trust package that contains the living trust, pour over will, durable power of attorney, health care power of attorney, living will, and funding instructions.

In establishing your trust, you identify yourself, heirs, your written intention and declaration to establish a trust and instructions for management and distribution. Who's Who in a trust are: (1) Trustor or grantor is the person who starts the trust. Usually you are the person who puts all your property in the trust; (2) Trustee is the person who manages the trust. The trust agreement is actually a contract between the trustor (you) and the trustee (also you); and (3) Beneficiary is the person who gets the benefits of the trust, income and principle (again you and eventually your heirs).

From the beginning, you are all three (trustor, trustee and beneficiary), except that a spouse may also be a co-trustee or beneficiary. You alone or you and your spouse are named as Trustees and Beneficiaries. If you and your spouse are co-trustees, either one of you can act and have control if the other becomes incapacitated or dies. If something happens to both of you, your successor trustee will step into your shoes to settle the estate.

A trust is relatively simple for an estate-planning attorney to set up and easy for you to maintain. After all the documentation is completed, the funding or transferring of all your major assets from your personal name into the name of the trust is the next step. The trust document does not really take effect until the creator transfers ownership of property to the trust. After the transfer of titles and funding, the legal owner of your assets is your trust. Not to worry, you continue to have complete and total control over your properties and assets. You can continue to buy, sell, give away or remove assets should you decide to do so. You manage your financial matters as you did before. Upon your death, your named co-trustee or successor trustee will instantly oversee your assets, pay any inheritance taxes and final bills and distribute your estate according to your exact instructions. In addition, in the event of a disability, your co-trustee or successor trustee can manage your financial affairs through the trust and power of attorney until you are able to resume as trustee.

According to your unique family, business and estate value situations, the attorney may suggest other advance planning techniques and Swiss army knife-like tools. These types of estate planning documents may be included as appropriate: By-Pass Trust; QTIP (Qualified Terminable Interest Property) Trust, Irrevocable Life Insurance Trust; Generation Skipping Trust; Grantor Retained Annuity Trust; Family Charitable Trust; Lifetime Gift Exclusions; Estate Equalization; Discretionary Support; Same Sex Couples; Life Estates; and Heritage or Legacy Trust. Ask your attorney if any of these type trusts apply to you, your family or financial situations.

Trustees

The trustee is the person holding property in trust. In establishing a trust, the person creating it is called the trustor, creator, grantor or settler. That same person becomes the trustee. The trustee or co-trustees are the ones in whom the estate, interest or power is vested, under an express or implied agreement to administer it for the benefit or use of the trustees and eventually the beneficiaries. Most likely, you name yourself as trustee or you and your spouse as co-trustees, so you will retain complete control over your estate assets. Successor trustees can be competent individuals like adult children, relatives or trusted friends. The successor trustees may or may not be beneficiaries. Sometimes people appoint financial institution trust departments or a law firm.

Be sure to name more than one successor trustee in case someone is unwilling or unable to carry out the duties. You retain the power to remove a trustee and appoint a new one. When you die, your successor trustee has a duty to pay your debts and distribute assets as the trust instructs.

The possibility of someone becoming incapacitated is six times greater than the possibility of death. If you become incapacitated, your co-trustee or successor trustee will oversee your care and manage your finances, until you recover and resume control. Before a successor trustee can take over the management of your trust, two doctors must sign affidavits that say you are not competent to handle your daily affairs. The definition of incapacity includes the inability to manage affairs and property effectively for reasons such as physical illness or disability, advanced age, mental illness, mental deficiency, chronic use of drugs, chronic intoxication, confinement or detention by a foreign power or disappearance.

Information Needed for Estate Planning and Strategy

The following is a sample of confidential information that you will provide the attorney as a basis for strategizing and preparing your estate plan:

Family Data: Full Legal Names, Addresses, Telephones, Emails, Websites, Birth dates; Occupations; Social Security numbers; Marital status; Date of marriage; Former marriages; Full legal name of spouse, with personal and contact information; Children, including adopted with their personal and contact information; Other beneficiary information.

Property and Asset Information: Real estate descriptions, locations, market values, balances; Cash Accounts, institute and ownership; Safe deposit boxes; Investments and brokerage accounts; Life insurance, company, beneficiary and amount; Retirement benefits and accounts; Business interests; Equipment; Notes, receivables and obligations; Funeral arrangements; and Major personal effects.

Advisors: Attorney; Accountant; Financial advisor; Primary personal bank; Life insurance agent; Stock broker; Business partners; and other professional service contacts.

Selection of Representatives, Guardians and Trustees

Selection of Health Care Representatives and Power of Attorney Representatives with their contact information.

Distribution Provisions: List the persons or organizations that you wish to give equal, specific or percentage bequests; Ages or circumstances of distribution; Advances that enable recipients to obtain educational, college or graduate school funds, purchase a home or start a business. List the charitable institution bequests; and Name those contingent beneficiaries to receive the residue of your estate after specific and charitable bequests are made or if all your originally named beneficiaries have predeceased you.

Specific Gifts: If a specific gift is unique or valued more or less over $5000, it can be listed in the trust gift section.

Family Questions: You and your attorney should discuss topics such as: citizenships; beneficiaries with disabilities, addictions, lifestyles; receipts of social security, disability or other government benefits; special medical, education or physical needs; divorces and settlement agreements; pre-nuptial or post-marriage contracts; state of residence; out-of-state or foreign property; gift tax returns; pets; and previous wills, trusts, powers of attorney or other estate plans to determine personalized planning and drafting aspects of the trust.

Funeral Instructions: Last arrangement instructions can be included in your trust documents, but additionally, that information needs to be in a detailed letter of instruction or last wishes binder.

Other Relevant Information, Documents or Comments

Transferring Ownership to Your Trust

Many people go to all the time, trouble and cost of preparing a living trust, and then make a major mistake of not 'funding' the trust, thus making it useless. Funding a trust means transferring or changing the ownerships held in your individual name into the name of the trustee and trust. If you have signed your trust documents and have not physically changed titles and beneficiary designations to transfer your individual assets to the trust, it does not control anything. Even a well-drafted living trust can only protect and control the properties and assets put into it.

Think of the trust as an empty vessel into which you, as the trust maker, pours property and assets. It is very important that you completely fund your trust so that everything applicable is in the trust name and positioned properly. Since one of the trust goals is to avoid probate and court intervention at incapacity, you are responsible for funding it as soon as possible. Typically, your attorney will review all your assets, explain the procedure and decide who will be responsible for what transfers.

Often the attorney will prepare new deeds, titles and record your residence and other real estate for you and provide instructions for the other transfers. It is important to remember that when you buy new property or open new accounts to register or title them in the name of your trust. If you forget to do the funding, a probate may be necessary to transfer assets into your trust or to named beneficiaries at the time of your death.

Assets That Go Into Your Trust

Assets to put into your living trust include: your home, land and other real estate, bank and savings accounts, certificates of deposit, safe deposit box, investment portfolios, mutual funds, money markets, business interests (sole proprietorship, general or limited partnership, closely held corporation, LLC or subchapter S corporation), intellectual property, patents, royalties, copyrights, annuities, expensive cars, boats and airplanes, valuable collectibles, web domains, club memberships, stocks, bonds, savings bonds, treasury securities, cemetery plots, oil and gas interests, foreign assets and owner financed mortgage loans or notes payable to you.

Re-titling real estate to put it into your trust does not activate a due on sale or transfer clauses, nor trigger a reappraisal or reevaluation of the property or effect property taxes. In fact, you will still be able to use the capital gains exemption when you sell your home. You should transfer property that you own in another state into your living trust to avoid probate in that state.

The assignment used to transfer business property to the trust should not trigger an event covered by a buy-sell agreement. Change business licenses and doing business as (DBA) to show your trust as the owner. Change your homeowners, title, business and liability insurances to reflect your living trust on the title and the trustees as additional insured.

Assets that are not allowed or that you may not want in your living trust include: IRA, 401(k) and other tax-deferred retirement accounts, Interests in professional corporations, some life insurance, Section 1244 stock, and incentive stock options. Personal property that typically does not have a formal title, such as jewelry, artworks, furniture, books, household goods, computer or camera equipment or sporting goods, can be transferred to your trust through an assignment, bill of sale or specific gifts section as part of your trust package.

Setting up a trust should not affect any loans or notes you owe or credit cards because these are not assets, so you don't need to do anything with them. Most state motor vehicle departments have an exemption to allow the transfer of car titles without probate. Instead they will ask for the presentation of the death certificate and completion of their signed affidavit form. You may not wish to put your vehicles into the trust unless they are very expensive or collectibles.

If you are leaving monetary gifts, it is best not to put in a specific dollar amount. Instead use a percentage of your estate. For example, rather than say, "I leave $50,000 to my Unitarian Universalist Congregation, put the gift in as a percentage of your estate and say "I leave ten percent of my net estate." That way, if you have extra expenses at the end of life or your resources are reduced, your trustee is not requuired to distribute a specific amount to the congregation and leave your other beneficiaries with a smaller amount than you intended or without a fair share.

Funding Process

The transferring and changing ownership titles or funding process may take some time, but it is not difficult. When your estate plan package is completed, the attorney should give you a special set of funding instructions unique to your trust showing you how to transfer titles and current assets as well as future purchases into the trust.

Since living trusts are becoming more common, financial institutions and investment firms are familiar with the transfer process and cooperative, so you should not meet with any resistance. Institutions often have their own standard forms that you will need to complete to change the ownership or beneficiary. Some may require written instructions to be notarized or guaranteed or assignment documents that can be mailed, emailed, scanned or faxed to the institution.

Agents and officers may ask for verification of the trust existence and identification of the trustees and successor trustees. A memorandum or abstract document your attorney prepares called the 'certificate of trust', which is an abbreviated summary version with only key points of validity will satisfy this requirement. You do not have to reveal any details about your estate or your beneficiaries. If you do encounter any difficulties, usually a quick call from your attorney will clear things up.

Some attorneys want to do or assist you with the funding work, especially re-titling the home, to make sure the trust is as effective as possible. However, it is usually a combination of the attorney doing some and you doing some of the funding work. You can save legal fees if you transfer many of the assets yourself. Remember that assets not formally transferred to the trust will not be part of the trust and might still be subject to probate. Make funding your living trust a priority and keep working at it until you are finished. Do not get distracted or lose your determination. It will take some effort and time, but as they say, "you can do it now, or you can pay the courts and attorneys to do it for you later."

If you do forget to transfer or title an asset, the attorney probably prepared a "pour over will" safety net meant to catch the forgotten asset and put it into the trust. There are no distributions listed in the will other than giving the remaining left out items to the trust for administration. There may be a probate required for the overlooked property if it exceeds the state limit for a small estate, but after that probate process, distributed according to your trust instructions.

Don't let the procrastination monster prevent you from holding up your end of the funding responsibilities. If you run into problems or want help in completing the funding process, ask your attorney or her staff for assistance. Look forward to the peace of mind you will have when the funding of your trust is complete.

When you are transferring assets and property titles, there are three important items in identifying your trust: (1) the Trust name; (2) the Trustees and (3) the date of execution of your living trust.

The correct format of registering a living trust looks something like:

The Brown Family Trust, Dated February 15, 2011, Andrew and Naoko Brown, Trustees (for a couple)

The Andrew S. Brown Trust, Dated February 15, 2011, Andrew S. Brown, Trustee (for a single person)

You may also see the title of a trust written similar to this: Andrew S. Brown Trust, Andrew S. Brown Trustee, UA DTD February 15, 2011.

The UA DTD stands for "Under Agreement Dated."

Maintaining Your Trust and Will

Once your estate plan is in place, you must maintain it. It is advisable to hold a living trust review with the professional that set it up for you if there are major life changes or at least every three years. Events such as divorce, marriage, remarriage, death, birth, blended families, disabled beneficiary, pet arrangements, early gifting, retirement, disability or financial changes could justify an amendment in your trust. If any of your successor trustees should move away, die, become incapacitated or just be unable or unwilling to fulfill their responsibilities, you should make designation changes accordingly. As a general rule, you have the power to amend your trust at any time it is no longer what you want or need.

Life is not static, and it is vitally important to analyze your estate planning documents periodically to be sure that they have not expired, continue to work together and reflect your current intentions. Anytime your net worth has increased or decreased due to retirement, new employment, receipt of an inheritance, change of business or winning the lottery, you should reevaluate and make the necessary changes. When there have been significant changes in the value of some of your assets, like those brought on by the recent fluctuations in the stock and housing markets, you may want to rebalance your bequests to specific beneficiaries. Perhaps your beneficiaries' health or circumstances have changed.

Make the appointment to take your will, trust and other estate planning documents in for a checkup as needs and time dictate. It is important that you do not attempt to alter your original documents yourself, since this might lead to questions of validity of the documents and bring challenges.

Advantages of a Trust

When you have a trust, you:

1. Avoid Probate. The fact that assets held in your trust are not subject to the complex, invasive, lengthy and costly probate process is possibly one of the most popular and greatest advantages. Because a probate court only has jurisdiction over assets personally owned in your name, if your trust owns the property, the court has no authority to validate, publish or oversee the distribution of your estate. Trusts save the greatest amount of taxes and post death administrative costs possible. Consider the example costs of probating a $1 million dollar estate at over $55,000, to the price of preparing and funding a trust for around $2000, and the savings are dramatic and obvious.

2. Have More Privacy. Probate files are a matter of public record. Anyone can access to the file and view your probated will, the list of properties, assets and their values, along with the beneficiaries and their shares. How do you think the salesman with the fast red sports car found and targeted your grandson heir and knew about his inheritance? There are notices to creditors published in the papers that seem to draw not only legitimate claims, but also fraud, con artists and other unscrupulous persons.

With a living trust, there is no listing of your assets and their values in permanent public records. No copies of your trust filed with the court. As a private document, the size and distribution of your estate remain confidential and not a matter of public record. The successor trustee quietly and seamlessly transfers trust assets to your named beneficiaries as you have instructed.

3. Reduce or Eliminate Estate Tax. Estate taxes are due on the transfer of assets because of the death of an individual. Trusts have built-in legal tax avoidance mechanisms. Since the trust is its own entity, it technically owns the assets rather than the person owning it. Therefore, when the person dies, the trust can continue and the distribution to the co-trustee or successor trustees are not labeled as a taxable transfer. With a living trust, title transfers into the trust. This eliminates the federal capital gains tax at death on increases in value, up to the date of the death.

The ability to pass assets to others is tax free only to a certain level determined by the federal and state governments. Couples with large estates and significant assets can greatly reduce or eliminate estate taxes aided by the way the written and funded trust. Trusts can legally preserve your hard-earned wealth for your heirs in the best possible ways.

4. Have no need for a new trust tax identification number. A trust has no special taxpayer identification number. The trust uses your social security number and you file a 1040 as always for income tax purpose. The trust does not require separate tax returns while you are living. File personal and business taxes the same way. A trust's purpose is not to save you any income taxes or avoid tax payments on any highly appreciated trust items during your lifetime. Only after your death, depending on how the trust is structured, it may be necessary for your successor trustee to obtain a new temporary EIN taxpayer number in order to manage the trust until it is closed.

5. Avoid Probate in Multiple States. If you have real estate in more than one state, you could face a potential probate in each state where the property is located. A revocable trust puts your property into trust and there are no multiple ancillary probates.

6. Avoid Guardianship or Conservatorship Proceedings and their costs. Guardianships are court proceedings held on your behalf in the event that you could no longer handle your affairs because of incompetency, perhaps due to a stroke, Alzheimer's or heart attack. Like probate, a conservatorship is necessary when a person can no longer sign due to physical or mental limitations. It is a public, emotional and sometimes humiliating process. Revocable living trusts provide an internal mechanism for the automatic appointment of a guardian of your choice in case you become incapacitated. This pre-determined guardianship avoids the need for your family to go to court and request that one of them be appointed guardian over your person and conservator of your estate.

With a trust, your pre-appointed successor trustee can freely manage your affairs such as pay your bills, protect and invest trust assets and oversee your care. A court imposed conservatorship results in expense, publicity and delays. The court also remains involved so your estate is required to pay court fees and costs each year for the conservatorship. Having a trust successor trustee or appointed guardian is extra protection to run the trust if you are disabled, you still need Power of Attorney for Financials and the Durable Power of Attorney for Health Care for non-trust decisions.

7. Control the Trustee Power. Use caution when choosing a trustee or giving power of attorney to an individual who will have the right to sign your name. The position of Trustee or Power of Attorney is not a completely free power. Civil and criminal law regulate trustee powers so that a successor trustee may not act in bad faith toward the trustee and must act as a prudent investor. Dictates must be followed for estate security and for the good of the heirs.

8. Have Continuity of Management. As the creator of the trust, you act as the trustee and manager in complete control of the all the assets. You can buy, sell or transfer properties as you wish. There is no exposure of your assets to the debts or liabilities of your children as there would be in joint tenancy or joint ownership. Sometimes a prolonged illness or accident can leave you incapacitated for months unable to conduct your affairs. In the case of temporary or permanent incapacity, your named successor trustee steps in as a fiduciary to oversee the trust on your behalf.

The successor trustee has no authority until your documented disability or death. The appointed trustee's powers are limited, but important to your peace of mind. Your estate is managed according to your wishes while you are disabled or upon your demise. The assets of the trust are not subject to probate, so the administration of the estate is much simpler, faster, private and more efficient.

9. Deter Challenges. It is much more difficult for an unhappy beneficiary to contest a living trust than it is for them to contest a will. In a probate court, anyone can easily challenge a will, even without a lawyer. Statistics show that one third of all will contests are successful. The trust can be drawn up to include an 'in terrorem' clause which threatens beneficiaries with forfeiture of their legacies and bequests should they dispute the validity or the distributions of the trust. With a living trust your wishes are carried out without interference. Additionally, in some states trusts are useful to deter scam-artists and creditors, as trusts in general are more difficult to access and attach than personal assets.

10. Preserve Benefits for Your Heirs. If there is a child or grandchild who is disabled, irresponsible or who has problems with addictive behaviors or substances, your trust can authorize your successor trustee to make special distributions so that the heir will not lose government assistance program benefit payments or so that the troubled heir does not squander their inheritance. A special child needs special planning.

Your trust controls when and how much your beneficiaries will receive. Additionally, in the same vein, a trust can arrange for support of a current spouse without disinheriting your children, which can be very important in second marriages.

Disadvantages of a Trust

Problems you may have with a trust include:

1. Problems occur when the **assets or property are left out of the trust** because of failure to change the titles and ownership to the trust. Once the funding transfers are complete, a living trust is easy to maintain.

2. Trustees may fail to make revisions as necessary. If death, marriage, births, tax law changes or other major events occur, it is advisable to review and revise the trust to keep it current. If your successor trustees or guardians have passed away or can no longer fulfill their responsibilities, you should make changes accordingly.

3. **Trustees forget to transfer or title assets.** It can be easy to procrastinate or get sidetracked in the funding of the trust. People can forget to title their assets in the trust name or forget to put the trust down as owner when they buy new property. As part of your trust, the attorney should prepare a pour-over will that acts like a safety net to catch the forgotten assets and send/pour it over into your trust. Depending on the size of the asset, there may have to be a probate for that item or small estate affidavit to clear up the trustee mistakes or oversights.

4. Myths and misunderstandings about trusts saving on taxes may give false security. It can be considered a disadvantage if people are relying on the trust as protection from income taxes, gift tax or litigation. A trust does not provide protection for assets against tax attachments, creditors, divorce, lawsuits or judgments.

5. A trust takes time and effort to fund by re-titling assets into the name of the trust. Putting the name of the trust on properties and assets to reflect the trust as owner or beneficiary is required in order to avoid probate. The disadvantageous problems arise when trustees do not complete the funding of the trust.

As you can observe, there are far more advantages than disadvantages to having a trust. Disadvantages of a properly prepared living trust have nothing to do with the trust itself. A living revocable trust offers significantly more protections and advantages than a will. The will alone may not be the best plan for you and your family because it does not avoid probate, only goes into effect when you die, provides no protection if you become mentally or physically incapacitated, becomes open public record and is easily challenged. The trust is a traditional and well-proven planning tool used in one form or another for over 400 years.

Trust Administration Upon Death

If your late husband had a trust, it is likely up to you as the trustee to oversee the administration of his trust and updates of your own trust. Upon the death of a spouse, trustee or family member, it is extremely important to consult your attorney as soon as possible to address the many estate administration issues.

When your spouse passes away, there are several extremely valuable options available to the successor trustee or executor to maximize the benefits to the estate's beneficiaries and minimize your liability as the successor trustee. These options may be lost by a trustee or executor's failure to take appropriate action or by taking the wrong action prematurely. Many law firms offer a complimentary consultation for you as the surviving spouse, successor trustee or executor. As trustee or co-trustee, you bear the ultimate responsibility for seeing the administration of the estate done in a timely, legal and proper manner.

You may be able to accomplish some of the administration tasks of the estate on your own, but an attorney, corporate trustee and/or accountant will provide valuable guidance and assistance that saves time, frustration and money. Following is an overview of the steps that are required in a typical trust administration.

Basic Trust Administration Steps

• **Call your estate-planning attorney** with notice of your husband's death. Many attorneys, like me, really care about their clients and would like the chance to attend the funeral to honor their friend, be supportive in your time of sorrow and assist you in proper adminsitration of the estate.

• **Make an appointment** to go over the trust documents, trust assets, the administration process and your trustee responsibilities. Together you will review provisions and specific instructions contained in the trust so that you understand the requirements in administration of the trust. Working with an attorney on the administration of the estate can save you immeasurable aggravation, bureaucratic red tape, years of work, liability for errors, fights with angry or estranged family members and even lawsuits. Do not accept, sell or distribute any assets or property before you meet with the attorney.

• **Make an inventory list of all the property and assets.** Gather documents that provide information on the asset types, account numbers, location, company or financial institution, estimated values and contact persons. This information will determine if an estate tax return needs to be filed (due and payable no later than nine months after the grantor's death). The trust may require its own IRS tax number. The attorney can help complete the SS4 form, apply to IRS and obtain one for you.

• **All beneficiaries of the trust and recipients of specific gifts need to be officially notified in writing.** Disputes can be avoided if the beneficiaries are kept informed of the process and progress. Ask the attorney to intervene, play referee or be the lightning rod if beneficiaries start to become confrontational or impatient. Partial distributions can be arranged if the estate is solvent and they are needed. The attorney will prepare receipts for distributive share, cover letters and return envelopes.

• **Under the instructions of the trust, you make claims and begin collections** of death benefits like the life insurance, retirement accounts, social security, bank accounts and such. You can place these funds in an interest bearing account to pay expenses and taxes, if there are any, until assets are distributed. Certified death certificates, trustee identification, forms and other documents will have to be submitted in order to receive the benefits. As trustee, you will transact the necessary business and keep accurate records.

• **Notification and change of the trust titles and beneficiaries** at various banks, investment or brokerage accounts, home and car titles, business ownership and more are arranged. Some of the assets' exact values at the date of the grantor's death are required. This may necessitate financial and stock account statements, collectible valuations, real estate comparables and appraisals.

• **You should revise your trust and other estate documents** to reflect the death, change of status, and to name successor trustees, beneficiaries and health care representatives for yourself. As the trustee, verify that all of the assets are within the trust. Review the investments in the trust to see if they still meet the objectives of income, growth and security. Depending on the size of the estate, there may be additional tax planning needed right away.

• **As the administrator of an estate, you must maintain careful records** of medical and funeral expenses, claims, bills and income received. If necessary, a trustee certainly can hire a team of professional advisors that are paid by the estate. An accountant should assist with the final personal income tax return for the estate and any possible federal inheritance tax form 706 returns if the estate is large enough to be subject to estate or inheritance taxes.

• **The trustee is entitled to reasonable compensation** for services, travel and out-of-pocket expenses. The trust documents provide trustee duties and compensation guidelines.

• **For the final distribution, the attorney prepares a trust package** that includes a copy of the trust, final estate inventory of assets and allocations spreadsheet, distribution checks, verification that designated accounts, property and personal effects were received, final distribution receipt, instructional cover letter and return envelope. After the final inventory of assets and accounting of expenses is prepared and given to the beneficiaries along with their distributions the estate is ready to close.

• **To close the estate, assets are gathered and distributed.** You as the administrator will collect all benefits and assets, pay all claims, taxes and expenses, divide the cash and personal effects and transfer property titles. After that, the trust dissolves and your administrator's job is complete.

• **If a trust is to stay in place** for you as a surviving spouse, for minors, for tax purposes or if the beneficiaries are to receive their inheritances in installments, the trust remains open. Separate bank and brokerage accounts, new tax identification number, bookkeeping and reporting procedures will need to be established.

The previous trust and trust administration information and pointers are not to be considered legal advice. The purpose of this section was to basically prepare you to work with your chosen attorney to settle your late husband's trust and estate and to make you an informed consumer when you contract for and manage your own trust.

Chapter Twenty-Eight

ETHICAL WILL OR LEGACY LETTER

Individuals do estate planning and prepare legal paperwork to ensure that their wishes, regarding the disposition of their property, be expressed in documents that are legally sound, understood and reflect their intentions. Wills and trusts state how you want your money and property distributed when you die. People also prepare living wills that outline any medical treatments to prolong their lives if they are unable to communicate.

There is also a third kind of will, the Ethical Will, that is much more philosophical and emotional. If you find the term 'ethical will' a bit archaic, the modern versions of the document are known as 'legacy letter' or 'ending note' or 'love will' or 'life letter' and 'spiritual-ethical will'.

In essence, legacy planning is the intangible spiritual dimension of estate planning. How do you want to be remembered after you are gone? When enduring words matter and you want to let your words linger, write a legacy letter. The ethical will/legacy letter is a personal communication to ensure that at the end of your life journey, your heritage and values are preserved for future generations.

> The real family legacy is in the stories, not the sterling.
> - Andrea Gross

Legacy of Intangibles

In addition to the tangible, monetary assets that one can inherit, there is a growing awareness that there is a legacy of intangibles transmitted in the form of an ethical will or legacy letter. While trusts and wills drawn up by lawyers convey the properties and assets, the legacy letter written by you lets your loved one inherit something vastly more personal and important than material possessions. Unlike a last will and testament or a living will, an ethical will/legacy letter is not a legal instrument. The legacy letter is a supplementary document expressing your last thoughts and wishes. This different kind of will voices your tributes to special people in your life, touchstones and lessons shared. Your personal letter is a vehicle of self-exploration and a precious heartfelt gift to loved ones.

The concept of the historic traditional ethical will was to transmit ethical instructions to future generations. Contemporary heirs resist orders given from the grave. They more readily accept an explicitly spiritual 'blessings' from elders. Though the content may be similar, the intention is to transmit learning, wisdom and love to future generations, which differentiates legacy letter writing from memoirs or an autobiography.

An ethical will/legacy letter is an expression of a philosophical and spiritual legacy that bequeaths your treasures of the heart, not your monetary treasures. Rather than just material goods, which we enjoy only temporarily, being passed on, it is time to give, devise, bequeath to your progeny and perhaps to their progeny, the conscious presence of a sense of ethics, values, traditions and a way of life. The ethical will takes an inventory of precepts instead of property, of concerns instead of cash, of love in lieu of material legacy.

An ethical will is a legacy letter to your spouse, children, grandchildren and future generations to sum up what you have learned in life and what you want most for them. Think of it as a love letter to your family. It lets your survivors know what has really mattered to you and why. Ethical wills may be one of the most cherished and meaningful gifts you can leave to your family and community. Imagine how priceless a handwritten letter to you from your great grandmother would be. A legacy letter reflects the voice of the heart. Words that come from the heart enter the heart.

Legacy letters are a personal way to share your family history, continuity, life lessons, values, blessings, joys, love, hopes and dreams for the present and future generations and the community. Think of an ethical will as a heartfelt letter describing who and what truly matters most in your life. Others can hold on, across time, to your connections and love. Your ethical will is a precious spiritual document, a true gift to the future.

History and Tradition of Ethical Wills and Legacy Letters

Ethical wills are nothing new. The idea of ethical wills traces to the first book of the Jewish and Christian Bibles over 3000 years ago. Initially, ethical wills were transmitted orally; with the first ethical will given by God himself to Abraham. Over time, they evolved into written documents. The dying Jacob gives his children what in Hebrew is called his *tzava'ah*, or spiritual estate. The *tzava'ah* or *zevaoth* is a document designed to pass ethical values from one generation to the next.

References to this tradition are found in the Bible in Genesis Chapter 49 and John 15-18. Passing along the wisdom, advice, and blessings of elders is a familiar tradition in Native American, Japanese, Muslim and other cultures as well. Four simple little words; "Tell me a story", have been the basis for the people who wrote the Bible, Quran, Talmud, Sutras and other great religious and spiritual texts and oral traditions.

Rabbis and Jewish laypeople have continued to write ethical wills throughout the centuries. During the nineteenth and twentieth centuries, the practice was widely adopted by the general public as additional aids to estate planning, in health care and hospice and as a spiritual healing tool.

The ethical will addresses a person's basic universal needs to be known, to belong, to be remembered, to have one's life make a difference, to bless and be blessed as described in Maslow's Hierarchy of Needs. The goal of writing an ethical will is to clarify a person's identity, life purpose, spiritual and ethical values, to link a person to both their family and cultural history, and communicate a legacy to future generations.

> The greatest use of a life is to spend it for something that will outlast it.
>
> - William James

Who Writes Ethical Wills, Why and When?

Women and men of every age, faith, tradition, ethnicity, economic circumstance, and educational level write ethical wills and legacy letters. Some recent examples include: President Barack Obama's legacy letter to his daughters January 2010, *The Measure of Our Success: A Letter to My Children and Yours* by Marion Wright Edelman and Randy Pausch, a Carnegie Mellon University professor's *Last Lecture* about facing terminal cancer.

Even though the legacy letter is not a legal document, estate attorneys and financial professionals are using the ethical will/legacy letter as a foundation in the preparation of the last will and testament to articulate the values to explain charitable and personal financial decisions. In my law practice, I help clients and others I coach prepare legacy letters as a way of creating a comprehensive will package. This is the financial and emotional side of communicating, as well as passing on your individual legacy.

The ethical will is used today as a spiritual healing tool in religious communities, hospice and in health care with seniors, the ailing, the aged, and the dying. *In Healthy Aging: A Lifelong Guide to Your Physical and Spiritual Well-Being*, Andrew Weil, MD, promotes preparing an "ethical will as a gift of spiritual health" to leave to family. Dr. Weil asserts that the ethical will's main importance is what it gives the writer in the midst of life. There are great healing powers in the creation of a personal narrative. Many feel that seniors have a responsibility to pass on their wisdom and blessings and to build relations among intergenerational family members.

> There is no such thing as an uninteresting life.
> - Mark Twain

Every ethical will or legacy letter is as unique as the person writing it. There is no one else in the world except you, who can create the legacy letter filled with your own personal experiences and wisdom. Your story is like a star, created in your past. It illuminates the present and continues to shine in the future.

The intent of your ethical will makes it unique and different from any memoir or spiritual autobiography you might record. The generic purpose of the ethical will is: to pass on your own life experiences, lessons learned, family history, personal stories, cultural and spiritual values, wisdom gained, blessings and expressions of love for, pride in, hopes and dreams for children and grandchildren, requests for forgiveness for regretted actions; your rationale for philanthropic and personal financial decisions; stories behind the meaningful specific items your heirs will receive and requests for ways to be remembered at the funeral and after your death.

Personal Reasons to Write an Ethical Will or Legacy Letter:

  • If you don't tell your life stories, the family history and about where you come from, no one else will and it will be lost forever

- It helps identify what you treasure most and what you stand for
- By articulating what you value now, you can take steps to insure the continuation of those values for future generations
- You learn a lot about yourself, your priorities and relationships in the process of writing your legacy letter
- You will come to terms with your mortality by creating something of meaning that will live on after you are gone
- It is natural that you want to be remembered, and that you leave something meaningful behind
- Personal memory letters provide a sense of purpose and place
- It provides a feeling of completion and fulfillment in your life.

Legacy letters are sometimes written by people at turning points and transitions in their lives and when facing challenging life situations. This transition period of your widowhood certainly is a life-changing time when you can use the writing exercise to help redefine yourself and your hopes for the future. Most legacy letters are not written just before a person's demise. Legacy letters are written at any life stage that writing a personal message is most fitting. It is a fun and insightful opportunity to harvest your life experiences, convert experience into wisdom, and allow for the fulfillment of the responsibility of passing this wisdom on to future generations.

> Every time an old person dies, it's like a library burning down.
> - Alex Haley

It is a chance to write down the emotions that you may not be able to express face-to-face. Legacy letters can be an excellent way to commemorate any milestone in life like births, weddings, holiday celebrations, accomplishments and more. If energy and time permits, writing an ethical will or legacy letter at the end of life adds a transcendent dimension to your life by providing a link to future generations. Your family and their issue may partake in some measure of your heritage, to a degree that a whisper of immortality becomes yours.

A personal legacy letter is one of the greatest gifts you can give to your children, grandchildren and beyond. Your letter has the potential to affect multiple generations perhaps even hundreds of years from now. Therefore, once you complete your legacy letter using the outline and questions in this section, it is important to put your legacy letter in a safe place. Choose someplace where those you love will be sure to find it such as with your trust and will and give copies to key persons.

Common Themes of Legacy Letters

There are common themes that run through many legacy letters. Older ethical wills or legacy letters generally contained blessings, burial instructions, instructions for the care of others, business and lifestyle advice and insights on personal and spiritual values. Some of the common themes seen in modern legacy letters include:

- Family history and traditions;
- Events and experiences that shaped your life;
- Important personal values and beliefs;
- Spiritual and religious values;
- Life's lessons;
- Hopes and blessings for future generations;
- Expressions of love; and
- Forgiving others and asking for forgiveness for actions or inactions

Ethical wills speak with such authenticity that they have the ability to make people take an accounting of their life, confront ultimate choices and consider what is important and what they are living for.

Please, do not use the legacy letter in a negative, guilt inducing or revengeful way. If unhealthy angry feelings toward another or unfulfilled dreams bubble up during the writing, deal with them now to repair the damage, make changes and restore peace. Forgiveness is something you do for yourself, not for the other person. Forgiveness doesn't mean the person didn't hurt you or that you should forget. You need to protect yourself, but you don't have to harbor the anger, guilt and hurt. Let go of bitter grievances and old grudges when you write your legacy letter. Remember the doctor's oath and buddhist tenet of "do no harm." Save any venting, anger or resentment for your private journal.

The past is not forgotten, but can be relegated to its proper place, leaving room for many new experiences. If the writer is terminally ill, a legacy letter lets the family know the person prepared for the end of life. It also gives comfort to the writer to know that they have passed on information of great and lasting value. Stories have to be told or they die. A legacy letter goes a long way toward preserving the writer's legacy and memory.

A mean spirited legacy letter can do as much harm as good. If it is hateful, a legacy letter might psychologically and emotionally cripple a person.

Cruel expressions of criticism and disappointment can destroy someone's capacity to live a meaningful life. Even in Star Wars: Return of the Jedi, Luke Skywalker forgives his father, Darth Vader for his transgressions; finding peace, renewing their bond of love and allowing Vader redemption. Though you may not live in a galaxy far, far away, granting forgiveness to others and yourself is something everyone should do and is quite relevant to future happiness.

Use your legacy letter so that others will remember you for your generous spirit and constructive positive messages. The legacy letter is supposed to be a love letter, blessings upon others and a message to future generations.

Any advice or requests contained in your letter should be to guide, not try to control like a puppet master from the grave. Words have the power to hurt or to heal, to incite or to inhibit. It is okay to express concerns, but do so with gentleness, respect and kindness. Intentionally use words that encourage, support and compliment. Go out of your way to use words for the benefit of all concerned, to heal relationships and instill confidence.

A legacy letter can be long or short, a few simple pages or an extensive missive or digital recording, so long as it comes from your heart and conveys your unique character, perceptions and the values accumulated over a lifetime. Writing your life story and insights can become an exciting adventure. It is a journey of self-discovery, unearthing gratitude, and acknowledging mistakes, leaving you to look ahead to the future with a clearer vision and direction.

Tips on Writing Your Own Legacy Letter

Writing a legacy letter is not difficult. The need to write a legacy letter is a deeply human impulse as well as sanctified by many cultural traditions. View it as the writing of a loving history and advice letter to your family. Legacy letter major sections include topics like: (1) Opening Paragraph; (2) Family History; (3) Personal History; (4) Lessons and Insights; (5) Ethical Ideals and Practices; (6) Religious Observances and Insights; (6) Overview of Life; and (7) Closing Thoughts.

The following outline structure of topics and fill-in-the-blanks questions will guide you right through the process of writing your own special legacy letter. It is a sequence of exercises to help you capture the memories and other thoughts. As you write about the elements of your life, you will find that they appear in turns as amusing, tender, intensely personal, self-examining and self-motivating and surely valued by all who receive them. Start a list of things you may want to write about in your letter. For example, topics like family, education, truth, beliefs, giving thanks, love, respect for self, healing/forgiveness, friendship, fear, money, success, little-big things, dreams and such. Having a list of topics and starter sentences is important because if you get bogged down on one topic you can go to another subject or era of your life.

Try not to think too much about it at first. Just let your thoughts become words, without internal editing or worries about spelling or grammar. As Mark Twain used to say, "I don't give a damn for a man that can only spell a word one way." In other words, write whatever comes to mind. You may write pages on one question or a few words on another. This simple approach can be both insightful and fun. Your confidence will build quickly as you fill in the blanks. You will probably think of additional subjects you want to share about what you have learned in life and what you want most for your loved ones.

Compiling the information and recording your thoughts can require a commitment of your time and resources. Composing your legacy letter is a deeper slower kind of remembering and framing of your thoughts. Don't try to write your entire letter at one sitting. Take as many sessions as you need.

As you embark on the process, enjoy answering the various questions and write down ideas about events, people, your memories, traditions and values. You may want to do some research, genealogy homework or pull out old photographs to stimulate the memories. The challenge is to evoke those thoughts and express them for your heirs and loved ones.

You will probably feel a sense of great accomplishment and relief when you are finished with your ethical will/legacy letter. You might even cry. It can be frightful journeying through your own life, opening up and being responsible in part for the future emotional, spiritual and physical health of other living beings. It's your legacy letter; do as much or as little as you wish. Please, just do it.

> There is no agony like bearing the untold story inside you.
> - Maya Angelou

Here are sample introductory topics and starter sentences format to help you enter this rewarding effort of sharing your own life story and values:

ETHICAL WILL/LEGACY LETTER

Opening
I write this to you, my _____, in order to:
I care for you very much and I thought it would be important to tell you how I feel.

The Family
My ancestors, parents, siblings were/are:
Events that helped shape our family:
Favorite sayings used in the family:
Old family recipes and traditions:
Characteristics that seem to run in the family:
Photographs and Memento Notes:

Personal History
This is the world into which I was born:
Here is data on my birth, education, family, work and activities:
Some of my experiences as a child include:
Hopes and dreams I had as a young person:
These were the formative events that helped shape my life:
Some people who strongly influenced my life:
These are some books, artworks and music that formed my thinking and brought me joy:
Some of my high points and larger than life experiences:
These are causes for which I and family members have felt a sense of responsibility, and I hope you might too:
I consider these my important highlights and accomplishments:
Some of the times I will remember most fondly are when:

Lessons and Insights
Some of the important lessons I learned in my life:
Special things learned from my parents, spouse, children or friends:
These are the mistakes that I regret having made the most in my life and I hope you will not repeat:
This is my definition of true happiness and success:
My hope and prayer for you is that you will always experience:
You may have tough times, but I want to encourage you to:

Ethical Ideals and Practices
Ideals that found expression in my life:
I would like to suggest to you the following:
Specific teachings that influenced me were:
People and experiences who taught me ethical lessons included:
My long-held beliefs and opinions include:
I dream that you find what makes you special and use it to achieve:

Religious Observances and Insights
Scriptural passages, books and music that move me the most:
The rituals and observances of most meaning to me:
Here are ideas for my memorial service and tombstone:
Please observe and remember me on these occasions and dates:

Overview of Life
This is how I feel as I look back over my life:
My most favorite possessions and the stories that explain what makes them so precious to me:
Treasure each day you have because it will teach you:
Don't you be afraid to:
Always remember:

Closing
I want you to know how special you are and how grateful I am to you for:
Time spent together was so special because:
Here are some of the things that I love about you:
I ask your forgiveness for:
I want to resolve and make peace regarding:
My ardent wish for you is:
Take good care of:
I hope you will remember your heritage and pass on a legacy of:

Signature _____

Date _____

Making Your Legacy Letter Special

In order to strengthen and personalize the themes, incorporate the use of fond nicknames; special words or sayings that will resonate with your loved ones; or make lists of quotes, books or music that were motivational for you. Go deep enough to make your life and the people in it come alive. Be descriptive; for instance, if your writing about the house you grew up in, be sure to describe what it looked liked, how it was furnished, who you lived with, what city or town was like in that era, what was special about growing up there and so on. The same goes for telling stories about family members and friends. Be specific as possible. Don't forget to use emotions.

The more uniquely personal the message is the better. As you write, clump related items together; patterns will emerge. Revise and expand the related categories into paragraphs, then arrange the paragraphs in an order that makes sense to you. Put this aside for a few weeks and then review and revise what you have written. Themes will appear from which you can create a coherent structure in your own voice and style.

There are attorneys, clerics and other services that will proof read, edit, ghost write and generally help you prepare the kind of memorial letter you want. The website at www.widowskey.com features legacy letter writing and coaching services available. Your legacy letter will leave a succinct package of heartfelt testimony of you being you, so that those left behind will know who you were and what you thought was important. The threads you weave become a lifeline for future generations.

Examples of Legacy Letter Wording

As you write you own legacy letter, here are some excerpts samples of legacy letters over the centuries from Riemer and Stampfer's *So That Your Values Live On* and other writers' sources. These examples from other people's letters may help stimulate composition and tone of your letter.

"First of all I want to say how important all of you are in my life journey and how much I love you. It was seldom that my full-blooded Irish father said the words, "I love you" but we never doubted it for a moment."

"I hope that my years will roll on, but prudence warns that this should not be taken for granted. Therefore, in this eighth decade of my life, let me start to leave my legacy of memories, opinions and conclusions."

"Somewhere among these papers is a will made out by a lawyer. Its purpose is to dispose of any material things that I may possess at the time of my departure from this world to the unknown adventure beyond. I hope its terms cause no ill will among you. It seemed sensible when I made it. It refers only to material things we enjoy only temporarily."

"All I needed was you to make my life complete. Wherever you are, I will always have my arms wrapped around you."

"The times have changed enormously during the brief stay of my life. They will for you as well. Yet you will find after many years that people change not so much. Thus, I feel free to provide some advice. This advice was not freely acquired and much of it learned late. I paid for it the hard way and hope you will do the better for it."

"Live together in harmony. Carry no ill will toward each other. Help each other in case of need. Honor and care for your mother. Make her old age happy as far as in your power. I have enjoyed your mother as a loving and appreciative wife. She always praised and told me how capable I was. Then I had to live up to her expectations. Any worthwhile thing I ever did was due to her urging and faith in me."

"I leave you not everything I never had, but everything I had in my lifetime: a good family, respect for learning, compassion for my fellow man and some four letter words for all occasions: words like help, give, care, feel and love."

"To the biblical tradition I owe the belief that man does not live by bread alone, nor does he live alone at all."

"I leave you the years I should like to have lived so that I might possibly see whether you generation will bring more love and peace to the world than ours did. I not only hope that you will, I pray that you will."

"I am writing this letter to share with you some things I find most important in life and to share some thoughts, dreams and hopes that I have for you. I hope that you will feel my support and my love for you in this letter. As a person who has children and also has a life-threatening illness, I have stopped trying to fix up you kids because my work is done in the world. I look at you with new eyes and delight in who you are."

"Always be listening. I'll always be saying hello to you through the cat purrs, lullabies, rainbows or when people are just generally acting nutty. You will find my hello in something that has special meaning to you."

"I believe in strong families and the need to stay together. As I've grown older I value family more. I enjoyed my study of the genealogy of our family and it's my hope that someone will continue my work and maintain our family information in years to come."

"Follow your heart. People must follow their heart in what they want out of life. Money doesn't always come hand-in-hand with what your heart tells you, but in the end the heart will benefit you the most."

"Finding a career you are proud of is very difficult but worth the search. You may need to try many different careers during your life. Don't be afraid of change, it's one of the things that can help keep you young at heart."

"Everyone must live their own life in their own way, as their values would have them live. Any variation of this is just a short-term diversion. Telling others how to live their life is not in anyone's job description."

"You were born of love. Let that be the nature and nurture of your growth. May it ever be with you. Know you are special and important."

"I'm sorry for some of the things I did, but very sorry for the many things I did not do."

"Your grandmother Mary was a very special lady who helped me greatly to believe in myself and to believe in the power of prayer. She loved me unconditionally. I hope you can say that about me."

"I have found that money can not buy true love or home-grown tomatoes."

"Being the father of you three wonderful boys was one of the most special things in my life. I always wished I could have helped you more and just "be" with you. I especially enjoyed our fishing trips together."

"Thank you for your love, being my children and your support of me through the years. You have been a great source of joy and strength."

"Give yourself for small things: small time to music, architecture, painting, sculpture and any uses of tones, colors, shapes and structuring space. See how it stretches and deepens you for other experiences. The beauty of nature predominates perhaps but man's imitations are not bad either."

"Some standard values that I have basically lived by throughout my life are that I have always believed in honesty and advocated truthfulness. I cherish my family with all my heart. I gave of myself to everyone in the family. The satisfaction and gratification that I received in return is in the accomplishments of my children. No father could be as proud to say "that's my daughter!" Throughout your lifetime so far, you have more than exceeded my greatest expectations."

"I leave the wish that my children have decency, sympathy, empathy, a sense of justice, respect for nature, outrage at man's inhumanity to man, assurance of the equality of all people, strength to oppose tyranny, belief that every life is invaluable, insight that those more blessed will share, tolerance for all, contentment in their being, joy in life and pride in each other and family."

"More than material possessions, I hope I will have left each of you: an optimistic spirit; fervor and enthusiasm for life; sensitivity to nature and esthetics; closeness and regard for one another; a sense of responsibility and concern for others; and a sense of worthwhileness about your selves. I wish that your life may be as good and satisfying as mine has been, and thank each of you for having contributed to it."

"Don't mourn for me. I have enjoyed my life. Carry on from here using the many blessings you have with wisdom and consecration to your family and mankind. Remember me affectionately as your father."

Your written words have absolute power because they have the power to affect others' emotions. Legacy letters can make your family and special people laugh hysterically, cry tears of joy or sadness, understand you and themselves better, or become thoughtful and turn their lives around.

Writing to others so intimately makes them feel important, loved and connected. It is imperative that you share your life and heartfelt message in such a way that you allow others to establish their own identity, yet be reminded that they are a part of you and those who came before. It is your duty to lovingly guide them and ensure that they develop a healthy sense of self. The carefully chosen words voiced in your letter can give loved ones a strong positive voice inside themselves, which will affect the choices they make. Additionally, make sure they know that they have choices. You can affect lives and future generations through one single legacy letter.

Preserving Your Legacy Letter

Once you have your draft finished, you might choose to have it typed up, word processed, printed, illustrated with pictures and nicely covered or bound. Remember, there is nothing like reading a long-hand letter in which someone actually took the time and effort to sit and write. If your penmanship is not the best, don't worry, as long as it is legible it won't matter to your loved ones. It's the message behind the words that count. Additionally, in this digital age, many read their legacy letter aloud and have it videotaped or recorded on a DVD compact disc. Cherished recordings can be prepared with home equipment or in a professional setting. Like with your trust, will and other documents, make sure you tell your heirs about your handwritten and typed legacy letters, CD, tapes or recordings and that they know where to find them.

Conveying Your Legacy Letter

The right time to convey the legacy letter/ethical will is your decision as the writer. Some choose to share it as soon as they finish writing it. A family gathering or reunion is a good time to present your letter to your family and friends while you are still alive. A legacy letter certainly can help clarify and communicating your feelings, exchange stories and laughter, provide insights into the writer's intellectual and emotional life and start healing wounds. Your letter enables greater empathy, understanding and harmony among those who read it. Many people make update revisions of this spiritual legacy letter and attach it to their trust and will materials. Some do both the early letter reading and a second caring message given after their death.

Make writing the legacy letter part of your 'bucket list' so there are no regrets or things left undone or unsaid. In my law practice, I have seen those receiving legacy letters cry and press them to their hearts in gratitude for a parting gift precious above all others.

For example, one client wrote, "About a month before he died, my dad gave me two handwritten pages in which he spoke about the importance of being honest, getting a good education, helping people in need, and always remaining loyal to family. That letter, his ethical will, meant more to me than any material possession he could have bequeathed."

John Donne, the poet, says that letters mingle souls. Beyond all your material wealth and possessions, your legacy letter may be the most valuable gift you could ever leave. A personal letter is one way of passing the torch, assuring that your history, wisdom, love and gratitude will live on forever. Only you have the power to bestow such a blessing on your loved ones and family that will last for generations to come.

> In life we need to be a little more like the farmer who puts back into the soil what he takes out.
> - Paul Newman

Chapter Twenty-Nine

LIFE ADJUSTMENTS - PROTOCOL

Dealing with the practical day-to-day problems of life after the loss of your loved one brings up numerous bereavement questions. Not only do you have to handle the physical, psychological and social responses to your loss, you also have to adjust to a drastically different new life. Learning how to honor and cherish a memory without letting it control you is a vital part of the grieving path. This section deals with some practical common-sense life adjustment problems you might be facing during times of mourning and includes insights and solutions to help work through them.

> Don't search for all the answers, which could not be given to you now because you would not be able to live them. The point is to live everything. Live the questions now. Perhaps then, someday far in the future, you will gradually, without even noticing it, live your way into the answers.
> - Rainer Maria Rilke

Thank You Notes

You should acknowledge all sympathy cards, letters, gift baskets, floral remembrances, checks, gift cards, assistance by funeral, clerics and participants, and donations to charitable or religious organizations in a short personally handwritten note. Even in these days of emails, Twitter, Facebook, commercial cards and countless types of telephones, old-fashioned etiquette dictates that you need to take the time and make the energy to respond appropriately.

An immediate expression of gratitude or telephone call might be sufficient to thank those who helped you with chores, brought food to the reception or house, or sent signed sympathy cards without written notes. Write to everyone who took the time and trouble to remember you and your family, write to you, made donations or supported you in your time of mourning.

Whatever the manner used to pay respect to your late husband, it deserves notice and an appreciative response from you. Those caring efforts and sympathy expressions are comforting and often treasured over time. Social etiquette suggests that you write thank you notes within the first month. Since you probably have no head or heart for correspondence, your thank you note can be as simple as "My family and I want to thank you for …" and then put in an additional remark or two. It is okay to duplicate some of the wording of your messages, but try to write a few words of personalize genuine appreciation in each letter.

If you feel overwhelmed by the job of writing thank you notes, you could start by writing a few each day and enlist the assistance of relatives or close friends. It is good to have company and help sorting through the tributes and memories. Don't turn the task over completely to others, because answering other mourners yourself is one of the cathartic healing exercises you need on the road to acceptance and adjustment. Actually, you will probably find solace in the renewed or continued connection with those who knew and shared memories with you and your late spouse.

Do not procrastinate, let correspondence pile up or avoid the duty until it becomes unmanageable or another dreaded chore. Apply yourself to the obligation of writing individual answers to all the outpourings of sympathy sent to you and your family. You will be finished with this necessary part of the funeral customs before you know it and feel better for it.

Appropriate Designation – Mrs. or Ms?

People generally don't know whether to refer to you in your widowhood as 'Mrs.' or 'Ms.' It is up to you as to what designation or prefix you wish to use in front of your name. Don't let anyone tell you it is not proper to use 'Mrs.' because you are no longer a wife. Would they dare tell you not to use your married last name either? You have earned the right to continue using 'Mrs.' or addressed as 'Ms.' if you like. You do not automatically become a 'Ms.' when you become widowed. Request that people address you in whatever way makes you the most comfortable. Nowadays, some widows go without using a prefix title at all. The letters in front of your name do not define you. As your individual identity immerges in the new world without your deceased husband, you will make the changes in thought.

Wedding Rings

The day the wedding ring was slipped onto your left hand is memorable; the day you decide to remove your wedding ring is an equally memorable day. Some widows never remove their wedding s rings and others take them off immediately. There is no appropriate or proper time, nor any rituals of passage around the removal of your rings. Taking off the wedding rings is very personal and symbolic for most widows. It can signify that you are accepting the reality of the death, putting aside visible evidence of a no longer existent marital status, beginning a new phase of life, are moving on or a new mate is ready to put a different ring on that important finger.

Those widows who choose to continue wearing their rings explain that they do it because: it has been part of their hand for so many years, they feel too bare without it; fear that others would judge them disloyal to the spouse or removal would dishonor the marriage; it was a symbol of being married forever and sealed for eternity; worn as a status symbol earned by years of marriage; keeping a part of the loved one nearby; serves as a link to precious memories; it is the most valuable best piece of jewelry they own; fearing that taking off the rings would signal a readiness to date other men; it also serves as a deterrent against unwanted attention from other men; or just because they are listening to someone else's advice on right length of time about continuing to wear the wedding rings.

To wear or not wear, is the question only answered by you. There are valid individual reasons on both sides of the discussion. Whatever personally brings you happiness and comfort or closure, is what you should do about your wedding rings. There is no right, wrong or proper decision. As with many adaptive aspects of the healing process, you may choose to take gradual steps.

Some options regarding alternate uses of wedding rings:

- Wear your rings on the right hand
- Wear your rings and your husband's ring on a necklace chain
- Reset and refashion your rings into a new style ring
- Melt your bands together into a new piece of jewelry or art
- Save your rings for one of your children or future generations
- Gift your rings to the oldest or most interested child
- Sell your rings to fund a memorial project or charity
- Return rings that were heirlooms from your husband's family.

Chapter Thirty

LIFE ADJUSTMENTS – HOME LIFE

Organizing and Removing Your Husband's Personal Items

Loving memories are stored in the heart, not in the closet. There is no set way or timeline for removing your deceased husband's personal items and property. Living with constant physical and symbolic reminders of your loss can work both ways. You should not prematurely rid yourself of all your late spouse's possessions, nor should you retain them in an unhealthy museum-like manner. There are family members and widows who, right after the funeral, go through the house like a tornado sweeping away every vestige of the deceased husband. This sort of manic rash action by the widow or her family is often regretted later.

Out of sight is not out of mind. Some widows leave everything untouched for a long time, as if they are in denial and waiting for the loved one to walk back through the door. Similar to the wedding rings question, there is no right answer or timeline when it comes to parting with the personal belongings of your loved one. You have to decide when you can deal with this gut wrenching but therapeutic part of the letting go process.

Simple everyday items like an old sports jacket, well-read books, a favorite chair, hand-written notes by the telephone, fishing gear with tangled lines, the pick-up truck driven for years or a pair of reading glasses on the nightstand can inexplicably offer comfort, as well as anguish, to you. You may avoid looking into the closets and drawers or visit them often to hold and inhale the last bits of after-shave aroma. Many widows sleep in the husband's t-shirt or wear an old sweater as a good-bye step.

Going through your husband's closet, drawers, desk, workshop or other spaces is an emotional trip down memory lane. The possessions are a part of who he was. The removal of items requires willpower over intense emotions. Maybe you could recruit a relative, good friend or another widow to help you do the sorting, boxing and taking donations to others who are in need of various things. Having the company of an understanding person who will encourage you to share the stories, memories, thoughts and hug you when you break down makes it less overwhelming and less lonely. Perhaps your children, grandchildren or others would like to pick out certain items that they might want to keep as special mementos. Passing sentimental or valuable items on to family members and friends can make them easier to part with.

In order not to go crazy or give up too soon, the key to organizing and clearing out is taking baby-steps. Prepare storage containers like file folders, shoeboxes, plastic bins and file boxes with labels to separate and identify. Little-by-little you can empty out the drawers, closets and remove many of the past-life objects scattered around the house. Divide stuff. First, there are the obvious items to throw in the trash (socks with holes). Second, keep the best and use it yourself. Third, set aside the still-useful donations for charity; and then, put the most symbolic special items that might be kept indefinitely or as heirlooms, like jewelry, photographs, diplomas, awards, letters, books, creative arts and such into sturdy boxes, frames or albums.

You might make gifts of some precious or valuable items right away or designate in writing who will receive them at your demise. Except for a few pictures or objects to stay in your living space, labeled boxes of remaining treasures can be stored in the attic or garage. One widowed client completely reframed her favorite batch of pictures and placed them in new locations around the home in honor of the deceased. You can donate clothes, shoes and other related personal items to a favorite church or charity so others in need can benefit from them.

Valuable marketable things like tools, extra vehicles, serviceable medical or sports equipment, that you will probably never ever use, can be sold at a garage sale, consignment shop, at auction or on EBay, Craigslist or given away at Freecycle.com. You could donate items or sale proceeds in your loved one's name. Somehow, it is comforting to know that things are put to good use and appreciated.

Letting go of an item does not devalue it. Even without the object, you always have the memories. Your cherished memories are stored in your heart and mind, not around the house. Sorting through belongings that remind you of the deceased, special events, your youth or other memories can bring up powerful emotions. The key to disposing of your loved one's possessions is how you integrate objects into your ongoing life rather than leave them in suspended animation. Items can easily become an untouchable shrine that prolongs your grief and interferes with healthy functioning. Realistically assess the consequences of your reluctance to let go. Don't live in the static past. You will continue to be traumatized by your loss until you come to accept it.

It can be emotionally difficult and fearful to clean out closets, workshops and boxes. But ask yourself if you are only keeping something because you think you should. Be careful not to make any 'thing' more important than moving forward with your life or healing. Be realistic about what you will actually need and use in the present and future. If you cannot decide about an item, wait a bit. It is your privilege to decide and act accordingly. There is no timeframe but your own. The right time will come.

One widow, Barbara Brabec, writes, "I cried puddles of tears as I framed pictures and the many small personal items in a glass-encased memory box. I hung it on the wall above his chest of drawers and his urn where I could look at it whenever I needed to feel his presence in my life. A funny thing happened as a result. Each day as I studied the contents of this box and recalled new memories associated with each photo or nostalgic item in it, I cried again, sometimes a little, sometimes a lot. It wasn't long, however, before I began to ask myself if I was crying for all that I'd lost forever, or shedding tears of gratitude for having had a great marriage and the love of such a dear man for so many years. All this is to say that it's a mistake to avoid remembering the good times because it hurts to do so, for these are the very memories you can stuff into that big hole in your heart."

There are many appropriate ways to keep your loved one 'alive' for you in your everyday life. Don't remove all indications that this person ever existed. It is important to indicate to the world and to yourself that you have not forgotten those you loved and lost. You can honor the deceased, while at the same time recognizing outwardly that he is dead and you are continuing to live and grow. You might need to make a few small changes to your home so that not everything reminds you of the loss.

Clearing out the majority of the physical personal items, with the exception of particular photographs or mementos, lets you relate to the place your lost love held. A healthy transition process includes learning to go on without needing constant physical reminders of your loved one. Be patient with the process. Change takes time.

Simplifying Your Life

Simplify is defined as 'to reduce to basic elements or to diminish in scope and complexity.' Current materialistic cultures never have learned what enough is. It is time to free your self from the never-ending buying, doing and being cycles and become more frugal with your time, person and finances. The concept of voluntary simplicity leaves you with that which gives you value and peace of mind. It is a matter of saying yes to what you want in your life and saying no to the things and situations you don't need, use or want in your new life.

Within a few months after the death of your husband is a very good time to begin to simplify your overall life. By organizing, simplifying and cleaning up clutter, you are clearing a path to a happier future. Clutter cause stress, drains your energy and generates feelings of uneasiness. Even if your idea of housework is to sweep the room with a glance, it is in your power to stop the constant strain by giving your abode a good cleaning and eliminating all but the essentials. Avoid chaos and instead spend time with people you love and doing what is important to you.

You are probably stretched to the limit, overscheduled and overstressed by work, family, your new roles and life in general. This is the time to review your systems (for shopping, paperwork, errands, banking, housework, laundry, mail, etc.) and try to make them more simplified and efficient. For example, you can automate so you don't have to do things or remember to do things. Use timers for watering, lights and install bill-paying options with your bank. Do a bit of up front work and then forget about it.

Get better at saying no to taxing obligations, needy people and time demands that are not serving you. Some other things that drain your precious time and energy are the Internet, email, telephone calls, television, radio, and printed materials that dominate modern lives. When you limit your media and information consumption, you will be less stressed, generally happier and have free time for self-nurturing.

Is your home crammed full, especially your bedroom? When you clutter up your living, sleeping and working spaces, you clutter your mind and your heart. Making room for positive change and even for love requires sorting your mess and getting rid of what no longer represents or supports you.

Benefits of organizing, de-cluttering and simplifying your life:

• Willingness to let go of extraneous possessions and make changes is healthy progress and helps you make a fresh start.
• If you have a buying problem, you may have duplicates, items you have never used or things you didn't realize you had, which reminds you to use what you already have before making future purchases.
• As you clean and organize, you'll no longer have to search for through piles and piles of stuff; a great stress reliever and time saver
• You won't be so hesitant to socialize and have people over if your home and life are tidy and organized.
• You will probably find great joy in giving objects to family and friends, making donations to worthy causes or putting the money you make from the sales of your trinkets into the bank.

While the average person is not defined as a classic hoarder, most households have an over-abundance of stuff that has been unused and stored for too long. Are you weighed-down and burdened with trash and treasures? Much human suffering comes from clinging to possessions for the sake of attachment. Just how many vases, shoes, towels, hammers, books, clothes, socks, craft materials and holiday decorations do you really need?

Do you really want someone else digging through piles of your old messes and garbage after you are gone? How embarrassing would that be? Don't pollute their good memories of you with resentful thoughts of doing the overwhelming job of sorting your things and house cleaning. More than likely your heirs will just toss the whole mess out and overlook what you believed valuable or important. The gift of preparedness on your part will make the task others face much less onerous.

You probably have numerous trash barrels full of old receipts, duplicate paperwork, out of style and unusable clothing, chipped dishes, soiled linens, frayed mats, ugly art, broken appliances, rusty tools, long forgotten programs and unlabeled meaningless photographs. Every home has its share. One woman's trash is another woman's treasure, but usually it is just trash. Start by getting things in order in your home and personal spaces. An organized home environment is the foundation for a clear mind. Make your home a haven and place of sanctuary. Spring clean and dispose of or donate things that have been sitting around or in storage for ages. Take down the sign that says, "This house is protected by killer dust bunnies."

The symbolic act of cleaning and simplifying becomes the catalyst for other positive actions. Even positive change involves losses. Learning to let go of things, places, people, attitudes and old beliefs becomes easier and more comfortable with practice. Physically and mentally releasing are key steps in making a place for the all the exciting new things and experiences that are waiting for you.

Don't think of simplifying your life as a large, indefinable task or one huge challenge. Reframe your task into a series of smaller tasks and take one action at a time. Make some time every day, whether you allot 10 minutes or a few hours, and complete one small task on your list. You know you can handle one room a month or one chest of drawers a week. Small bites will make it feel that much more manageable and achievable.

As you sort through objects in your life, put the keepers in frames, photo albums with labels, and scrapbooks. Instead of watching television, you will find the cleaning out, sorting and organizing of your memories far more entertaining than any sit-com or movie. You will laugh and cry.

Use birthdays, holidays and special occasions to give meaningful items to family and friends. Enjoy their smiles, appreciation and pleasurable use of the early inheritances. If you have become the family Smithsonian repository, read as dumping ground, for everyone else's old boxes of stuff, it is time to put out the word that they need to come get their loot within three months or you will dispose of it or put it in storage with their name as the payee. It is time for them to assume their responsibility. Follow through with this mandate. You don't need to explain or apologize to anyone.

If your objects have any historical value or significance, you can sell, donate or loan them to a local historical society, museums or libraries. Then visit your donations while letting others benefit from insights into different eras. One of my clients set up a foundation to to renovate a historical home to for his family's antiques and feature his grandmother's collection of oil paintings. What a valuable gift to the city and honor to his ancestors, not to mention the tax break.

If you were packing for a cruise or trip, you would probably take only your finest things. Use that kind of selective thinking when simplifying your home and life. Keep your best quality things and use them. What are you saving the 'good' china, silver, crystal, perfume or towels for, if not for yourself, family and friends? When is the Queen of England going to come for tea? Treat yourself and loved ones like royalty. Appreciate and enjoy the best you have everyday.

When you finally lighten your load or pass the torch, you will experience a sense of relief and freedom to pursue hobbies, travel, share or make different living arrangements, entertain and be open to much more. Simplifying lets you shrug off unnecessary burdens and responsibilities.

The past and your accompanying memories have their place, but you need to live in the heart of this moment right here and right now. Eliminate, automate, delegate, donate or hire help. Live free and fully.

> Be content with what you have; rejoice in the way things are. When you realize there is nothing lacking, the whole world belongs to you.
>
> - Lao Tzu

Changing Living Arrangements

A common question among widows is whether they should downsize or make different living arrangements. Do a careful analysis before making a major move right away. Status quo really is okay.

However, if you want to make lifestyle or location changes, some of your options include:

1. Selling your residence. Consider the reasons and the pros and cons of selling. Think rationally about topics such as: financial investment and return in the current market; familiar area; supportive neighborhood friends; nearby facilities and activities; monetary factors; necessity for money to pay expenses and live on; size of home and yard to maintain; sentimental reasons; need for daily assistance; and your ability to find a suitable comfortable replacement. Consult with family friends and market experts before making such an irreversible decision. Changing housing arrangements may be too physically and emotionally demanding, since you are dealing with so much change the first year. Do take measures to make your dwelling more secure with new locks, lighting and security-medical systems.

2. Living with relatives or children. If you are physically, mentally and financially healthy, it is better to resist the urges of others to live with family members, as was tradition in the past. Comingling homes is difficult on all parties in today's mobile busy society. Often a move to multi-generational homes means relocating to distance places without the usual familiar environment, church, social circles, medical caregivers and other support systems. Moves can increase loneliness and confusion. Compromise with visits, but try to maintain your location, independence and growth through the grief to a new life of your own.

3. Downsizing to an apartment, condominium or senior living facility. Due to financial constraints, inability to keep up with housekeeping and landscape maintenance, fear of living alone in case of illness or injury, or wanting to be away from sad memories are the most common reasons widows give for downsizing to apartments, condos or care facilities. Sometimes it is possible to delegate or hire others to perform the necessary care services so that you can stay in your home if you wish.

It is important to maintain a comfortable familiar home setting like you had before so your energy is directed toward healing. Living arrangements in senior complexes with different levels of care have greatly improved over the years. Having a place to live that provides security, activities, meals, programs, on-site medical facilities, 24 hour assistance and other people with similar interests may be appropriate for your situation.

4. Shared housing. More popular than ever, for companionship and financial considerations, is the arrangement of having a friend or family member move into your home. There is no substitute for your lost spouse. Sharing a home will diminish your privacy, however it has been proven satisfactory to have a trusted, caring friend or relative share your home, especially if you have similar values, daily habits and interests. You must be aware that whatever environment, surroundings, housing and relationships you may select; nothing will be quite the same as when your spouse was alive.

Sometimes just a few small changes in your home make it so everything doesn't remind you of the loss of your loved one. Try rearranging or reupholstering some furniture, place living plants and flowers throughout the house, add new bath accessories or freshen up the paint colors. Any of those subtle adjustments will lighten your spirits. If you need help with rearranging, painting, repairs or landscaping, check with your family or neighbors to make good on their previous offers of help. Small changes can stop the automatic glance to the right expecting to see your spouse on the old green sofa in the den. You will feel better in your nest as you change or rearrange things to suit your own needs and preferences. Home surroundings, seen as your individual safe haven, are an important element of healthy resilience, adjustment and adaptation.

Regardless of what housing decision you make, be sure to consult with those who know and care about you as well as professional advisors. A word of precaution is not to make drastic change decisions immediately after the death of your loved one. Many decisions, often made during a confusing and emotional time, can have long-ranged financial consequences and unintended consequences. When things are a bit more settled, listen to your head, heart and intuition trinity to assure your overall well-being, happiness, stability and sense of security.

New Roles and Responsibilities

Through no action, fault or desire of your own, you find yourself a widow, facing life on your own. Your life partner, confidante, best friend, provider, co-parent, and more often than not, financial mainstay and decision maker are gone, leaving you to assume all the roles. Now that you are a widow, responsibilities and playing parts that culturally, traditionally or by mutual decision were reserved for your husband, are thrust upon you. That system worked for the both of you until the 'managing partner' was no longer there. Normal is forever changed. When your spouse dies you need to find a new balance and rhythm which includes role reorganization.

You will soon begin to recognize what the loss means to you in actual day-to-day life. You become your family's new chief cook, bottle washer and CEO, having to wear many hats and learn to be a jack-of-all-trades. Your late husband took on numerous roles and performed a variety of functions inherent in being a husband and father. As a widow, you and your family must compensate and reassign obligations to accommodate changes in the family dynamics. It can be a struggle to reestablish stability in the face of the death and subsequent imbalance.

Other types of losses have also occurred. There is an end of your co-partnering place in the family and interruption of a well-choreographed dance of family routine. All the newly unoccupied roles and undone functions are important secondary losses that affect you and your family significantly and they need to be mourned. Being forced to deal with an unbalanced personal, social and family situation compounds grief. You grieve for the loss of your husband's role as lover, handy man, accountant, cheerleader, confidante, dance partner, trip navigator and best friend. You have to forgo, adapt and often take on the unfamiliar roles yourself.

If you are a mother, you have to bond with your children where the other parent was the primary player. For example, you will need to understand and get involved in the son's sports events, hobbies, activities, video games and other interests. Children need to feel continuity in support and security from the remaining parent. There are lots of reassignments and compromises involved. All you can do, is all you can do.

All of a sudden, in forging your new role, you are doing all the parenting, taking care of the house, yard, cars, finances, repairs, health concerns, care of parents, and much more. There are chores you must now begin to do, decisions that must be made, paperwork that won't wait, and skills to learn in order to accomplish even simple tasks. For couples, often one partner would have been in charge of doing the driving, getting groceries, keeping track of doctor's appointments and medications, being the caregiver or just confronting life challenges together.

There are loss-oriented sorrows and stresses related directly to the death of your spouse. These include the lack of companionship and social interaction, ending of the physical relationship with your husband and disintegration of plans of the future together. Yearning for your lost love is common as you are weaned into solitude. It can be frightening to come home to an empty house. Grief support group frequently advise you not to let the house be completely quiet unless you are ready to deal with your feelings. Often widows will leave a radio or television playing.

Dealing with daily routines at home and social activities by your self are constant reminders of your gaping loss. Even if there are loving family members and supportive friends surrounding you, you learn the meaning of primarily being on your own. There are places or events you now have to attend alone. You will miss and ache for many of the things you used to have and do together. Don't be surprised when feelings of abandonment, anger and pain rear their heads as you try to cope.

During the process, you will learn to release the past, connect with the present and reorient to the future. Part of this growth is deciding how to redefine your new roles and what they mean to you. It may be time and a relief to let go of the things and habitual activities that you never liked much in the first place (attending his alma mater football games in the cold, meat and potatos barbeques, Tuesday bridge nights with the Drakes again, clogging classes). Instead this is your chance to take up different activities (destination travels, return to school or work, RV camping, tap dance classes, reading to children at the library, photography and the like) and build networks of additional or new friends (church groups, look up high school buddies or support group acquaintances). You are never too old to be what you might have been, according to George Eliot.

Over time and with practice, your confidence in making decisions, taking necessary actions or finding resources will grow in all arenas. Mistakes are inevitable, but they are each learning opportunities. You cannot fail; you can only learn and grow. Few things are irreversible or affect the whole for long. Honor your decisions, choices and mistakes. Embrace the menial tasks as well as the big-picture situations.

Think about what small steps you can take to move forward in your redefined roles. Before you can run, you need to stand up and walk. Once you get up and running, one of the most significant rewards is to be able to say to yourself, "I can do this. My new life works." You are stronger than you seem, braver than you believe and smarter than you think.

Where to Turn When You Need Help

Changes and challenges are always easier when you let other people assist. There is always someone or a team of folks who are ready, willing and able to help you, each in their own way. Build up your resource team of relatives, co-workers, clergy, church members, friends, neighbors, counselors, support groups, medical staff, spiritual mentors, handy men, nursing services, government agencies and anyone else that comes to mind.

Don't worry about being seen as helpless or weak. Instead, people will admire your courage under the circumstances and your determination to grow and learn. People are inherently good and want to be of assistance. Often your resource network folks are just waiting to be asked and for an opportunity to be of service. Don't you feel good when you are able to help someone else or guide her through a change? The key to getting others to assist you through this time lies in three little words: "I need help." It is a simple non-confrontational non-apologetic reminder of your legitimate need. Don't let false pride keeping you from asking for help in dealing with your newly assumed life roles and responsibilities.

You can learn to live a healthy functioning new life without your loved one. After working on your grief and making practical readjustments demanded by your new responsibilities and roles, carry on in a renewed and productive fashion.

Chapter Thirty-One

LIFE ADJUSTMENTS - FINANCE

The emotional effects of your husband's death can be debilitating, and the financial impact of the death can also be equally devastating. You may have lost your primary income provider, have limited assets or just not know anything about the status of your family money matters. The financial security of most widows is reduced by at least half. Regardless of your actual income or assets, financial uncertainty is the basis of many early fears and concerns. While you are attempting to get your own financial house in order and under control, you are also trying to settle the estate and deal with grief. You face many kinds of transactions, paperwork, making independent decisions and learning new skills in a relatively short time.

Finances

The largest obstacle to resolutions is often your state of mind about finances. About half of widowed women admit to fears about losing their money, being indigent and becoming bag ladies. Irrational fear that money could evaporate anchors in inexperience. Lack of knowledge is the biggest barrier to women getting involved in managing their money and any investments. Now is the time to develop the confidence and some basic knowledge you will need to make the decisions that will affect your financial well-being in the future. Women learning new ways and working with financial advisors feel more responsible, confident and optimistic.

Learning to understand and navigate the financial world toward stability will support emotional recovery. Taking care of financial matters can be one of the most challenging jobs during the estate settlement process. Although the business end of things seems inconsequential during the grieving period, it is important to get your financial matters organized and under control in order to secure a quality of life in the future. The sooner you get hold of your financial situation, the easier it will be for you psychologically and also prevent problems down the road.

Most widows are capable, intelligent and competent people. In their past, many also delegated the role of family financial manager to their husbands. It won't be too much of an adjustment if you were the person who handled the bills and were involved in financial investment decisions. However, if your loved one was the 'managing partner' who handled all of the money matters, you may feel overwhelmed at first sorting through the accounts, assets and finite resources. A first step may be to learn a bit more about budgeting, accounting, credit and investing basics.

Would you rather watch paint dry than deal with financial planners, budgeting or face credit card debts? There are basic understandable organization steps in addition to finding people who are capable of helping you with complex financial matters. You may want to consult a family member, trusted friend or financial planner to help you on a short and long-term basis. Keys in gaining control of your financial matters are to: simplify your organization and decision making process; identify the depth and magnitude of the situation and any problems; find a confidante and sounding board; and let others help or guide decisions for you.

Getting Your Financial House in Order - Primary Steps:

1. Gather all significant documents and records on expenses, income, bank accounts, investment accounts, tax returns and forthcoming benefits. You need to know exactly what assets you own, what debts

you owe, where accounts are located and how to access them. Refer to the checklist of important documents in chapter eighteen.

2. Pay documented regular expenses to keep the mortgage current and the utilities running. Perhaps you can start automated payments of reoccurring bills to simplify the money management process. Set up systems to keep up-to-date records and bookkeeping.

3. Develop a system of money management. Start with a list or spreadsheet of all policies, accounts with numbers, balances, debts, locations and access information. Organize, sort, file and label important documents. Keep your system simple and accessible.

4. Estimate how much money you need to sustain a comfortable lifestyle. Do not make any investments or spend lavishly until you get a firm grip on the current and future financial situations. Use a standard budget ledger to work out incomes and estimated expenses. With visual references and records, you will make informed choices about what you can live with or do without.

5. Make careful choices upon the receipt of large sum payments like insurance or benefit disbursements. It may be advisable to hold on to your house, but a strategic mistake is paying off the mortgage. It is better to have some liquidity than tie it all up in real estate, quick investments or annuities.

Park any financial windfalls in interest bearing money market accounts or rolling CDs until you have the large picture in focus and are more comfortable with the mechanics and terminology of investing. If you are the beneficiary on your late husband's 401(k) plan, you may be able to roll that into your own 401(k) for tax reasons. Ask the experts before you act.

6. Transfer ownership of various accounts, titles, credit cards, insurance and other legal or financial items to your own name or trust. Get professional advice from your attorney, tax advisor or financial consultant before making these changes. You will probably have to provide a copy of the death certificate and, possibly, a copy of your marriage license, a copy of the trust or some other documentation proving you are the executor of the estate. Be aware of tax consequences before you make changes in accounts or titles.

Saving for Emergencies

Statistics show that women control over fifty percent of the wealth in the United States. This can be misleading, because you will also find that women are most often the poorest segments of the population, especially women over 65 due to death of a spouse or divorce. No widow can afford to lose any of their capital, income or inheritance. Most women do not even have investment portfolios or savings. You may be in the majority of widows who face working longer/harder/smarter and learning how to live frugally. Don't think of frugal as doing without. You can live well on lots less cash. Often the best memories and bonding experiences come from the simplest times.

Are you between a rock and a hard place with little or no insurance money, too young for Social Security, can't find a decent paying job, or face age and training discrimination? If you are having difficulties providing the most basic housing, food, utilities, or telephone services for yourself or your family, it is advisable to immediately seek assistance from social, government, religious, family, friends and community practical support groups and systems.

No matter what your financial situation, move forward with the big long-term picture, use common sense and spend your money wisely. Federal Reserve reports that forty percent (40%) of people spend more than they earn. Widows, especially young ones, admit that they continue to spend at the same rate as when their spouse was alive so they could pretend he was still around, even though they could not afford it. This cycle of buying material goods for a temporary jolt of joy does not last and only multiplies the stress of being strapped financially or in debt.

This is not the time to spend lavishly. Don't rush out and buy a new BMW, but do visit your local beauty salon for a bit of pampering, have your family over for a special dinner each month or take a long-dreamed-of trip. Be done with financial folly. After what you have been through, you deserve to be on the right track with finances and spending and stay there.

Saving for a rainy day is very important. Regularly putting aside a small amount adds up quickly. You are well aware of how unforeseen situations invariably come up in life. The car transmission goes out, someone needs immediate medical care, a windstorm damages the house, your computer crashes or there were debts that you didn't know existed before your spouse's death. When such possible financial setbacks occur, your savings, frugal lifestyle and being a wise consumer will buffer the impact an emergency can have on your quality of life. It is easier to focus on your healing process when you aren't being distracted by financial problems and worries.

Financial Planners and Counselors

Whether you inherit inadequate or abundant funds, do not rush into financial, investment or insurance changes. At first, take time to assess your situation without becoming consumed or overwhelmed by financial concerns and strategies. You should consider hiring a financial advisor if you are not familiar with or do not have the time for taking care of any of your money or investments. It is advisable to keep your own financial portfolio if you can.

For many widows, money matters are the last bastion of privacy, with all sorts of trust and control issues involved. Even if your children are financially responsible, their objectivity may be slanted or their positions on your investments may be too conservative or too aggressive for your circumstances. After you engage a planning advisor, you may wish to ask the children to go with you if they have questions. A professional investment counselor can assist you on insurance, investment portfolios that match your needs, asset allocation, and other planning tools.

Hiring the right financial advisor to assist you with investments, insurance products, and retirement accounts is rather like the princess in search of true love. You may have to kiss many frogs before you find Prince Charming. To minimize your amphibious encounters, look for financial experts who have the training, testing, experiences, continuing education and certification.

Look for professional designations such as Registered Investment Advisor (RIA), Certified Financial Planner (CFP), Chartered Retirement Planning Counselor (CRPC) or Certified Financial Analyst (CFA). You can find out about fee-based financial advisors at such sites as the National Association of Personal Financial Advisors (NARFA.org). NARFA and others recommend reputable salaried or fee-based advisors rather than the commission-based brokers. USAA and other financial institutes have Certified Financial Planner practitioners ready to help widows. Some key questions to ask your financial advisor, include: Is your money earned by commissions or fees? Have you ever had complaints filed against you?

When you decide on an investment counselor that you know and trust, here are four preliminary suggestions to consider for improving your investment and retirement accounts:

1. Review investments to determine if they still meet your current objectives of growth, income and security. Could assets be reinvested to provide you adequate income and serve as a hedge against inflation? Get help developing a financial plan that allows you to live comfortably, without worrying about your money running out.

2. Consolidate your accounts to a single financial service provider. It not only saves on fees, but also gives you a consolidated view of your account for management and correspondences. Consult with your financial advisor first to see if there is any tax consequence associated with the transfer of assets.

3. Consider rebalancing your investment portfolio allocations to help you reach your goals. Let's say you set up your investments with 70 percent in stocks and 30 percent in bonds. If bonds have been more secure and outperformed stocks, you can discuss this change with your advisors and request that they shift your portfolio to different percentages. Diversity is usually wise. Again, check beforehand for possible tax consequences.

4. Periodically review your beneficiaries on your insurance and retirement accounts including IRAs, 401(k), 403(b) and annuities. The specific named beneficiaries will inherit your accounts after you die, so be sure they reflect your situation, status, wishes and that contact information is current.

Trust yourself in managing the investment portfolio. The myths about women not being good at finance have been busted. According to *Wall Street Journal*, women are naturally more cautious, take a more conservative approach and consistently bring in better returns. Men aren't as concerned about risk and often trade without fully researching the issue. Overall, women's risk-adjusted investment results make them better investors than men. Use your innate gender skills and complementary certified financial agent help to provide for your current and future monetary security. Study books like the *Wall Street Journal's Guide to Understanding Money and Investing* so that you will be an informed manager of your finances.

Beware of Predators

Get referrals or work with someone you know and trust because there are plenty of disreputable sales and advisory people who take advantage of grieving widows or those who are not knowledgeable in financial matters. Widows often become victims of unethical unprofessional predators. In the early stages of your new status, you may be stuck in an emotional state of paralysis and unable to focus on the multitude of decisions challenging you. While in a vulnerable state, you may tend to be overly trusting and follow the lead of whoever is being nice to you. Remember that charm is not character and that charisma has no market value. Always question the sales person and the product or services they are trying to sell you.

In one case, a widowed client uninvolved in her late husband's financial matters told the broker to go ahead and do what he was doing for them before. The unscrupulous broker immediately flipped the account to the highest commission schedule that the firm allowed, invested in high-risk areas and started churning the account. The portfolio ended up being totally unsuitable for her situation and current cash flow needs, plus it costs her substantial amounts in market losses and fees.

EXCLUSIVE READER ONLINE RESOURCES

A password hidden in *Widow's Key* allows you to receive extra reader resources. You can now get access to items, checklists and other valuable resources not in the book.

Here are a few related topics available to *Widow's Key* readers only:

* How to Find an Attorney or Financial Planner

* Easy to Make Holiday and Special Occasion Recipes

* Widows Small Group Tours to Sacred Places

Visit the *Widow's Key* companion website at www.widowskey.com. Follow the simple instructions to find your password in the book and get your extra reader-only information.

Chapter Thirty-Two

LIFE ADJUSTMENTS – SOCIAL ACTIVITY/RELATIONSHIPS

"My husband was my constant companion and we did everything together, not really needing other people. Now I need to relearn social skills and interacting with others all over again," bemoan widows. *Living with Loss: Meditations for Grieving Widows* by Ellen Sue Stern, encourages using the loss and resulting changes in your life as a meaningful catalyst.

A deeper appreciation for the blessings you still have in your life: health, family, friends, employment is often a part of those changes and growth. Be fully present in the lives of others and always end any conversation with your loved ones by saying, 'I love you'. Every experience, even the death of your husband will make you stronger and more appreciative of life itself.

> The best way to move on from a loss is to live the best life we're capable of, a life in which our essential gifts are maximized, a life full of joy, gratitude and grace. In living your best life, you honor not only the process of grieving and growth it inspires, but also the one you've lost.
>
> - Ellen Sue Stern

"I know that my husband would want me and the kids to live and be happy. I try very hard to keep that in my head when I'm doing things," said one of my widowed clients. As you pick up the pieces, your emotional and social life poses one of the greatest challenges. Perhaps a great void created when your husband died because he was your best friend, confidant, provider of emotional support, connection to mutual friends and events, and the go-to decision maker for major situations or your social lifeline.

There are constructive and sensitive ways to rebuild your social life while honoring your loved one's memory. There is no reason to feel guilty about wanting to be around other people after your loss. Right now socializing does not mean dating; that topic is covered in chapter thirty-three.

Make time for talking to your children, family and friends. Socializing with relatives, friends and colleagues has a significant impact on your happiness and health. A good friend's attentive ear and open mind can provide priceless insights. After a long confidential talk, you'll find yourself refreshed and infected with the trust only a strong bond of friendship can provide. Positive, honest and supportive people can act as incubators for healing and happiness. The quality of your relationships makes seemingly unbearable situations bearable. You feel best when you stay in connection and in harmony with others. Companionship is your treasured reward.

Don't isolate yourself at home and distance yourself from family and friends. Three weeks have passed; or is it four? As you sit at the kitchen table over another cup of coffee with memories of him continuously looping through your brain, you need to get up and get out of the house. You need to do something active and positive for and by yourself. If the number of social exchanges and outings has decreased dramatically, try setting up at least one get together or activity a week to keep you socially interactive.

If you just aren't quite able to face going out and socializing in groups, call some of those people who offered to help and ask them to come over and assist you with a specific task. Invite a friend over for a simple meal, cup of coffee, to watch a movie, for a walk, ride to services together or just chat. People are waiting for an opportunity to be supportive, but mistakenly 'don't want to bother you', so you sometimes have to be the one to reach out and suggest a meet up. Sometimes it isn't the partner or friends you are missing, but the activities and hobbies you shared. Take yourself out for a nice dinner or to a movie. Don't hold back or isolate yourself.

If you do or do not feel quite like going back to all the normal routines at work, school or social circles, listen to your own mind and body needs, not the expectations or demands of others. If you are not up to it, do not let anyone tell you that you must get back to work or other activities. Likewise, do not let anyone tell you that you should not go back to your daily social and business routine, if you feel it is important to return. Structure and happiness at work can satisfy your need for order and purpose during your transition. People at your workplace will probably offer condolences, but they secretly hope you will pick up the pace and get back to business as usual. Assure your supervisors that you may need time to regain your efficiency, but that your performance will be returning to normal.

Everyone's circumstances, grief and resiliency are different. Working or socializing to run away or distract your self from grief will not be the cure or magic potion. There is no avoiding or rushing grief. Remember that your work or life will never be the same way it was before your loss. You don't need to be self-sacrificing or heroic. You are a heroine by merely living day-to-day with what life has thrown at you and dealing with all the changes. Be gentle with yourself and others. Stop the disapproving inner dialogue and treat others with patience and caring, just as you expect to be treated.

> Nobody gets to live life backward. Look ahead; that is where your future lies.
>
> - Ann Landers

Holidays and Traditions

Holidays and special dates are, without a doubt, some of the most difficult times for you as a widow to endure. For many, not just widows, holidays are a time of isolation and depression. The associated sadness is referred to as "holiday blues." During the holidays, everyone wants you join in the family gatherings, festivities of the season and at least act happy. The added stress and pressure of holidays and traditions can make your grieving process more difficult. Be prepared for birthdays, anniversaries, and other special occasions to trigger an emotional time for you. You will be reminded of the painful absence of your loved one who is not there to celebrate with you.

Don't try to run from your grief; it will only follow you wherever you go. You may feel sadness, intensified loss, lonely, fear, dread, anger or the desire to avoid it all curled up alone with containers of your favorite ice cream. My clients and I call this 'ice cream therapy, the five flavors of healing.'

During the holiday season, everyone is telling you to be happy, grateful and count your blessings. Those emotions are all valid, but you may still be feeling sorrow and loss. There are constructive ways to express some of your sadness other than telling the laughing Santa to "stuff a sock in it." Helping others helps. Hiding from a holiday never makes it go away. Being all alone, dwelling on the fact that your mate is not there, can makes things worse. Consider some of the following suggestions that might help get you up, out and through special dates and the holiday seasons.

Knowing that a difficult date to reckon with is approaching, you should plan accordingly. Let people know that you will probably need their extra support during that time. Don't hesitate to ask for what you need or want from others during the holidays. Assure them that you don't want them to shy away from talking about the deceased or sharing remembrances of special times together. His absence is on everyone's mind anyway. Warn them that you may need a shoulder to lean on, a friend to listen to your stories, someone to laugh and cry with or just company on those days.

Together or alone, you will be able to muddle through holiday or anniversary dates much better than you think you will. Usually the anxious anticipation of pain, especially between November and January 2nd, always looms larger and is worst than the actual events or days. Having the special dates spread throughout a calendar year helps to deal with the loss one-by-one.

Observe the holiday seasons, but perhaps in a more subdued manner with gaiety a bit curtailed. Do not ignore special occasions entirely, especially if you have children. They need to know that even without your loved one around, life continues and that you will still commemorate events in their lives. Depending on how recently the death occurred, you can cut back or drop some of the responsibilities and traditions, but be careful not to throw out all your rituals and observances. Subconsciously, the structuring and participating in ritual activities around special dates is actually an effective method of facing and adjusting to your loss.

Valentine's Day, when the whole world focuses on love and romance, may amplify your solo status. Universally one of the most dreaded holidays, you can turn it into one of love for your fellow humans. This is a time to step outside your individual pangs of grief or loneliness and be of loving service to others. Call or send Valentine Day cards to others who may be alone. Help your grandchildren bake a heart cake for their parents. Babysit for a friend so she can go out. If you will fall apart like a jilted sixteen-year-old if you don't get the usual Valentine Day present, be a little self-indulgent and buy yourself therapeutic flowers, earrings or a fancy box of candy.

> The truth is where the truth is, and it's sometimes in the candy store.
>
> - Bob Dylan

Non-profit and church organizations seem to have many volunteers around Thanksgiving and Christmas, but this could be the time to help. Consider taking plates of decorated cupcakes or cookies to senior centers, hospitals or women's shelters. To many forgotten people, a simple gesture can bring renewed hope and warmth to their hearts. Generally, getting outside of yourself and volunteering your talents or time to be of service to others just makes you feel better. It also reminds you to be grateful for all the love you've had and the blessings that still exist in your own life.

If this is the first Thanksgiving without your husband, you may think that you have nothing to be thankful for or that the motions of celebrating are pointless. A few ideas for getting through Thanksgiving include:

- Letting someone else cook this year or go to a restaurant
- Donate food to a needy family for Thanksgiving in his name
- Make your husband's favorite dish or dessert
- Propose a toast to your spouse, "To Stu who is with us in spirit."
- Light remembrance candles at dinner
- Share and have others share recollections about the lost loved one.
- Gathering and sharing positive memories of the past and plans for the future will be healing for everyone. Don't lose the opportunity to remember or leave words unspoken.
- Honor, love and be grateful for those present and remember those gone who will never be forgotten. There are many who miss him.

Christmas, New Years Eve, Hanukkah, Kwanzaa and other various traditional family gatherings can be a double-edged sword. You want to honor the deceased and carry on past traditions, but you also have a hard time handling the season without your mate. The moment when you feel joyful, suddenly an equal sadness for what your deceased partner is missing strikes you. This dual reality is normal and is a sign of progress, not regression. It is okay to smile and laugh. You are not being disloyal to your deceased husband by moving on with life, enjoying the company of family and friends or observing holidays like when together.

You can make your own decisions regarding any special days or holidays. Demands, pressures and unrealistic expectations fill most holidays. After the death of your husband, you should think primarily of your own needs, limits and comfort level. Give yourself the gift of simplicity. It is acceptable to say "No, thank you" and not have to explain anything to anyone. You do not have to accommodate or placate anyone.

Take control of the situation. Give yourself the option of not hosting the family feast or attending holiday events or parties. Depending on your physical and mental health, you may want to cut back on the decorating, shopping, wrapping, cooking, home-made gifts, cleaning, entertaining and other activities that filled previous holiday seasons. Do not over-commit or overwhelm yourself. Take it easy this turn around. Give yourself permission to let others help you for a change. Maybe this is the time to pass the 'making it all happen' torch to another generation. You can always resume or pick up the rituals or traditions at a later date.

Try marking the holidays in new and different ways. Remain flexible and willing to try alternative plans and traditions. Some holiday observations may have to be eliminated, shared or reassigned. Go to someone else's home for Christmas or Hanukkah meals and celebrations. Whip up your or your late husband's famous recipe as a contribution to the gathering. Perhaps you might alter a few details, such as opening the gifts on Christmas Eve instead of Christmas morning. Take time to do something symbolic like lighting a candle at the meal, having a special song sung at church services in honor of the deceased or making a charitable donation.

> There is no monster like silence. It grows faster than children, filling first a heart, then a house, then history.
> - Roger Rosenblatt

Most of all, don't allow yourself to be totally isolated and besotted in your deepest grief over the holidays. It is a curse to be walled in by silence. Tear down those walls and get yourself out of the house and regular routines. You don't have to entertain, attend parties or do all the usual activities.

Treat yourself to some special holiday baked goodies, indulge in a spa treatment, take a walking or driving tour of the Christmas lights, attend the holiday music programs at your church or local cultural center and sing along, visit the mall and watch the others rush about doing their last minute shopping or children at the ice skating rink, hike along a snow cover forest trail, or just enjoy the glory and beauty of the season. You can do any of these or more things alone or invite a friend to accompany you.

Buy your own special-occasion gift, as your loved one would have done. Some widows who don't want to be around home with all the memories, obligations or responsibilities, will take advantage of the wonderful deals and take a holiday travel break. Consider an all inclusive cruise or travel to a sunny warm beach destination or go play in the snow for a Currier and Ives White Christmas. Travel and adventure are one of the greatest gifts you can give yourself. What will it take to make the holiday meaningful and more comfortable for you?

If you are motivated and have the strength to continue some of your past traditional rituals, do so. Just as you can say no, you can say yes. It is good therapy to do whatever you want to do for the day. Holidays become more bearable, especially when you consider the needs of others. Volunteer for organizations who are trying to feed, clothe and shelter those in need. Visits to hospitals, nursing homes, or shut-ins will brighten their spirits as well as yours. Joy is contagious. Find a tree of giving that provides anonymous ways of adopting a child or family for the holidays. Food and gift boxes are caring wonderful ways to help an unfortunate family celebrate the season.

During the holidays, you need people around you who care and understand how difficult it may be to face the holidays alone. Friends, relatives and co-workers can be called on to relieve your loneliness during the holidays. Let them know that you would like them to help you by:

- Acknowledging your grief during stressful times
- Being kind and thoughtful to you. No one needs kindness and thoughtfulness more than you do
- Extending invitations to regular holiday activities

• Not pushing you into joining in festivities if you don't feel ready
• Mentioning your late husband by name when relating sympathies and stories
• Recalling happier holiday memories that included the deceased
• Giving a plant, not a holiday one, but flowering, living budding plants or spring bulbs, so that you have something to look forward to after the holidays
• Sending someone over to help you with home winterization, shoveling or holiday decorations
• Inviting you join them for coffee or a meal or bringing you some special foods or treats
• Asking if you would like them to shop with you or for you
• Getting together for an old-fashioned afternoon of baking treats, making holiday candies or wrapping gifts
• Giving you a hand-made coupon book redeemable for yardwork, household chores or fun outings
• Preparing a list of contacts and phone numbers for people such as carpenter, electrician, plumber, painter, landscaper, car mechanic to help with your odd jobs
• Offering to be a travel companion if you want to get away
• Helping you find a widow's support group and perhaps accompanying you to the first few meetings
• Putting their telephone number on a card and encourage you to call night or day as needed

You can acknowledge and celebrate significant days for as long as you may wish. The mind's calendar remembers your deceased husband anyway. Holidays, birthdays, anniversaries and special occasions no longer need to be dreaded, avoided, forgotten or endured alone. It is normal to feel some distress about the holidays and other significant dates. Countless other widows have experienced what you feel right now. They will tell you that when you survive those milestone dates for the first time, the subsequent times though them were less traumatic. After a while, you will begin to focus more on where you are going rather than where you have been.

Travel

While the only trips you seem to manage soon after the death of your husband are to the supermarket, church, concert in the city or dinner with family and friends, you need to get out. Soon folks may extend invitations or encourage you to start thinking of going somewhere more distant and out of your area filled with too many poignant memories. A good beginning might be travel to visit relatives or friends around the state or across the country. It is taking the journey that matters, not the destination.

Travel teaches us how to see. - African proverb

Depending on your level of adventure and finances, you could: Set sail on a Caribbean cruise, join a group excursion to see butterflies in Mexico, become a pilgrim on the Camino de Santiago across Spain; visit famous gardens of England, swim with pink dolphins of Brazil, walk along the Great Wall of China, take that African safari you always dreamed about, photograph Machu Picchu, see the brilliant fall foliage in Canada, tour Europe with your granddaughter, take an educational Elderhostel program, volunteer at a widows hostel in India, attend a cooking school in Italy, sip cocktails on a Rio beach, hike through Turkey's archaeological ruins, help build a school for Mayan children in Guatemala, or all of the above.

Today, magazines, books, movies and other media inspire women to travel. A very popular book and movie, *Eat Pray Love* by Elizabeth Gilbert, describes a divorcee who takes a year off to travel to Italy, India and Indonesia for a healing self-discovery journey. Other insightful funny accounts of women traveling alone have been written by Frances Mayes' *Under the Tuscan*

Sun, Susan Orlean's *My Kind of Place: Travel Stories from a Woman Who's Been Everywhere* and additional brave globetrotting ladies. Rita Golden Gelman, author of *Tales of a Female Nomad,* says, "I move throughout the world without a plan, guided by instinct, connecting through trust, and constantly watching for serendipitous opportunities." You'll be touched, delighted, encouraged and inspired by their stories.

Start your own folder or visualization board with colorful pictures and articles of your dream travel locations to get the imagination sizzling. Buy or subscribe to travel magazines to explore the possibilities. Although you may need to take a conservative approach with your investments, it is possible to make your lifestyle adventurous. Your unwillingness to push the boundaries can limit you more than your budget.

If your family or friends are not able to accompany you, you should not be afraid or hesitate to travel alone. If your join a tour, take a cruise or RV around the country, you will make instant friends with similar interests, have tons of fun and think "Wow! Look at me!" Your friends and family will be so proud (and envious) of you for living boldly with such a sense of adventure and zest for life. Be careful, travel, new friends and experiences can become a habit.

> If a woman be gracious and courteous to strangers, it shows
> she is a citizen of the world, and that her heart is no island
> cut off from other lands, but a continent that joins to them.
> - Francis Bacon

Numerous adventure and expedition clubs and groups such as National Geographic, Sierra Club, GAP Adventures, Smithsonian Institution, Journey Women, Elderhostel, Gutsy Women Travel and others have prearranged relaxing or wanderlust-satisfying journeys. When traveling alone, at first many prefer to have professionals organize their travel plans and make advance arrangements. There are positives and negatives to tour groups, but it is preferable to not venturing out at all.

There are many delightful travel spots and itineraries to suit every desire, taste, budget and physical ability. Do you prefer: to stay at one destination, cover many cities/countries, outdoor excursions, water sports, shopping, museums, golf, fishing, skiing, nightlife or relaxing beach days? Do you want emphasis on historical, religious, art, nature, culture, volunteering, education, music, sports, activities or parties? How long do you want to travel? There is a difference between traveling to see the country, to see the people or immersing yourself in the country's culture.

Nothing in life is to be feared; It is only to be understood. The physical act of travel can be a slow unfolding of discovery, like the gentle spiritual path, or it can be a sudden realization, full of excitement and learning. Travel, learning about, volunteering or serving other people is a powerful healing medicine. The whole world is yours to explore.

Magazines, web sites, newspapers, travel agents, blogs and books are full of travel advice and advertisements for trips of all kinds. Travel agencies, airlines or cruise companies, discount outlets and online sites offer vacation specials and discounts. Some trips can seem like the ark, priced per person based on double occupancy. Always ask if the cruise or tour or accommodations charge the dreaded single supplements or penalty for being a solo traveler. Inquire about roommate matching services and sharing a room with another single female traveler.

Take advantage of off-season bargains or last minute travel opportunities. The *Widow's Key* site (www.widowskey.com) features customized group trips to exciting unique locations with a personal guide. Additionally, you can use your AARP, AAA, Vacations to Go, SERVAS, Educators Bed & Breakfasts, hotel, cruise, airline and other discounts on rooms, transportation, car rental, optional sidetrips and things that make your trip complete.

If you are going to travel, you need to get your passport. A passport is a document, issued by a national government, which certifies the identity and nationality of its holder. The elements of identity are name, date of birth, sex, and place of birth. Of itself, a passport does not entitle the passport holder entry into another country, nor to consular protection while abroad or any other privileges. It does entitle the passport holder to return to the country that issued the passport. If you plan to make international trips, even on cruise ships, a passport is required.

You can get the form (DS-82) and apply for a passport at many post offices around the country. Some offices may require an appointment to take your application, so call first. The cost of a passport is $25 acceptance fee and $75 application fee for a total of $100. To renew a passport it cost $75. Some of the offices will also take your passport photograph for an additional $15. If you are in a hurry, you may request the Department of State's Expedited Passport Processing Service for an additional $60.

It has been said that "One who does not travel is like someone who only read one page of a book." However, there are those souls who have no interest in other locations, traditions or cultures. Some just naturally have lower risk and curiosity levels and are quite content to stay close to home and family. Just don't become house bound, closed up or try to get through your grief alone.

There is more than one way to do life. In travel, the world seems to expand and so do you. Through travels you will regain faith in yourself and faith in the basic humanity and goodness that is common to everyone in the world. So if you are up for it, you go girlfriend!

> A journey always begins in a place called here. Pack your bags and imagine your journey. Unpack your bags and imagine that your journey is done. If you're afraid of a journey, don't buy shoes.
>
> - Mark Strand

Chapter Thirty-Three

LIFE ADJUSTMENTS - DATING AND REMARRIAGE

Questions of dating and remarriage are a common topic among widows. Compared to women of like ages, the majority of older men are married or remarried. U.S. Census figures show that there are only about a third as many widowers as widows each year. Male widowers remarry much sooner after the death of their wives, customarily within a year of the loss.

In social scientists' studies of surviving spouses, the loss of a mate is a great deal harder psychologically and physically on men than women. Widowers' mortality rates were almost sixty-one percent (61%) higher than the rates for married men. The good news is that committed relationships and remarriage by widowers dramatically lowered their mortality rates by at least 70% over those who did not remarry. Therefore, the percentage of widowers who re-couple is greater and their time single is much shorter.

The same physiologic and psychological differences that give females greater longevity also acts to make women more resistant to the stresses of widowhood. A study published in the *American Journal of Public Health*, says the death of a husband has almost no effect on women's mortality rates. Women may have more of a sense of survivability, have supportive circles of friends and are more adaptable. Widows generally remarry within five years or often not at all. An increasing number of widows say that they do not wish to remarry or take care of a man again. Some folks say, "Don't remarry unless you need a purse or a nurse." Additionally, Joseph Campbell wisely says that "marriage is a recognition of a spiritual identity."

Dating

Dating should be less about matching outward circumstances and more about meeting your inner necessity. It does not matter if you are an older widow or a young widow; there is always room for companionship, friendship, love and joy.

> Grief can take care of itself, but to get the full value of a joy
> you must have somebody to divide it with.
>
> — Mark Twain

There is no timeframe for when someone might be ready for new male companionship. The general traditional waiting period before dating falls somewhere around one year. You will have your own instincts about when it feels right or respectful. Starting to date or getting remarried before your deep grief work is complete, or because you are afraid to be alone, are never good reasons or foundations for future relationships. It is better to be single and happy than married to the wrong person and unhappy.

The idea of dating, marrying or having sex with someone other than your late husband, may make you quite uncomfortable, shy and insecure at first. You need to be in a phase of your grief recovery path where you are comfortable about resuming social interactions and intimate relations with men. Don't feel guilty, embarrassed, ashamed or worried about what other people will think if you are ready to move forward into the dating world.

Before you jump back into the dating pond, it is advisable to take the time to clarify your own thoughts, needs, goals and hopes with regard to any future partner. Any 'replacement' mentality is doomed to fail. All people want to be loved for their unique selves and not compared constantly to a former spouse or an idealized prior marriage. Trying to fill your gap of loneliness by getting involved with someone new right away may be a detrimental substitute to working through your grief. It results in double loss and double grieving if it does not work out.

It may sound trite, but you need to be happy with yourself first before you can be happy in any relationship. When you exude self-confidence, wholeness and happiness during your search for a new partner, you will be more satisfied with the results. If you come across as desperate, miserable and act like you need someone or something to make you happy or a whole person, you are going to chase away good prospects. Relationships don't define you. Your special personality, interests, attributes, spirituality and character define you. Try replacing widowhood with selfhood. The more you know yourself and love your life, the more people will be attracted to you and seek you out. Starting a new relationship that is healthy and joyful requires both individuals to be happy and complete.

Women in their 30s and 40s become widows everyday. It is likely they will eventually start dating and remarry. Finding love and romance can happen at any age, whether you are 45, 65 or even 95+. Middle-aged through late eighties dating is a wonderful time for exploration, freedom and happiness. So if you feel ready to start dating and give love a second chance, do it. Keep your hopes high and your expectations reasonable about finding 'the one' right away.

As you begin to date, if you know the connection or chemistry is not there, don't force it. Both you and your date will be better off for your honesty. The key is to continue to visualize the general sort of person you would like to find and remember that the person you want to build a new life with does exist. Don't let yourself get discouraged on the path to finding romance. Listen to your heart to decide when you are ready to step out into the dating world. As Dr. Wayne Dyer says, "Love cancels out fear, and fear cancels out love."

John Gray, Ph.D., relationship expert and author of *Men Are From Mars, Women Are From Venus*, says the most important thing people can do to find romance is create a series of positive dating experiences and have fun visiting. A date doesn't have to feel as uncomfortable as a job interview. For exciting dates, come prepared with interesting conversation starters and questions about the other person that flow effortlessly. Arriving with topics on your mind unique to each date increases your chances of really getting to know a potential partner. By asking specific questions about your date's interests, you show that you actually do want to get to know the person. Allow yourself to be present, open and caring. When you expect a good time with a wonderful person, that is usually what you get.

Some widows say they feel caught in the middle of two relationships. You don't want to feel like you are being unfaithful to your late husband's memory and on the other hand, you don't want to betray the new partner by still feeling love and holding that special place in your heart for your late husband. Dealing outright with mixed feelings of guilt and betrayal is crucial to forming a healthy new relationship. It is best to talk openly about this with a counselor, support group and the new love interest. Amazing what airing certain feelings can do to resolve and dissolve the concerns about them. Remember that your obligation in a relationship is to the new person you are dating. You will always have a place in your heart for your late husband, but you must also take care not to make comparisons, feel guilt or neglect your new relationship.

> When one door of happiness closes, another one opens. But often we look so long at the closed door that we do not see the one that has opened for us.
> - Helen Keller

Online Dating

If you have not met anyone to date through the normal channels of friends, church, interest groups, travel clubs or social gathering, take a proactive step and put yourself out in the world and cyberspace. Online dating is very common today, with millions of people looking for friendship, love, romance or companionship for activities or travel. In this computer age, one in five marriages started with Internet matches.

There are dozens of online match and dating services, several specifically for widows and widowers or seniors. It isn't just for the twenty year olds; all ages from 18 to 88 are found online chatting and meeting others twenty-four hours a day. Website dating service fees range from free to monthly paid membership subscriptions. Some popular sites include Match.com, EHarmony.com, SeniorPeopleMeet.com, and NewJourneyDating.com. Additionally, there are Widow Meet Up groups in over 100 U.S. cities.

Many widows would like to date someone who is a widower because they would know first hand their unique situation, offering support, company, patience and understanding. If nothing else, you will get in touch with some diverse and interesting people. In writing a profile and corresponding, you will discover a lot about yourself and others.

Do you believe in computer dating? Only if the computers really love each other.

- Groucho Marx

When you first sign on with an Internet dating service, you write up and post a profile and a picture. This assists the service with matching you with potential dates that have the same key indicator words or interests. Some tips on profile basics include:

- Be honest and truthful
- Do not disclose specifics like where you live, work or telephone
- Watch out for grammar and spelling mistakes
- Stay upbeat and away from too serious or gloomy topics
- Don't be too generic. For example, if you like water sports, be specific and share a short true story
- Note desired types and deal breakers (i.e. you want a certain religion, no smokers, within a certain geographic area, etc.)

• Post current pictures. Profiles with good photographs in different settings will get ten times the viewings
• Take time to fill out as much of the categories as possible. Like you, people want a good idea of who you are and dislike those writings that show no effort or use the phrase "Ask me later".
• You can always update and change your profile and pictures, so don't worry about what you offer the first time out.

Your contact information will remain anonymous. The only one who gets any more of your personal information are those you chose to give it to as you correspond. Putting together your profile is a great way of clarifying a lot about yourself in your own mind and your capabilities. It also gets you to think about what you want out of a new relationship and how much you have to offer. You will probably discover that you are a terrific person with a loyal heart, many talents, great personality and actually ready to meet new people and excited to move on with your life.

You can take your time browsing through profiles of potential matches and even check out the competition. If you find someone of interest or someone contacts you by email, you have the chance to get to know the person long before you meet him, if ever. It can be fun to correspond in a private non-threatening environment with whomever you choose. There is an online courtesy of responding to incoming messages politely, even if to quickly say you are not interested and wish him well in his search. If someone is overly disagreeable, gets aggressive or says things rude or crude, you can instantly block them and report them to the service.

If you use online dating sites, observe common sense privacy and security guidelines. Stay anonymous and vague about personal locations and details until you have corresponded with the other person for a while and perhaps even after you have met them in person. Don't trust anyone who rushes you to divulge information too soon or asks intrusive questions about your financial status, bank, business or credit matters. Never ever send money to online friends, no matter how convincing their sob story. There are scam artists in the chat rooms and dating sites mixed in with those who are there for the right reasons. Use your intuition. Throughout the dating process, it is up to you who gets the green light and who does not.

If your online communications are progressing well, you may decide to talk on the telephone or meet in person. If you use common sense precautions, meeting a match service date is no more dangerous than going on a blind date. When you decide to meet in person, you can remain safe if you meet in a public place, drive yourself to the location, let others know where you are and check in when you return home.

You already know some life story and personality traits about an online buddy, so use that to your advantage. Many cyber-pals already feel like old friends, at least in spirit, by the time they meet in person. Dating later in life is different from your prior youthful experiences. This time around, you can relax, have a good time and enjoy the new experience without teenaged anxiety or unrealistic expectations. Let your wise beautiful powerful woman self come out. To build rapport, pay attention, keep eye contact, smile and talk about some of the common interests that made you compatible in the first place.

Keep the date upbeat, simple and positive. Remember the subtle art of flirting, a playful way to get to know someone better. On the first series of dates, it is best to avoid conversation black holes that can cause offensive, like politics, religion, the former spouse, loneliness or marriage. If the time together does not go well or there is no connection, it is okay to honestly say that you were pleased to meet, but don't think things will work out between you. You have plenty to offer and it is only a matter of time before the right person comes along and notices.

Allowing the wrong person into your life can damage you and destroy your tender self-confidence. If a relationship looks like it might be going somewhere, reasonably gather all the information you can on the new person in your life, ask friends, Google the guy and keep your eyes and ears open. Stay clear of anyone who is not one hundred percent free and clear of past relationships or too raw with grief. If your new friend can only see you on his schedule, seems to telephone you within a two-hour window, whispers and hangs up suddenly during your chats, or won't give you his home information, beware he may have a significant other or still be married. Additionally, when someone is vague about his education or job field or if any information doesn't make sense or seems to be contradictive, dig deeper. One gal client has a criteria of not dating anyone who is married, gay or has a waist smaller than hers. Trust your instinct if something doesn't seem right. It is better to wait or move on to someone else that can give you the attention, honesty and respect you deserve.

Embrace each step and even each misstep of finding romance. No one said finding a new meaningful relationship was easy. You can just decide to have fun with the process. Companionship is a treasured reward. Try to remain open to possibilities and optimistic that your ideal partner will manifest. Hey, princess, you may have to kiss lots of frogs before finding your prince, but the trouble and wait will definitely be worth the rewards of finding a lasting loving relationship. Learning about the Internet dating process is another instance where you can ask friends or family to help you get started. Take it slow and make it right.

Sexuality

There is substantial research data to show that despite myths to the contrary, mentally and physically healthy persons remain sexually active into their eighties and beyond. When it comes to getting physical in a new relationship, the rule about trusting your intuition still applies. During the early stages of dating, do not feel obligated to go too far physically and only proceed as far as you are comfortable. It is fine to just hold hands, hug, cuddle, kiss and enjoy the moment. New relationships are still romantic, especially if they start out slowly and in consideration of the sensitivity and vulnerability of you as a widow.

Don't buy into one of the biggest myths women have perpetuated on them. That is the belief that a man won't date you more than three times if you don't have sex with him. If that is the kind of teenage pressure you receive from someone, dump him. Anyone who is seeking a mature respectful relationship knows that it requires an entirely different level of assessing, building trust and patience. Good men worth your time and consideration are absolutely on the same page.

It is a universal longing to have love in your life, to be held and feel physical closeness with another person. Not to say that you and others should believe the other myths that say all widows are lonely, sex starved and desperate to find a mate. Statistics from AARP show that a relatively low number, twenty-two percent (22%) of 45-plus single women were sexually active in the past six months. But also, they were not hung up about it or thought it was any big deal. Many agreed that after menopause they may feel the desire for closeness but no longer feel the need for sex. Self-satisfaction is a normal, less complicated method for relieving physical tension. One can be celibate without sacrificing sensuality and sexual without sacrificing independence. In fact, sexuality studies show that after age fifty, single women are more easygoing, sexually adventurous and want to have fun sex, if, and when it comes along. Joy and ecstasy link with health and well-being. Women tend to be better informed on topics like STDs, AIDS and how to practice safe sex. The main driving force for older women or widows dating is not sex urges, at least in the same way it is for men. Older widowed men also admit to sex taking a new dimension, as they are not necessarily seeking penile penetration for amorous satisfaction. Men want and enjoy caressing as much, because it relieves the pressure to achieve an erection to please his partner or himself. Society today openly discusses erectile dysfunction and hormone replacement and advertising touts many products to relieve performance anxiety.

Remarriage

The death of a husband produces dramatic declines in the physical, social and economic well-being of the surviving widow. While you go through your own timelines of grief work and resiliency about getting into current and new activities, the time comes when you begin to long for the love and intimacies that exist for you only in a marriage or committed relationship.

Widowers really experience greater loneliness, sadness and begin to ask, "Who will care deeply about my well-being" or "Who will care for me day-to-day or if I become ill?" Widowed men discover sooner that they want the stability of a marriage and the knowledge that someone is near and there for them. Statistics indicate that when a widower is stuck in his ways, stays shut up in the house rather than reach out into the world for new challenges, or if he clings to old routines and experiences complicated grief after he loses his wife, he becomes more depressed, vulnerable to illness and dies within a short time of his wife's demise. Widowers and widows are able to mitigate these adverse effects by remarrying.

Many dying spouses told their widow that they wanted to them to move on, remarry when they are emotionally ready and most of all they want them to be happy again. It is a compliment to your late husband and your marriage if you later wish to remarry. After a personally determined period of bereavement, you may consider the possibility of sharing life and love with another. Attitudes about how a widowed woman should behave have changed over the past several years. In western cultures, there are no set mourning periods, strict bans on remarriage or scriptural notions that a widow is obligated to marry her deceased husband's brother to keep the property in the paternal family.

At first, you may not be able to imagine remarrying or life with another man after you have lost your mate. However, after a few years, you may find yourself deeply in love with someone very different from your first husband, but who is perfectly suited to you at this time and stage of life. Never underestimate your heart's need and capacity for love. Remain open to the possibility of another long-term partner. You have many good years left to contribute to someone's life and let them contribute to yours.

> The heart has its reasons which reason knows not of.
>
> - Pascal

Grief advisors suggest that the first six months or more of your widowhood should be deliberately spent on you, your health, your grief work, your recovery, your family, your life adjustments and finding your way into your new life. Ultimately, in today's world and the western culture, it is your decision how and when to fill your life with a new loving relationship or to remarry. Many well-adjusted widows choose not to remarry. You may instead find a partner for companionship, social, physical, financial and emotional reasons.

If you are a single widowed parent of younger children, advisors say to take at least a year to begin thinking about dating or remarriage. A child's timeline for grief and ways of processing loss and enormous changes are different from those for an adult. After a death, sufficient time for taking stock of what has happened, healing, making life adjustments and figuring out what is wanted out of life is needed. It takes you and your children time to get used to the unsettling new reality and its challenges.

Before you commit to remarrying, counselors, legal advisors and other widowed persons speaking from life experiences (like the Cushenbery coauthors of *Coping with Life after Your Mate Dies*) offer some practical aspects to consider, each vital to the success of any new marriage. You do not want any big surprises. Go into any marriage with your eyes wide open.

Questions for in-depth pre-nuptial discussion may include:

1. Do you have the same interests, value systems and common ground on major issues of life?
2. Do you share religious beliefs and spiritual values? Will you become more or less involved in your religious practice as time goes on or as there are children?
3. Are personal habits of the other person similar and agreeable?
4. Is your prospective mate attentive, open-minded, trustworthy and understanding?
5. Are you able to communicate openly and resolve differences?
6. What is the financial status of each and do you agree regarding spending, saving, donations, tithing and helping others?
7. Do either of you have tax problems or debts like child support or alimony that will impact your life together?
8. Are there past encounters with the law or convictions that might cause trouble getting a job, renting property or volunteering?
9. Should you wait before your remarry or live together?
10. Have you agreed on your living arrangements?
11. Are there family or financial obligations to consider?
12. What is the physical and mental health of each of you?
13. How is your sexually compatibility?
14. If you are younger, do you plan to have children or add to your existing family?
15. If there are children, how do they feel about the person and how do they feel about you remarrying?
16. Are there family members or relatives with issues, addictions or dependancies that might affect you or your marriage?
17. If you have grown children, what will be your time, social and financial involvement with them?
18. How will you manage your family traditions and holidays?
19. Are a prenuptial agreement and new estate plan needed?

After you start dating and find someone you think is compatible, there is the task of including your children and determining if there is a fit. There must be a commitment on your part to ensuring that your children are making a healthy transition, which includes healing from the loss, before asking them to make another big transition of accepting someone new. Let your children become acquainted with your new romantic interest and his family before you announce any permanent plans. You are marrying this person as well as his family members and children, so any negative reactions or discomfort on either side require serious discussion.

It is important to recognize that it is common for your family, friends and children (both younger and grown adults) to be very concerned or conflicted about you dating or marrying someone else. Children, still economically and emotionally dependent on you, might fear abandonment or neglect if you remarried. They may feel threatened with emotional, physical and financial losses. If children think they are losing you, it revives and compounds the loss they already experienced.

Children and some others may see your dating or remarriage as a betrayal to your deceased husband. They might see any change in the status quo or any relationship you enter as negative. This new development should be discussed and explained from your point of view. However, on the other hand, if your older children, relatives or close friends pose objective loving concerns about your possible new mate, be open to their observations and consider those matters carefully.

You must seek a sensitive balance between recognizing the difficulty others have in accommodating this new situation and your own rights and needs to move forward. Having respectful, open and trusting conversations about your transitions will help with gradual acceptance and support. When customs, traditions and others' expectations and demands become a prison, it is time to free yourself in order to heal and grow.

The final decision as to what is the best for all concerned rests with the two of you. Once you are both comfortable with your decision, let your children know your intentions privately and ask for their love, blessings and involvement in the future plans.

He who finds a wife finds what is good.

- Proverbs 18:22

Chapter Thirty-Four

LIFE ADJUSTMENTS – PERSONAL

Your life is changing dramatically. The road to recovery includes learning to adjust to and integrate your loss, restoring your ability to function and creating your new life accordingly. After the death of your loved one and your old life, you can arise, like a phoenix. You may never fully recover from the sad events or ever forget your deceased husband, but you need to start reinvesting yourself in new purposes, goals, ideas, roles, activities, people and other pursuits.

Don't fall into the bear trap of self-pity. There is not much juice in just hanging on. Get back to dreaming about what you are moving toward. Find new ways to integrate the treasured parts of the past with the new opportunities, experiences and adventures of the present and your self-designed future. So that creative good comes from your loss, channel your suffering and anger into meaningful efforts for the benefit of all.

Designing Your New Life – Change, Value and Purpose

We are all apprenticed to the same teacher, reality. You were born with a core of strength that has helped you survive difficult changes in the past and will surely help you get through whatever you are encountering now with the death of your loved one. Being a strong individual is a necessary tool in your transformational toolbox. Explore the fierce aspect of your being. Even though you incorporate the best of what you experience, always come back to yourself. Believe in yourself and your ability to progress through change. The knowledge, talent, ability, inner strength, resiliency and tools to handle any challenge that comes your way are already yours.

A reptilian part of the brain focuses on safety, protection, avoiding change and keeping things the way they are. Even good change is about loss. As a primal human, you are not good at letting go of anything because during change you are out of control of what might happen. You gain an acceptance of what is as soon as you recognize sources of resistance within yourself. It is only by allowing life to lead you through change and letting go of the control that solutions start showing up.

Be patient, change depends on your endurance and on your ability to wait for the next phase of your life to progress at its own pace. Organized activity and maintained enthusiasm are the wellsprings of your power. Plan your life and time carefully hour-by hour, day-by-day, month-by-month.

> It takes as much energy to wish as it does to plan.
> - Eleanor Roosevelt

There is much more to being a widow than just overcoming grief and suffering, coping with the changing circumstances or getting through this particularly difficult life passage. During this time, pain is inevitable, but suffering is optional. In the wider perspective, this is a pilgrimage journey into selfhood. Buried under multiple role layers of having been a wife, mother, daughter or profession, there is a real you just yearning for discovery. You can become the archaeologist excavating the true you. Stop waiting for someone else to unwrap you. Don't hold yourself back. If you get stuck or struggle to discover what you want and need empowering strategies for making it happen, there are books, tapes, CDs, DVDs, blogs, web sites and even personal coaching for widows.

Value

In an insightful, "believe in your self-worth" story, a known speaker started his seminar by holding up a $20 dollar bill. In the room of 200, he asked, "Who would like this $20 bill?" Hands started going up. He said, "I am going to give this $20 to one of you, but first let me do this." He proceeded to crumple up the $20 dollar bill. He then asked, "Who still wants it?" Still the hands were up in the air. Well, he replied, "What if I do this?" And he dropped it on the ground and started to grind it into the floor with his shoe. He picked it up, now crumpled and dirty. "Now, who still wants it?" Still the hands went into the air. "My friends, we have all learned a very valuable lesson. No matter what I did to the money, you still wanted it because it did not decrease in value. It was still worth $20. Many times in our lives we are dropped, crumpled, and ground into the dirt by the decisions we make and the circumstances that come our way. We feel as though we are worthless. But, no matter what has happened or what will happen, you will never lose your value. Dirty or clean, crumpled or finely creased, you are still priceless to those who do love you." The speaker finishes with, "The worth of our lives comes not in what we do or who we know, but by who we are and whose we are."

As someone of value, you must make good use of your time. In a graduation speech, Apple Computer founder Steve Jobs told graduating students, "Your time is limited, so don't waste it living someone else's life. Don't be trapped by dogma which is living with the results of other people's thinking. Don't let the noise of others' opinions drown out your own inner voice. Most important, have the courage to follow your heart and intuition. They somehow already know what you truly want to become."

During stressful changing times, your intuition and calm heart center seem to become like antennae that receive signals and signs. Be open to and value your external and internal guides. Don't let your rational mind dismiss these intuitive feelings. They can provide you further directions along the new paths you are taking. It is essential to trust your own intelligence and intuition in order to believe that you are innately capable. Always listen to your internal knowing intuition. No matter how uncomfortable the message may be, your intuition will subtly nudge you in the right direction with universal wisdom, clarity, knowledge, inspiration, support and love.

Nobel Laureate Toni Morrison explains how you are the great author of your own life. "You are your own stories and therefore free to imagine and experience what it means to be human. What it feels like to be human without domination over others, without reckless arrogance, without fear of others unlike you, without rotating, rehearsing and reinventing the hatreds you learned in the sandbox. And although you don't have complete control over the narrative (no author does), you could nevertheless create it."

Purpose

Don't give up your power and lose energy on fear and guilt. Power is not necessarily will, force or domination. Power is actually the ability to do work and get things done. What do you care about and want to get done? Martin Luther King, Jr. and others believed that love is the most powerful and available source of power in the universe. Power is internal and self-rejuvenating, like a hybrid car recharging while in motion. Learn to be the embodiment of power and energy fields that affect others. What life design or purpose do you want to give your energy to?

It is time to explore new self-images, purposes and experiences in order to push the boundaries. What would you create or do if money were no object? How old would you be if you didn't know your age? Where would you visit if you won a free trip around the world? If you were appointed chairperson of a multi-million dollar foundation, what charities or causes would you support? What is the subject and title of your best selling book? What genre would a movie of your life fall into and which stars would play the leading roles? If you had Aladdin's magic lamp, what would your three wishes be for the future?

> If you don't have a dream, how are you going to make a dream come true?
>
> - Oscar Hammerstein

You can certainly rewrite and renegotiate new meaning and purpose into your life without minimizing your loved one's memory. Your life with the deceased helped to define your reality and sense of self. Your grief experience affirms the ongoing significance of your loved one to you and in your life. His death inevitably and permanently changes you. That bit of you created and validated by the old relationship is no longer the same. Discover who you are right now and start defining your life and aliveness in the present.

Constantly set new goals for yourself. If you are getting close to one goal or objective, move it and change it, but keep moving in a general desired direction. Every small step you take forward on your journey will prepare you for the steps ahead. Everything matters. Keep on trucking despite the bumps in the road along the way. Good choices can help you heal and gain control of your life.

Great healing and happiness will come from pursuing your unique life purpose, path and dreams. You don't need to do anything drastic, but when you start paying attention to your own inner compass and listening to your inner voice you will be more fulfilled and happier. All life asks of you is that you to be the best person you can be. In order to do your best, you need to isolate the things that are getting in the way of moving on after a loss. Investigate what may be stopping you from changing and pursuing your own life's purpose. Make a firm commitment to push through any impeding fear, doubt, shame, impatience, guilt, blame or insecurity, and replace them with better patterns of thought and behavior that move you into a higher phase of life.

The key is to clarify your goals and make sure they are consistent to your values. Once you have a clear image of your life purpose and objectives in your mind, then you work at making it happen as if you can't possibly fail. No dream is too big, exotic, or unrealistic to go after no matter what your current situation may be at this time. Study and adopt the philosophy, habits and actions of successful people. Be decisive and focused. Develop your own blueprint for success and prepare for whatever it is you want.

When you prove to yourself that you can plan, commit and succeed, you will build the self-confidence necessary to aim for even higher aspirations. Don't block the way with lame excuses. Your dreams are not less realistic or attainable just because you are a senior citizen, single raising children, handicapped, don't have a college degree, lack funds or currently doing a job you dislike. You deserve to have your deep dreams fulfilled…by you. After you accomplish one dream, you are more prepared and inspired to create and pursue other dreams. Always set new goals for yourself so that you can continue to achieve new personal bests in all aspects of life. Go from good enough to world-class kick-ass great.

Happiness Attitude

Being happy is a process that begins with a belief that you can be happier and knowing that you deserve to be happy. There is even a book called *Happiness is an Inside Job*. It is up to you to choose and adopt positive attitudes that lead to inner happiness. A simple but effective way to increase your happiness is just to remember how much you have and to be grateful for small blessings.

An attitude of gratitude can make you happier, but how do you remain grateful in the midst of loss or adversity? The broader perspective of gratefulness toward life in general helps in times of grief. Realize that there something in every situation to feel grateful for in some way. There is nothing bad from which good doesn't come. Gratitude for small favors might make you feel better and it certainly won't do any harm. This might be a good time to read *The Art of Happiness* or *Open Heart* by Nobel Peace Prize winner, the Dalai Lama of Tibet.

Count your blessings and actively appreciate everything in life that you take for granted, including life itself.

Forgive yourself for mistakes. As you progress through this major life change, you will make mistakes such as giving up too quickly, not manifesting and acknowledging changes in yourself and not making your recovery a priority. See mistakes as lessons, time for discovery and opportunities for growth. You can avoid making the same gaffes after you face and recognize your occasional misjudgments.

Use your heart, head and soul sword to cut away what no longer works, does not serve you, or holds you back from your potential. Forgive yourself for being human and move on to manifest a great life.

Believe in yourself. The average person criticizes herself 55 times a day. You don't criticize nature or art, but you put yourself down for not being perfect. Watch out for that nay-saying inner voice. Women crave assurances that they matter and are loved. Be full of grace and kind to yourself first. Know that you are a beautiful powerful woman.

Embrace your essential force, archetypal essence, universal voice, intensity, joyfulness, wholeness of self, energy for good and much more. You are an expression of the divine nature inherent in all women. You have the strength of your ancestors running through your blood. Value and trust your wisdom, inner voice and intuition. Use positive affirmations about yourself to clarify and set intentions. What gives you the deepest joy? What is your greatest hope? What most calls to your heart? "If you do not hope, you will not find what is beyond your hopes," says St. Clement.

Empowerment

Sometimes it seems hard to believe in yourself as a woman. There are gender and status (widowhood) stereotypes in the world that try to limit and discriminate against women. In the media, women are seldom represented well. They are often trivialized, objectified, sexualized, demeaned, belittled, and shown as powerless. In Washington, D.C. of 210 statues, only 9 are of women. Less than twenty percent (20%) of the U.S. Congress members are women. Women compromise 52% of the population, and they take care of the other 48%, so you would think that they would have more say in the laws that govern them. Women need to gain more visibility and be honored. Women are the real untapped resources and wealth of nations.

It is up to everyone, including yoursef, to stop the institutional biases and other forces portraying and making women feel inferior and inadequate. Break the barriers and you will find doors you did not know existed. Women should believe in their own strengths and also support those trying to make a difference. How can you blow wind into another's sail? It is important to your positive self-image and to the world that you speak out, step up, get involved, mentor others and support changes to the system and to your life. Take risks to blaze trails, widen paths, open doors and achieve.

Where in your life are you willing to take a greater role in helping others and leadership? Just getting better, after your great loss, is being a role model for other widows. This is how you make changes and manifest new beginnings. A popular phrase holds, "If you aren't standing on the edge, you are taking up too much room." Be bold because, as they say "well behaved women rarely make history."

> Life is a grindstone. Whether it grinds us down or polishes
> us up depends on us.
> - Thomas L. Holdcroft

You create your own self-imposed limitations. So much depends on the ABCs of attitude, balance and courage. Do you want to be an example or a warning to other widows? After all you have been through, you know you are resilient and an expert in change, so make some positive personal changes today. Ask your inner self what wants to be received, known, released, realized and done. Do not get stuck on what, how and when you will change. Look for why you want to change and the rest will follow.

Conquer Negative Thinking

Do not let negative thinking limit you and your plans. Use any lack of knowledge and your fears as a catalyst in the change process. Ask questions and ask for help. Make written lists of your concerns, what you need to learn, your expectations, goals and priorities. You will gain a greater sense of forward movement and control as you replace fear and worry with planning and action. You would not build a house without plans. The outer world really does respond to inner intention and direction. Decide what you need, break tasks into manageable pieces, stay energized, keep your focus, use humor, have patience and celebrate even the smallest victories.

Put seeds of faith in the right place and stop those self-limiting thoughts. Step into greater miracles. Even Jesus had to master his negative thoughts and fears. His most famous test was when he went to the desert alone for 40 days, where Satan tempted him with his negative egos. These types of spiritual tests are very similar in many ancient cultures and mythology. You have to master your negative attitudes and beliefs to become enlightened and regain access over your God-given natural abilities.

Positive results come from positive thoughts and positive actions. It is risky to try new things, but the greater risk is to do nothing. You will be stronger by going forward to new beginnings. Take the time and mentally celebrate each milestone and accomplishment. By acknowledging progress, you can stay motivated for what lies ahead and believe in the attainability of other tasks. Write down your successes, no matter how small, in a notepad to which you can refer later. Keeping track of accomplishments is a great source of encouragement when you are going through tough patches. Some widows write in their joy-nals to celebrate their joys, achievements and transitions. Embrace your growing strength. You will find that not only does grief close doors, it also opens doors that let you access joy.

Forgiveness

When you are going through tough times, difficult past experiences with family and others seem to amplify. There may be problems forgiving and letting it go. People carry around past hurts that are extremely painful and weigh on them. Lack of forgiveness for past transgressions can be like a festering sore that never heals, often throbs and opens easily. Relationship and personal issues that are left unresolved can manifest into other problems for you such as stress, anxiety, unresolved anger, and poor self-esteem.

Forgiveness is a very powerful tool for self-healing. You are free from any self-imposed bondage of angst by letting go and forgiving the people who hurt you. If some past misgiving has been weighing you, while you are doing all your other grief and recovery work, include forgiveness in your emotional house cleaning.

Everyone, at one point or another, has done or said things or made mistakes they wished they could go back in time to change. It really is liberating when the person who harmed you or whom you harmed is able to find forgiveness. Yes, forgiveness is a two-part deal. When you are able to forgive someone, you need to offer yourself the same courtesy and forgive yourself. The only one you hurt with lack of forgiveness is you. Once you internalize that, you should be able to forgive family members and others for past offense without needing to drag the subject up again.

An important part of relationships is closeness and sharing. However, limit time spent with negative or self-absorbed people. There may be those insecure folks who think a single widow is out to steal someone's husband or some other such nonsense. Sometimes, to avoid feeling like a fifth wheel, you have to create a new interests and a new life with new friends. Do your best to deflect or ignore any negative energy or statements others might send your way. Most of all, ignore other people's judgments of you. A state of mind consciousness is contagious, so stay away from toxic people.

Remember at this time you are vulnerable and need to keep healthy boundaries so that you remain your own defined person, not co-dependent on someone else. You can maintain appropriate boundaries if you: Respect yourself, honor your own needs, tell and expect the truth, have time alone and for other friends, learn to say no, and are able to remove yourself from any situation that is verbally, mentally or physically abusive. The number one addiction is not drugs; it is seeking the approval of other people. Believe in yourself and stay focused on your own priorities. As Shakespeare said, "do not suffer fools gladly."

Time Alone

During the first days and weeks of your grief, family and friends were probably around solicitously helping you move through the shock and funeral process. Eventually they have to return to their everyday lives. Do not allow yourself to get into a negative mindset of feeling abandoned, lonely, angry or unloved.

Just because you are alone does not mean you are lonely or that loneliness is something for you to suffer. It is a shame, that in our society, solitude is regarded as a something to be avoided. Being alone is no more a sign of being unwanted as is being surrounded by people a sign of popularity. Furthermore, loneliness is only a state of mind. In the Tibetan language there is no concept or word for 'lonely' since they believe that all humans are interconnected. Many Christians, who believe in an omnipresent God, express similar sentiments. Also, the Phillippine language does not have the linguistic structure for the phrase 'I grieve', they can only say 'we grieve.'

The concept of being alone or answering the call of solitude is a basic need as essential and universal as the need to bond with others. Studies show that downtime by yourself, meditation, rest and relaxation bolster the immune system. When you deny yourself periods of solitude, you get very out of touch with your inner self, anxious, angry and depressed as well. Perhaps because solitude in today's modern world is less available (i.e. email, cell phones, express mail, 300 channel cable television, crowds everywhere), it is more needed than ever and defending time alone has become something of a trend.

Periods away from other people, preferably unstructured and unplugged, is essential for you to achieve physical and mental harmony. Revel in your newly found "just me, myself and I" quality times as much as you enjoy time spent with others. Solitude is valuable time to ponder the world around you, dream or just be in the moment.

> Though you have made me see troubles, many and bitter,
> your will restore my life again.
> - Psalm 71:20

Recognize your private time as another necessary part of the mourning and healing process. Time alone is just as important as connecting with others during grief. It takes energy to visit with and entertain others; energy that you need to conserve for yourself. Try to take advantage of this initial time alone to reflect, pray, cry, or whatever you feel you want or need to do. Face and sort through the feelings that you may not ready to share with others. Your mental and physical being requires times of tranquility and solitude. Constantly being busy or in the company of others can turn into a postponement or repression of your grief. Look for the balance between the social support of others and your own personal needs for time alone.

Explore your thoughts in your art, letter writing, journal keeping, music or dreams. There may be a list of activities or projects that you've wanted to do with your time alone over the past few months but haven't had the opportunity. Take precious time for yourself, whether it is walking in the park, indulging in a spa treatment, organizing family photographs to remember the good times, seeing the latest movie, visiting an art gallery, browsing in a library or book store for hours, taking a day trip to historical sites or starting a new project. Time alone is precious well-spent time.

The worst loneliness is not to be comfortable with yourself.
- Mark Twain

Health

It is important for you to have good physical health and sufficient energy in order to endure the difficult grief and change processes that face you. Of course, a balanced diet, exercise, plenty of rest and regular doctor and dental appointments are very important. Work to maintain good physical and mental health. Get medical examinations and treatments as your symptoms warrant them. If health problems are acute or persist, you may require professional care. Store current ICE ("In Case of Emergency") speed dial information on your telephones.

Get rid of and avoid the negative habits that you may use to avoid uncomfortable feelings, situations, and activities. For instance food, TV, alcohol, smart phones, drugs, shopping, risk-taking, drama and over-scheduling should be reasonably limited or eliminated. According to many ancient and modern thinkers, breath ties the human spirit to its physical body. So incorporate deep breathing and its benefits into your life. The key to getting you past the physical pains of grief are natural diet, sufficient exercise, rest and other stress-relieving activities.

After a significant loss, there are high risks of adverse physical consequences. Stress depletes calcium, vitamin D and phosphorus, cause insomnia and create eating disorders. Physical symptoms of grief may also include muscle and joint pain, headaches, dizziness, digestive problems or chest pains. Be sure to check with your doctor if you are experiencing chest pains. Be aware that during your bereavement, many pre-existing condition may become exacerbated.

If you are suffering from a disease, such as diabetes, cancer or heart disease, and you feel traditional medicine is not helping you, you might consider alternative approaches to your health care. Each year, more than 80 million Americans utilize some form of complementary and alternative medicine (CAM), and 68% of adults have tried at least one kind of CAM therapy. Read up on different types of natural therapies. Alternative therapies include Chiropractic; Acupuncture, Deep Massage, Aromatherapy; Reiki; and Qi Gong. Yoga is also good way to relieve stress and remove toxins from the body. It is one of the physical exercise methods that can be done at home or a fitness center. If yoga is not your first choice, find workouts that provide you a therapeutic opportunity to enjoy nature such as hiking a wooded trail or taking your dog for a walk in the park.

Physical benefits of walking are a good cardiovascular exercise. There are also spiritual benefits as well. Even as you are on a daily walk, running, hiking, in route to a specific destination or running errands, that can be a time for prayer or meditation. At the same time, you are moving and doing something good for your body, exercise gives you time to work out your thoughts. It is a win-win experience.

Nhat Hanh, a Buddhist monk has taught walking meditation for many years. Walking meditation is like eating; with each step, your body and spirit are nourished. The objective of meditation is not to stop the mind; meditation's purpose is to be present fully and cultivate awareness.

> The miracle is not to walk on water. The miracle is to walk on the green earth in the present moment, to appreciate the peace and beauty that are available now.
>
> - Nhat Hanh

During a period of great change, even good change, physical and emotional energies are constantly building up. Any bit of positive movement you make will actually help dissipate the lethargy, depression, tension and anxiety you are feeling. Whenever you feel sad or stuck, just start moving. Start with simple tasks or activities like taking a shower, washing the laundry, watering the plants, walking the dog or writing a few thank you cards. Another day when you feel ready, join an exercise class, walk through a park or the neighborhood, take a bicycle ride, work in the garden, or wash the car. When you move, healthier emotions tapped into will make you feel better and raise your confidence. The best cure for sorrow and grief is action. Relaxation and joy are links to your good health and well-being.

> To keep a lamp burning, you have to put oil in it.
>
> - Mother Teresa

Spiritual Growth

After a great loss, like the death of your loved one, you start seeking out the purpose of your own life. The quest for a more religious or spiritual life naturally leads you to exploring the eternal questions on the meaning of life. You may seek out established religions or philosophies. By praying or meditating upon scriptural quotations, sutras and anecdotes and by emulating the examples of great spiritual leaders of the past, you look for personal help and spiritual growth.

There are many pathways to connect with the soul and spirit, but the destination is the same. Core lessons and convictions emerge from all religions, teachings and traditions. Your present life has great potential. You should never waste even a single minute of your precious human existence. Spiritual growth comes from realizing the rarity and value of life and capacity for service to humanity.

> Great awareness comes slowly, piece by piece. The path of spiritual growth is a path of lifelong learning. The experience of spiritual power is basically a joyful one.
>
> - M. Scott Peck

In your spiritual growth, the definitions of wealth and success previously held by you; notions like achievements, material goods and fame, make way for a new vision of what it means to be truly happy and to live a fulfilled meaningful life. Your concepts of happiness may shift to those people and states of mind that center around family, honesty, spirituality and leads to peace, contentment and renewed self-esteem. You can live a more spiritual life by turning your focus away from external temporary sources of happiness, like tangible goods, physical attractions and professional success. Put more energy and attention to non-material, intangible, subtle sources of joy and contentment. Suffering ends and happiness results when you let go of grasping, clinging and material attachments.

> When the heart weeps for what it has lost, the soul laughs
> for what it has found.
>   - Sufi aphorism

When everything around you is changing, take a time each day to go inside to tap into your spiritual center. Use the outlet that works best for you like sitting in silence, praying, taking a quiet meditative walk or expressing your

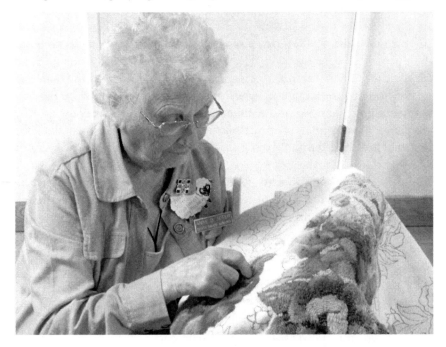

faith. Close your eyes and let your scared and tired mind take a rest. Find that safety point within yourself that is untouched by what is happening around you. Once your natural center becomes quiet and attune, you are more open to stability, guidance and gentle suggestions to help you move through change with hope and optimism. When you tap into this real and spiritual side of yourself, you are connecting with invisible forces, higher-frequencies, angels, your father upstairs, saints, prophets, ancestors or whatever is preparing your way and assisting you. You can access this resource at any time simply by focusing inward.

One exercise my clients have found entertaining and insightful is to imagine that they are sitting at their kitchen table sharing stories with some of history's famous widows like Eleanor Roosevelt, Jackie Kennedy, Joan Didion, Queen Victoria, or Mary Lincoln or whoever else comes to mind. Think what memories, tales and advice they would share with you.

Start looking at people from a place of spirit. They will realize that you are recognizing their soul energy and spirit, seeing them as worthwhile and inviting them to be true. Support and empower others by commenting on their manifestations of spirit. The greeting 'namaste' means 'I recognize the sacred within you.' You need recognitions and connections that nourish you and your relationships. There is a tribal feeling of being embraced and re-empowered by the joyful spirit of others. Common humanity and experiences bind you together more than differences. If you help and heal one woman that means she can heal a family and so on around the world. The spiritual world responds whenever asked.

No matter how you categorize your religion or spirituality, you can turn to prayer, ritual and meditation in these times of unfortunate circumstances, finding that you need more spiritual guidance and comforting traditions than usual. Whether it is just communicating with a higher power or articulating your needs, prayer is a way of reflecting and clarifying your thoughts. If prayer fits into your idea of spirituality, try to work it into every day, not just the difficult ones. Prayer makes you more aware of what and how you are feeling, so try to include it in your daily schedule or write out your thoughts and prayers in a notebook or journal. Cultivate your individual sacred space.

On life's journey faith is nourishment, virtuous deeds are a shelter, wisdom is the light by day and right mindfulness is the protection by night. If a woman lives a pure life, nothing can destroy her.

- Buddha

Quiet time, prayer and meditation sessions are about reaching greater levels of relaxation, clarity and consciousness. In order to get to know yourself better, write down the experiences, people or things that make your heart feel nourished, more open, positive, alive, vibrant, loved and healthy. Maybe you feel most in tune with the world being in nature, listening to music, working on your art and craft or dancing.

Who are the people that make you feel the most loved, nurtured and accepted? Get together with them this week. For you, homemaking, playing with your child, working on meaningful tasks, helping a lonely friend, group activities, volunteering or caring for loved ones may replenish your spirit. You may approach the spiritual through music and movement that unbinds your heart. Whatever you do, make your life have a greater and higher purpose. You cannot do much to control the length of your life, but you can do something about its depth and width.

> It is only with the heart that one can see rightly. What is essential is invisible to the eye.
>   - Antoine de Saint-Exupery

The fastest path to a spiritual connection to the divine is through nature. Take time each day to look for inspiration and comfort within with your natural surroundings. The ever-present power and beauty of nature are all knowing, trusting, and in tune with the rest of the universe.

Simply taking a walk, swimming in the ocean, cruising along on a bike ride, or working in a garden, counting stars or playing with a pet is enough to connect you with the energy of nature and something higher. Even if you are a city dweller, you can add an environment of living plants to your home and office. Spend some time each day being grateful for all your blessings.

Life is about doing more of what keeps you positive. Taking a more Polly Anna positive approach to each day will help you feel more alive and involved in the world. Reconnect with the lightness and humor in life. You were not put on this earth to be negative, dark and angry. Spirituality means to experience immense inspiration and bliss.

Children are continually laughing and tapping into their innately understand that life is about joy. As you pursue healing and spirituality, give yourself permission to be playful and silly. Do whatever makes you smile and laugh. Remember, it is okay to be happy and smile, even if that smile is through tears.

YOU KNOW YOU ARE GETTING BETTER WHEN:

- Old photographs, certain colognes or favorite songs make you smile instead of burst into tears.
- When you feel someone else's pain in your heart and gut and it hurts you more than your own for a change.
- When you can tell someone else going through the first pangs of grief that life really does go on and life can become better than ever...and really believe it.
- Some day you wake up and don't reach across the bed or miss your departed love until after 10:00 A.M.
- You do not have to remind yourself to breathe or keep moving.
- You recognize when an old familiar fear or insecurity shows up and replace it with positive emotions.
- You successfully get through tax season and try online trading.
- You want to and find a way to honor your great love
- You are able leave grief in the past and think about your future.
- You find you are productively busy and enjoy living and learning.
- You are beyond the tangle of guilt, worry and fearful thinking.
- Marathon, Conservation and other forward looking websites are your primary computer bookmarks.
- Your home, files, estate plan and life are in order.
- Your home has your unique signature and you feel comfortable coming back to an empty house or content doing things by yourself.
- When someone says "sorry for your loss," you answer, "I've only had a year of loss. I had xx years of gain."
- You have learned to trust yourself and to trust life again.
- You stop the lone wolf act and let the shepherd's love fill you.
- You can watch your children or grandchildren playing, smile and say, "Micheal would have loved this pandemonium...and then turned down his hearing aids!"
- You are known for your glorious selfhood rather than your widowhood.
- Sentences begin with progressive "Tomorrow...." instead of past tenses "back when...." You use the word "I" instead of "we".
- You are dedicated to living life out-loud and in gratitude for life.
- Your journal of the recovery process becomes a run away best seller on the *New York Times* list and you counsel other widows.
- The words 'guilty' 'lonely' 'hopeless' or 'what if' don't enter your mind or conversation.

- You wear stilettos, kiss a new guy, feel tingles and start planning.
- You get your Citizen of the World travel merit badge.
- You have taken up the passions and projects of your mate and you share the abundant gift with others.
- It is a week past your old wedding anniversary or the date of his death before you remember.
- Prayers and meditations are full of gratitude instead of bargaining, anger, pleas or complaints.
- You are the first to laugh and tell stories about your old doubts, fears and mistakes.
- Peace and serenity enter your life and you discover what a resilient, strong and courageous person you have become.
- Your children, family, friends and others dealing with life-changing experiences look to you as an inspirational model and mentor.
- Your story and quotes appear in the next edition of *Widow's Key.*

Conclusion

From the beginning, just by reading this book, you have shown that you possess an open curious mind, positive outlook and the precious faith and belief that your life can be better. Since life stepped in and changed your plans, you have been learning how to use your heart, mind and soul's deeper powers to heal yourself. You acquire phenomenal insights and strength that comes from going through the grieving process after the death of your loved one. Your journey is full of physical, mental, emotional, spiritual and social peaks and valleys. Despite what may seem like a constant state of flux, you move through each experience more keenly aware of your feelings, your strengths and your resilience. You are better prepared and awaiting the life journey ahead.

Widow's Key was created because I felt a tremendous sense of heart and soul connections with my widowed clients. Their struggles and successes moved me deeply. Every widow had a unique story to tell and multitudes of memories to share. Each deceased husband was a special person---a man with loves, dreams, passions, hopes for the future, visions, projects to complete and perhaps unborn children or grandchildren. While the sting of your loss is still great, you realize the tremendous gift that you had in knowing your beloved.

I had to create a practical guide for my clients that would help before, during and after the death of their loved one. Hopefully, *Widow's Key* offered you support as you progressed through your own life changing experiences. Similarly, you have the opportunity to share that gift with others through the choices you make in the coming months and years.

As you continue your journey of healing, do not forget the lessons learned or the challenges overcome. Have faith in your own resiliency and strength. If you need help, *Widow's Key* is always here at your side as a guide.

I hope this book gave you the comfort of an understanding heart and was a source to turn to during your challenging times. Always share your insights and wisdom with someone else along the way. Please recommend *Widow's Key* or pass it on if you know someone else who may need it. Remember that it is not the power of the events you are going through; it is the power that you give the events. I trust that your new life is everything you wished. You have so much more to explore, learn, experience, write, give and become. Rethink what is possible for your life.

Linda Lindholm

References

Adams, Kathleen, 2005, *The Complete Estate Planning Guide*, New York, New American Library.

Alter, Robert M. and Alter, Jane, 2000, *The Transformative Power of Crisis, Our Journey to Psychological Healing and Spiritual Awakening*, New York, HarperCollins.

Anderson, Megory, 2003, *Sacred Dying: Creating Rituals for Embracing the End of Life*, New York, Marlowe & Company.

Bonanno, George, 2009, *The Other Side of Sadness: What the New Science Of Bereavement Tells Us About Life After Loss*, New York, Basic Books.

Bowlby, John, 1980, *Attachment and Loss: Loss, Sadness and Depression*, New York, Basic Books.

Bridges, William, 1983, *Transitions, Making Sense of Life's Changes*, Reading, Massachusetts, Addison-Wesley Publishing Company.

Buckingham, Robert, 1996, *The Handbook of Hospice Care*, Amherst, New York, Prometheus Books.

Calhoun, Lawrence and Tedeschi, Richard (Editors), 2006, *Handbook of Posttraumatic Growth: Research and Practice and Clinical Applications of Posttraumatic Growth*, East Sussex, UK, Routledge.

Chaline, Eric, 2000, *Zen and the Art of Travel*, Naperville, IL, Sourcebooks.

Colgrove, Melba, Bloomfield, Harlod H. and McWilliams, Peter, 1993, *How to Survive the Loss of a Love*, Los Angeles, Prelude Press.

Corey, G., 2001, *Theory and Practice of Counseling and Psychotherapy*, Belmont, California, Brooks/Cole.

Cushenbery, Donald C. and Cushenbery, Rita Crossley, 1991, *Coping with Life After Your Mate Dies*, Grand Rapids, Michigan, Baker Book House.

Dalai Lama, 2002, *Advice on Dying and Living a Better Life*, New York, Atria Books.
_____, 1998, *The Art of Happiness*, New York, Penguin Putnam.
_____, 1997, *The Joy of Living and Dying in Peace*, San Francisco, Harper.

Davis, C.G., Wortman, C.B.,Lehman, D.R. and Silver, R.C., 2000, *Searching for Meaning In Life, Death Studies* 24.

Deits, Bob, 2004, *Life After Loss, A Practical Guide to Renewing You Life After Experiencing Major Loss*, Cambridge, Massachusetts, Lifelong Books.

Didion, Joan, 2005, *The Year of Magical Thinking*, New York, Alfred A. Knopf.

Dunnan, Nancy, 2003, *The Widow's Financial Survival Guide*, New York, Perigee Book.

Dyer, Wayne, 2010, *The Power of Intention, Learning to Co-Create Your World Your Way*, Carlsbad, California, Hay House.
_____, 2009, *101 Ways to Transform Your Life*, Carlsbad, California, Hay House.

Easwaran, Eknath, 1996, *God Makes the Rivers to Flow, Selections from the Sacred Literature of the World*, Tomales, California, Nilgiri Press.

Freud, Sigmond, 1957 (original 1917), *Mourning and Melancholia* in the standard edition of the complete psychological works of Sigmond Freud (Vol 14), New York, Basic Books.

Friedman, Russell and James, John W., 2008, *The Grief Recovery Handbook and When Children Grieve*, New York, HarperCollins.

Gelman, Rita Goldman, 2001, *Tales of a Female Nomad*, New York, New York, Three Rivers Press/Random House.

Gilbert, Elizabeth, 2006, *Eat, Pray, Love, One Woman's Search for Everything Across Italy, India and Indonesia*, New York, Penguin Books.

Gilbran, Kahlil, 1923, *The Prophet*, New York, Alfred A. Knopf.

Ginsburg, Genevieve Davis, 1997, *Widow to Widow: Thoughtful, Practical Ideas for Rebuilding Your Life*, Cambridge, Massachusetts, Da Capo Press.

Herskowitz, Suzan D, 2001, *Wills, Trusts and Probate*, Boston, Massachusetts, Pearson Custom Publishing.

Kalish, Richard A., 1985, *Death, Grief and Caring Relationships*, Monterey, California, Brooks/Cole Publishing.

Kilcrease, J. Worth, 2009, *End of Life Bereavement Counseling: What Do You Do When You Lose Someone You Love?*, Austin, Texas, www.kilcrease.com.

Kubler-Ross, Elisabeth, 1969, *On Death and Dying*, New York, MacMillan.

Kushner, Harold S., 1981, *When Bad Things Happen to Good People*, New York, Avon.

Lewis, C. S., 1976, *A Grief Observed*, New York, Bantam.

Lord, Janice Harris, 1992, *Beyond Sympathy, What to Say and Do for Someone Suffering an Injury, Illness or Loss*, Ventura, California, Pathfinder Publishing.

Mayo Clinic Staff, 2009, *Complicated Grief*, Mayo Foundation for Medical Education and Research, MayoClinic.com.

Mitsch, Raymand, and Brookside, Lynn, 1993, *Grieving the Loss of Someone You Love*, Ventura, California, Regal Books.

Neimeyer, Robert, 1998, *Lessons of Loss: A Guide to Coping*, New York, McGraw-Hill.

_____, 2001, *Innovations in End-of-Life Care*,

_____, 2001, *Meaning Reconstruction & the Experience of Loss*, Washington, D.C., American Psychological Association.

_____, and Prigerson, H.G. and Davies, B., 2002, *Mourning and Meaning*, American Behavioral Scientist 46(2) 235-251.

O'Brien, Michael J., and Shook, Larry, 1998, *Profit from Experience, A Handbook for Learning, Growth and Change*, New York, Berkley Books.

Plotnick, Charles K. and Leimberg, Stephan R., 2002, *How to Settle an Estate, A Manual for Executors and Trustees*, New York, Penguin Putnam.

Rando, Therese A., 1991, *How to Go on Living When Someone You Love Dies*, Lexington, Massachusetts, Bantam Book with Lexington Books.

_____, 1995, *Grief and Mourning: Accommodating to Loss*, in Wass and Neimeyer (Eds), Dying, Washington, D.C., Taylor & Francis.

Riemer, Jack, and Stampfer, Nathaniel, 1991, *So That Your Values Live On: Ethical Wills and How to Prepare Them*, Woodstock, Vermont, Jewish Lights Publishing.

Rinpoche, Sogyal, 1993, *The Tibetan Book of Living and Dying*, San Francisco, Harper.

Rupp, Joyce, 1990, *Praying Our Goodbyes*, Ave Maria Press.

Servaty-Seib, Heather, 2004, *Connections Between Counseling Theories and Current Theories of Grief and Mourning*, Journal of Mental Health Counseling.

Shelton, Mary Murray, 2000, *Guidance From the Darkness, The Transforming Power of the Divine Feminine in Difficult Times*, New York Penguin Putnam.

Sissom, Ruth, 1990, *Instantly a Widow*, Grand Rapids, Michigan, Discovery House.

Thurman, Robert, 1994, *The Tibetan Book of the Dead* (translation), New York, Bantam Books.

Viorst, Judith, 1998, *Necessary Losses, The Loves, Illusions, Dependencies, and Impossible Expectations That All of Us Have to Give Up in Order to Grow*, New York, Simon & Schuster.

Volkan, Vamik D., and Zintl, Elizabeth, 1994, *Life After Loss, The Lessons of Grief*, New York, Collier Books.

Waterman, Deborah Boles, 2010, *Before (I die), During (The process), and After (You're gone)*, Eugene, Oregon, Deborah Waterman.

Weenolsen, Patricia, 1996, *The Art of Dying, A Comprehensive Guide to Your Physical, Emotional and Spiritual Concerns*, New York, St. Martin's Griffin.

White, E.B., 1952, *Charlotte's Web*, New York, Harper & Row.

Worden, J. W., 2002, *Grief Counseling and Grief Therapy: A Handbook for the Mental Health Practitioner*, New York, Springer.

Zaleski, Philip and Kaufman, Paul, 1997, *Gifts of the Spirit, Living the Wisdom of the Great Religious Traditions*, San Francisco, Harper Collins.

Zurak, Gary, 1990, *The Seat of the Soul*, New York, Simon & Schuster.

Acknowledgements

There have been numerous people who have assisted, encouraged and inspired me. In gratitude for your unwavering belief in me and my book:

Dora Lee Eldred-Roelofs
Mhaire Merryman
Dawn Lindholm
Robert J. Newton
Emily Grosvenor
John K. Larson
Joseph Micheal Rice
Timothy Singler
Stuart Hellebrand
Samuel J. Comouche
Stefano Lalwani
Vin Morley
Walter Lane

Index

CPSIA information can be obtained at www.ICGtesting.com
Printed in the USA
LVOW071529200812

295097LV00002B/88/P